Really Interesting Stuff You Don't Need to Know

Mega Edition

Over 3,000 Fascinating Facts

David Fickes

Introduction

I have tried to ensure that all information in this book is as accurate as possible. This book is intended for people who prefer to read interesting facts rather than quiz themselves. Since the information isn't in a question and answer format, it also allows different types of facts that aren't as well suited for a quiz format.

There are over 3,000 fascinating facts with illustrations covering a wide range of topics including animals, arts, history, literature, movies, science and nature, sports, television, U.S. geography, U.S. presidents, world geography, and more.

If you enjoyed this book and learned a little and would like others to enjoy it also, please put out a review or rating. If you scan the QR code below, it will take you directly to the Amazon review and rating page.

Contents

Facts 1-500

1) Alexander the Great, Julius Caesar, Genghis Khan, Napoleon, Mussolini, and Hitler all suffered from ailurophobia, a fear of cats.

2) Pringles aren't really a potato chip because they are made from dehydrated potato flakes pressed together rather than thinly sliced potatoes, so they are a crisp and can't be marketed as a chip.

3) Bears don't urinate while they hibernate. Their body converts the urine into protein, and they use it as food.

4) President George W. Bush was a head cheerleader in high school.

5) Giant anteaters eat up to 30,000 ants a day, and they still have time to sleep 16 hours a day.

6) More than 80% of marriages in history might have been between second or closer cousins. Ancient times had fewer people dispersed over wide areas, so inbreeding was inevitable.

7) Rats can't vomit; this makes them particularly vulnerable to poison.

8) The ancient Greeks drank their wine diluted; it was usually mixed three-parts water to one-part wine. If you drank undiluted wine, you were considered a drunkard and someone who lacked restraint and principle.

9) Quincunx is an arrangement of five objects with four at the corners of a square or rectangle and the fifth at its center, such as the number five on dice.

10) The earth is the densest planet in our solar system.

11) President Barack Obama's mother had the first name Stanley.

12) With 1.5 crimes per citizen, Vatican City has the world's highest national crime rate per capita. The reason is that the population is so small, only about 800 people, with millions of tourists, and the crime is mainly petty theft.

13) The Aztecs played a game called ollamalitzli, which was like basketball. They had to get a hard rubber ball through a stone hoop.

14) Reaching only about two feet in length, the cookiecutter shark's name comes from its unusual feeding method where it gouges out round plugs of flesh from larger animals.

15) *The Mousetrap* is the longest-running play in history; it is an Agatha Christie murder mystery and has been running in London's West End since 1952.

16) Beijing was the first city to host both the Summer and Winter Olympics. It hosted the 2008 summer games and the 2022 winter games.

17) Walter and John Huston were the first father and son to win Oscars for the same film, *The Treasure of the Sierra Madre*.

18) Dr. James Naismith, who invented the game of basketball in 1891, is the only Kansas Jayhawk men's basketball coach in history with a losing record. He founded the University of Kansas basketball program, where he became the Kansas coach and athletic director.

19) If something is napiform, it is shaped like a turnip.

20) Recent research suggests that ice is slippery because there are loose water molecules on the surface that act like marbles on a floor. Prior theories that it was due to pressure creating a thin layer of water on the surface have been disproven since the pressure would have to be far too great.

21) Martin Van Buren is the only U.S. president that did not speak English as their first language. Van Buren, who was president from 1837 to 1841, grew up in the Dutch community of Kinderhook, New York, and spoke

Dutch as a child; he learned English as a second language while attending school.

22) Roman gladiator fights started as a part of funerals. When wealthy nobles died, they would have bouts at the graveside.

23) Jimmy Carter was the first U.S. president born in a hospital.

24) Humans are the only animals with chins; scientists don't know why.

25) Potassium-40 (K-40) is the most common radioactive element in the human body. It makes up about 0.012% of the potassium found in nature, and we ingest it in foods containing potassium.

26) Mongolia is the only country that has entirely wild horses that have never been domesticated by humans. The endangered Przewalski's horse is native to the steppes of Mongolia; all other wild horses are feral horses that are descendants of domesticated horses.

27) In the Bible, Lake Kinneret is known as the Sea of Galilee.

28) Ancient Greek men didn't wear trousers; they thought men from other cultures who wore them were barbaric and effeminate.

29) Flamingos are naturally white; their brine shrimp and algae diet make them pink.

30) The current population of Ireland (Northern Ireland and Ireland) is still about 20% less than it was before the great potato famine started in 1845.

31) For the longest recorded successful sniper shot of 2,475 meters, the bullet took 6 seconds to reach its target.

32) In Greek mythology, they believed redheads turned into vampires when they died.

33) At 2,700 miles wide, Alaska is the widest state from east to west.

34) Stars don't twinkle; the light they emit is steady and constant, but the earth's atmosphere interferes with what we witness and makes them appear to twinkle.

35) The Diomede Islands, located in the middle of the Bering Strait, consist of two islands that are separated by 2.4 miles and have a 21-hour time difference. Big Diomede is owned by Russia; Little Diomede is owned by the United States. They represent the closest distance between the two countries; the time difference is due to the international date line passing between the islands.

36) In 1928, the first automatically sliced commercial bread was produced in Missouri.

37) Frank Sinatra inspired the name for the cartoon dog Scooby-Doo; Fred Silverman suggested naming him Scooby-Doo based on the refrain "Scooby-dooby-doo" from Sinatra's song "Strangers in the Night."

38) About 1850 BC, the earliest known contraceptive devices for women were invented. They were objects or concoctions inserted into the vagina to block or kill sperm; Egyptians used concoctions made of crocodile dung, honey, and sodium carbonate.

39) Rock paper scissors originated in China about 2,000 years ago.

40) On a per weight basis, spider silk has a tensile strength five times greater than steel. Each strand is 1,000 times thinner than a human hair and is made up of thousands of nanostrands, only 20 millionths of a millimeter in diameter.

41) All humans are about 99.9% genetically the same.

42) King Louis XIV, who ruled France from 1643 to 1715, was offered plans for the first bacteriological weapon by an Italian chemist; he refused instantly and paid the scientist to keep the deadly discovery a secret.

43) At up to 30 feet long, the reticulated python is the longest snake.

44) To help minimize the number of accidents caused by miscommunication, aviation English is the language used by pilots and air traffic controllers around the world. It consists of about 300 words that are a combination of professional jargon and plain English.

45) In the opening credits for the first season of *Gilligan's Island*, the U.S. flag is at half-mast as the *Minnow* pulls out of harbor because of John F. Kennedy's assassination. The scene was filmed in November 1963 in Hawaii; the cast and crew learned of Kennedy's assassination on the last day of filming.

46) Most of the fat you lose is exhaled. About 84% of fat loss is converted into carbon dioxide and exhaled; the remaining 16% is converted to water and exits through urine or sweat.

47) Before getting married in the White House, Grover Cleveland had his sister perform the duties normally done by the president's wife.

48) All the gold ever mined would fit in four Olympic swimming pools.

49) Juneau, Alaska, is the least accessible state capital; you must fly or take a boat.

50) The Great Wall of China's mortar contains the standard mixture of lime and water plus an additional ingredient, sticky rice. It was the world's first composite mortar.

51) In 2010, a tiny shark, Mollisquama mississippiensis, was discovered in the Gulf of Mexico; it is only 5.5 inches long and looks like a tiny sperm whale.

52) In 1998, speed dating was created by Jewish Rabbi Yaacov Deyo. At a Beverly Hills, California, matchmaking event, he brought along a gragger, the noisemaker used during Purim; he twirled the gragger when it was time to switch partners. They decided on 10 minutes for each date because it was an easy number.

53) Sapphires are the second hardest gem after diamonds.

54) The most common team name for U.S. college football teams is Eagles.

55) The word oxymoron is itself an oxymoron. It derives from the Greek "oxys," meaning sharp or pointed, and "moros," meaning stupid. The word itself is composed of a contradiction in terms, and it also means a contradiction in terms.

56) Zimbabwe has 16 official languages, the most of any country.

57) Juliet is 13 years old in Shakespeare's *Romeo and Juliet*.

58) The Mississippi River has the largest drainage basin of any U.S. river; it drains 1,245,000 square miles, including all or parts of 31 states.

59) Abraham Lincoln is the only U.S. president ever awarded a patent; it was for a device that helped buoy vessels over shoals.

60) Ancient Egyptians were very tolerant of genetic and medical disorders. For example, dwarfism was quite common, and dwarfs were highly respected. Pharaoh Amenemope wrote that caring for the old, the sick, and the malformed was a moral duty.

61) At 5.5 million square miles, the Antarctic Polar Desert is the world's largest desert.

62) Sewer manhole covers are round, so they can't fall through the opening. The cover rests on a lip that is smaller than the cover; no matter its dimensions, a square or rectangular cover could always fall through.

63) The four states of matter observable in everyday life are solid, liquid, gas, and plasma.

64) In 1975, Kodak created the first digital still camera; it weighed 8 pounds and took 0.01-megapixel black-and-white photos. The pictures took 23 seconds to render onto a cassette tape that displayed the image on a television set.

65) Barnacle geese chicks must jump off cliffs, sometimes hundreds of feet high, when they are as little as one day old and can't fly. Barnacle geese, which nest in the Arctic, protect their young from predators by nesting on high ledges and cliffs. They can't feed the babies in the nest, and the chicks must eat within 36 hours. To get to the grass they need to eat, the chicks must jump from their nest and hope to survive. Fortunately, the chicks are light and fluffy, and usually survive the fall, even after bouncing off rocks.

66) The human eye can distinguish about 10 million colors.

67) Snails are almost completely blind and don't have any mechanism to hear either, but their sense of smell is extraordinary.

68) The word idiot derives from the ancient Greeks. In ancient Athens, contributing to politics and society was considered the norm and desirable; most people participated in politics in some form. Those who did not contribute were known as "idiotes," which came from the word "idios," meaning the self, and were considered apathetic, uneducated, and ignorant.

69) Bananas are the most frequently sold item at Walmart.

70) With 800 languages spoken, New York City is the world's most linguistically diverse (highest number of languages spoken) city.

71) During the American Civil War, the novel *Les Misérables* was given to all officers in the Confederate army. Robert E. Lee believed the book symbolized their cause.

72) The oldest Summer Olympics medalist was 72; he medaled in shooting in 1920.

73) Green is the first color mentioned in the Bible. Genesis 1:30 states, "To every thing that creepeth upon the earth, wherein there is life, I have given every green herb for meat: and it was so."

74) The United States has the most dogs of any country; Brazil has the second most.

75) In the television show *Have Gun - Will Travel*, the lead character's name, Paladin, comes from the Paladins, the 12 knights in Charlemagne's court in the 8th century. Over time, a paladin has come to mean a knight, warrior, or chivalrous person.

76) White Castle is the oldest hamburger chain in the United States; it was founded in 1921.

77) A polar bear's fur isn't white. It is transparent and appears white only because it reflects visible light.

78) Without a visual reference point, humans are incapable of walking in a straight line. If blindfolded or lost in terrain devoid of landmarks, we tend to walk in circles. Scientists have yet been unable to determine why.

79) The oldest known recipe is an 8,000-year-old recipe for nettle pudding.

80) Murmurations are the patterns starlings create when they flock together in the sky in swooping, coordinated patterns.

81) At age 48, George Blanda was the oldest player ever in an NFL game.

82) The prop used for Dr. McCoy's medical scanner in the original *Star Trek* television series was a salt shaker.

83) At their closest point, Europe and Africa are separated by nine miles between Spain and Morocco.

84) A ship's speed is measured in knots because they historically used real knots to measure speed. By the late 16th century, sailors measured a ship's speed by throwing out a piece of wood attached to a length of rope with knots tied at regular intervals. They allowed the rope to go out as the ship moved forward, and after a set length of time, they pulled the rope back in, counted the knots that had gone out, and calculated the speed. A knot eventually came to mean one nautical mile per hour.

85) With an annual average temperature of 29.7 degrees Fahrenheit, Ulaanbaatar, Mongolia, is the world's coldest national capital city.

86) The Mediterranean Sea is referenced in the Bible as the Great Sea.

87) Only the nine-banded armadillo and humans are known to be infected with leprosy.

88) Maine is the closest state to Africa; Quoddy Head, Maine, is 3,154 miles from Morocco. It is almost 1,000 miles closer than Florida.

89) Only about 2% of the islands in the Caribbean are inhabited.

90) Junk email is called spam because of Monty Python. The 1970 *Monty Python's Flying Circus* sketch where a waitress reads a menu with an endless variety of Spam options and a chorus of Vikings sings "Spam, Spam, Spam, Spam" resulted in spam being used generically for something that drowns out or overrides everything else as junk email does.

91) In 1845, Portland, Oregon, got its name when Asa Lovejoy and Francis Pettygrove flipped a coin. Lovejoy was from Massachusetts and wanted to name the new settlement Boston; Pettygrove was from Maine and wanted to name it Portland.

92) Our own Milky Way Galaxy is estimated to contain at least 100 billion planets and 200 to 400 billion stars.

93) Between 1935 and 1945, the secret German government program Lebensborn encouraged suitable women to bear children and create racially pure Aryans for the Third Reich. Women in the program were required to hand their children over to the SS to be raised; the program originally started in Germany but spread to other occupied European countries during WWII. Estimates are that there were about 20,000 Lebensborn children born; the most famous is ABBA singer Anni-Frid Lyngstad, who was born to a Norwegian mother and a German sergeant.

94) A baby owl is called an owlet.

95) Woodrow Wilson is the only U.S. president with a PhD; he had a doctorate in history and political science.

96) Slave-maker ants will take over the nest of other ants, and when the new ants hatch, they become slaves of the colony.

97) If you could fold an average thickness (0.004 inches) paper in half 42 times, it would be thick enough to reach the moon; if you could fold it 103 times, it would be 109 billion light-years thick, thicker than the observable universe is wide.

98) In 1898, Nikola Tesla created the first remote control that could control mechanical devices at a distance with radio waves. The first electronic television wasn't invented until 29 years later in 1927, and the first wireless television remote wasn't created until 1956.

99) Relative to its weight, the strongest organism known is the gonorrhea bacterium. They can pull with a force of 100,000 times their body weight, comparable to a 150-pound person pulling 7,500 tons.

100) Adolf Hitler described Switzerland as "a pimple on the face of Europe." He hated it and thought it had no right to exist; he had a planned invasion but never initiated it.

101) *Peyton Place* (1964-1969) was the first U.S. primetime television soap opera.

102) Based on active enrollment, Indira Gandhi National Open University is the world's largest university. It is a distance-learning university in New Delhi, India, and has over 4 million students.

103) In ancient Greece, women would go to great lengths to have a thick, swarthy unibrow. To the Greeks, a unibrow signaled beauty and brains; women would line their brows with soot or use tree resin to attach fake eyebrows made of goat hair to their foreheads.

104) About 1 in every 200 people is born with an extra rib, called a cervical rib, that forms above the first rib, just above the collarbone. You can have a cervical rib on either or both sides, and it can be a fully-formed bony rib or a thin strand of tissue fibers.

105) Denmark has the world's oldest operating amusement park; it started in 1583.

106) Washington has the only state flag that has an image of a president.

107) A domestic cat shares 95.6% of its DNA with a tiger.

108) The state name Idaho was proposed by a lobbyist, who claimed it was a Shoshone word meaning "Gem of the Mountains"; in reality, he just made it up.

109) Warren Moon is the first player ever in both the Pro Football Hall of Fame and the Canadian Football Hall of Fame.

110) The Wright brothers only flew together once in 1910; otherwise, their father made them promise they would never fly together in case an accident would take them both.

111) Playwright Tennessee Williams choked to death on the cap of a bottle of barbiturates.

112) Missouri and Tennessee share the most borders with other states; they each border eight other states.

113) Scientists have found that humans are born with two innate fears, the fear of falling and the fear of loud sounds. All other phobias are acquired.

114) At an international competition, the longest table tennis rally (single point) lasted for 2 hours and 12 minutes, with an estimated 12,000 hits. It was the opening point of a 1936 world championship match; game time limits were later put in place.

115) President Martin Van Buren helped to make the word "ok" popular. Based on the town he was from in New York, one of his nicknames was "Old Kinderhook"; during his presidential campaign, people held up signs and chanted "OK."

116) The Mayans and the Aztecs used cocoa beans as a form of currency.

117) Taking cocaine increases the chance of having a heart attack within the hour by 2400%.

118) The earth receives more energy from the sun every hour than the entire world uses in a year. The earth receives about 430 quintillion joules of energy from the sun every hour; annually, we use about 410 quintillion joules of energy.

119) President Andrew Johnson was an indentured servant as a child. When he was three years old, his father passed away, and Johnson and his brother became indentured servants to a tailor and worked for food and lodging. They both eventually ran away, and Johnson taught himself to read and worked as a tailor.

120) In protecting their hives from outsiders, bees will sometimes sting other bees.

121) While only 3.1% of the world's children live in the United States, they own 40% of the toys consumed globally.

122) Hilary Clinton was the first U.S. first lady elected to public office.

123) At 2,640 miles, the Irtysh River in Russia, China, and Kazakhstan is the world's longest tributary river. It is the chief tributary of the Ob River.

124) The technical term for a cat's hairball is bezoar. The term also applies to a mass of indigestible material found in the gastrointestinal tract of other animals, including humans.

125) Eight U.S. presidents were born as British subjects: George Washington, John Adams, Thomas Jefferson, James Madison, James Monroe, John Quincy Adams, Andrew Jackson, and William Henry Harrison.

126) Nine U.S. presidents never attended college: George Washington, Andrew Jackson, Martin Van Buren, Zachary Taylor, Millard Fillmore, Abraham Lincoln, Andrew Johnson, Grover Cleveland, and Harry S. Truman.

127) In 1863, Venezuela was the first country to abolish capital punishment for all crimes.

128) A human sneeze travels about 100 mph.

129) Modern humans appeared about 200,000 years ago, but recorded history only dates back about 5,000 years, so about 97.5% of human history is unrecorded.

130) There are 88 constellations in the night sky.

131) When glass breaks, the cracks move at speeds up to 3,000 mph.

132) All the bacteria in an average human body collectively weigh about four pounds.

133) While the United States has about 4.4% of the world's population, it has about 22% of the world's prisoners.

134) Windsor Castle employs a fendersmith, who just tends and lights fires.

135) Bees have five eyes; they have two large, compound eyes on the sides of their head and three simple eyes on the top of their head.

136) During the 1960s, Canada employed what was known as a fruit machine that was supposed to be able to identify gay men. The subjects viewed naked or semi-naked images of men and women, and the device measured their pupil response to see if the pupil enlarged as an indication of attraction. It was employed as part of a campaign to eliminate all gay men from the civil service, the Royal Canadian Mounted Police, and the military; although the device didn't work, a substantial number of workers did lose their jobs. Funding for the project was discontinued in 1967.

137) The giraffe has the longest tail of any land animal; its tail can be up to eight feet long.

138) In the same house within 11 hours, President Theodore Roosevelt lost his mother to typhoid fever and his wife to kidney failure after giving birth to their daughter.

139) *I Love Lucy* is generally credited with inventing the television rerun. During Lucille Ball's pregnancy, they had to rerun episodes.

140) About 90% of drownings take place in swimming pools, bathtubs, and rivers.

141) The worldwide life expectancy at birth is 69 years.

142) Reindeer eyes change color from gold in summer to blue in winter. During bright, summer light, their eyes reflect most light and look gold; during winter, the tissue behind their retina becomes less reflective, and their eyes appear blue. This increases their light sensitivity and vision in the low winter light.

143) Technically, U.S. Independence Day is July 2, 1776, which is when Congress voted America free from British rule. July 4 is the day the Declaration of Independence was adopted.

144) Before the words were changed and it was published in 1935, "Happy Birthday to You" was originally called "Good Morning to All."

145) The Great Pyramid at Giza was the world's tallest man-made structure for over 3,800 years.

146) Due to anti-German sentiment during WWI, the British royal family changed their name from Saxe-Coburg and Gotha to Windsor, so the family is named after the castle and not the other way around.

147) A group of pandas is called an embarrassment.

148) As seen in *Game of Thrones*, dire wolves existed in the Americas up to about 10,000 years ago. At about 150 pounds, they were about the same size as the largest modern gray wolves, but their teeth were larger with greater shearing ability, and they had the highest bite force of any known Canis species.

149) The tradition in the White House Roosevelt Room has been to hang Franklin Delano Roosevelt's portrait over the mantel during Democratic administrations and hang Theodore Roosevelt's portrait above the mantel during Republican administrations. Whichever painting is not over the mantel is hung on the south wall of the room.

150) At age 32, Sally Ride was the youngest American astronaut in space.

151) The adult human body has about 100,000 miles of blood vessels.

152) The hippopotamus produces its own sunscreen. It produces a mucus-like secretion that keeps them cool and acts as a powerful sunscreen.

153) The average person has four to six dreams per night.

154) The British pound is the world's oldest currency still in use; it is 1,200 years old.

155) Isaac Asimov is the only author to publish books in 9 of the 10 Dewey Decimal categories.

156) The world's most poached (illegally hunted) animal is the pangolin, a small mammal covered in large overlapping scales. It eats ants and termites and is found in Asia and sub-Saharan Africa. It is poached for its meat and for its scales that are used in traditional medicine.

157) Manny Pacquiao won world titles in the largest number of boxing weight divisions. He held titles in eight divisions: flyweight, super bantamweight, featherweight, super featherweight, lightweight, light welterweight, welterweight, and super welterweight.

158) For countries that share a land border, the distance between Brasilia, Brazil, and Paris, France, is the greatest distance between any two national capital cities. French Guiana borders Brazil and is part of France, just as Alaska is part of the United States, so France shares a land border with Brazil. Paris and Brasilia are 5,424 miles apart.

159) The cornea is the only part of the human body without a blood supply.

160) At 64 degrees north latitude, Reykjavik, Iceland, is the world's most northern national capital city.

161) Along with other benefits, a U.S. Medal of Honor recipient gets a retirement pay increase of 10%, a special Medal of Honor pension, a supplemental clothing allowance, and free travel on Department of Defense military aircraft.

162) President James A. Garfield could write in Greek with one hand and Latin with the other. He was ambidextrous and taught both languages while attending college.

163) Pluto hadn't even made one complete revolution around the sun between its discovery as a planet and its demotion to a dwarf planet. Pluto was discovered in 1930, and it takes 248 years for it to complete one rotation around the sun, so its first birthday (one Pluto year) since discovery won't be until 2178.

164) Hippopotomonstrosesquippedaliophobia is the fear of long words.

165) A cat's jaw can't move sideways, so it can't chew large chunks.

166) Hippopotamus skin is two inches thick; it is difficult for even bullets to penetrate it.

167) Worldwide, there are about 2.5 human births for every death.

168) The St. Louis Cardinals' name originally referred to the color of their uniforms and not the bird. Willie McHale, a columnist for the *St. Louis Republic*, overheard a woman in the stands describe the uniforms as a shade of cardinal. He began using the nickname rather than their previous name, the Perfectos, and it caught on. The bird logo didn't appear until the 1920s.

169) By the number of members, the United Kingdom has the world's largest two-house legislature, with 1,435 members.

170) The highest fall that a person ever survived without a parachute is 33,330 feet. The fall was the result of a 1972 airplane explosion, and the survivor spent several days in a coma and many months in the hospital but made an almost complete recovery.

171) Shortly after the American Civil War, one-third to one-half of U.S. currency was counterfeit. This was a major threat to the economy, and the Secret Service was founded in 1865 specifically to reduce counterfeit money.

172) Lobsters do not have blood like vertebrate animals. The liquid found in their body that acts as blood is called hemolymph; it is colorless and turns blue when exposed to air due to oxygen reacting with the copper in the fluid.

173) The jawbone is the hardest bone in the human body.

174) To get the stunning detail in his bird paintings, John James Audubon would often kill the subject and pose it, so he could create realistic paintings without the subject flying away.

175) The Russian October Revolution took place in November. It was October in the old Julian calendar but November in the current Gregorian calendar.

176) The pound or number symbol (#) is also called an octothorpe; the name is believed to have been made up by workers at Bell Telephone Labs, who needed a name for the symbol on the telephone keypad.

177) Palau, an archipelago of over 500 islands in the western Pacific Ocean occupying 177 square miles with just over 20,000 people, is divided into 16 states; each state has an elected legislature and a tribal chiefdom.

178) Rodents account for about 50% of all mammal species; bats account for about 25%, and all other mammals make up the remaining 25%.

179) The Amazon rainforest produces more than 20% of the world's oxygen.

180) Bamboo is the fastest growing plant. Bamboo can grow 35 inches in a day, a rate of 0.00002 mph.

181) Frances Folsom Cleveland is the youngest U.S. first lady ever. She was 21 when she married Grover Cleveland in the White House; he was 49.

182) In 1457, King James II of Scotland banned golf and soccer because they interfered with archery practice needed for national defense.

183) In 1935, Jesse Owens set world records in three different events in 45 minutes. At a Big Ten track and field meet, he set world records in the long jump, 220-yard sprint, and 220-yard low hurdles and tied the 100-yard dash world record.

184) There are 108 stitches on a regulation baseball.

185) The average American home has 300,000 things in it.

186) The Buddha you often see in statues is a Buddha and not the Buddha. The Buddha, Siddhartha Gautama who founded Buddhism, is not the same person as the typical fat, laughing Buddha that is based on an eccentric 10th-century monk. In Buddhism, the term Buddha is used for a person who has attained enlightenment through meditation.

187) Joseph Priestley, who later discovered oxygen, invented carbonated soda water.

188) A blue whale's heart is so massive that you can hear its heartbeat two miles away.

189) James Madison was the first U.S. president to wear long pants; previous presidents wore knee breeches.

190) The Los Angeles Dodgers MLB team got their name from the trolleys in Brooklyn, New York. The team was established in Brooklyn in 1883 and went through several different names before settling on the Trolley Dodgers. At the time, the Brooklyn trolleys were a major cause of accidents, so people were familiar with dodging trolleys. When the team moved to Los Angeles after the 1957 season, the shortened Dodgers name was kept.

191) Oysters can change their gender based on environmental conditions; they are born male but can change back and forth based on conditions.

192) President Thomas Jefferson kept a pair of grizzly bear cubs in a cage on the front lawn of the White House for a few months; they were a gift. He decided they were too dangerous to keep and bequeathed them to a museum.

193) Before he went solo, Barry Manilow was Bette Midler's piano player.

194) In 1818, the treadmill was created as a machine to reform stubborn and idle convicts. Sir William Cubitt, an English civil engineer, created a large paddle wheel with 24 spokes that prisoners would climb. As the

spokes turned, gears were used to pump water or crush grain. Prisoners would work in grueling eight-hour shifts, climbing the equivalent of 7,200 feet; combined with poor diets, this often led to injury and illness. Prisons all over Britain and the United States used the machines.

195) At 8,200 feet deep, Kings Canyon in California is the deepest canyon in the United States.

196) Presidents Thomas Jefferson and John Adams both died on July 4, 1826.

197) A mononymous person is known and addressed by one name.

198) Silver is the best conductor of electricity of any metal; it is slightly more conductive than copper but much more expensive.

199) Since the British Centurion tank was introduced in 1945, all British tanks and most armored fighting vehicles come equipped with tea-making facilities. The equipment is known as a boiling vessel and draws its power from the tank's main electrical supply; it can make tea, boil water, and heat food.

200) The Red Sea is the world's warmest sea.

201) At the age of 85, Tony Bennet was the oldest living artist to have a song on Billboard's Hot 100.

202) Tsutomu Yamaguchi is the only recognized person to survive both the Hiroshima and Nagasaki atomic bomb blasts. He was in Hiroshima on business for the first bomb and then returned home to Nagasaki.

203) Even though it is the same size, the moon appears to be larger when it is nearer the horizon than when it is higher in the sky. This is known as the Moon Illusion and has been known since ancient times. There is no consensus on what causes the illusion, but the most important factor is likely that terrain and other objects are in view along with the moon and impact the perception of distance and size when it is nearer the horizon.

204) About half of all people can remember at least one instance of lucid dreaming, where they realize they are dreaming but are still asleep.

205) At its peak in the 1990s when it was mailing out CDs to get people to sign up for internet service, AOL was producing 50% of the world's CDs.

206) The first item bought and sold across the internet in 1971 was marijuana; Stanford University students were buying from MIT students.

207) The Motel 6 and Super 8 motel chains both got their names from their original room rates. When it started in 1962, Motel 6 charged $6 per night, and Super 8 charged $8.88 per night when it started in 1974.

208) At 142 feet in diameter, the Roman Pantheon's dome is still the world's largest unreinforced concrete dome; it was built in 125 AD.

209) New York City is further south than Rome, Italy.

210) When Disneyland opened in 1955, Tomorrowland was designed to look like 1986, the distant future.

211) Austin, Texas, is the largest population city in the United States that doesn't have an MLB, NFL, NBA, or NHL team; it is the 11th largest city in the United States.

212) Blue whales give birth to the largest young of any animal; newborn blue whales are about 23 feet long and weigh 5,000 to 6,000 pounds.

213) More than 90% of the world's jury trials occur in the United States.

214) An elephant has 40,000 muscles in its trunk; there are about 640 muscles in the entire human body.

215) The sperm whale dives deeper and stays underwater longer than any other whale. They can dive for more than an hour and can go more than 4,000 feet deep.

216) At its closest point, the distance between the United States and Russia is 2.4 miles.

217) The most used punctuation mark is the comma.

218) To allow visitors to travel safely to Olympia, a truce, or ekecheiria, was put in place before and during each of the ancient Olympic games. During this time, wars were suspended; legal disputes were put on hold, and no death penalties were carried out.

219) In the 1920s when insulin was still harvested from animals, it took 10,000 pounds of pig pancreases to make 1 pound of concentrated insulin.

220) Huh is the closest thing to a universal word. It means the same thing in every language, and everybody in almost every language says it.

221) The ketchup used by McDonald's annually would fill 50 Olympic swimming pools.

222) The material that became Kleenex was originally used for gas mask filters in WWI.

223) Based on volume, Lake Kariba, on the Zambezi River in Zambia and Zimbabwe, is the world's largest man-made lake; it contains 43.3 cubic miles of water.

224) At about 17 pounds, a sperm whale's brain is the largest of any animal; comparatively, a human brain is about 3 pounds.

225) It took over 200,000 years for the world's human population to reach one billion, but it only took 200 more years to reach 7 billion.

226) In 1892, Juan Vucetich was the first person to solve a crime using fingerprints.

227) Although the triggering mechanism is different, dead people can get goosebumps. As rigor mortis sets in, muscles contract, and the arrector pili muscles attached to the hair follicles also contract to produce goosebumps.

228) In the wild, there is no such thing as an alpha male wolf. Wolves act like families, with older members as leaders. There is no fighting to move up the hierarchy, and they aren't born as leaders or followers.

229) In 1857, Harrods in London was the first store to ever sell toilet paper; it was individual wipes that were rough on one side and shiny on the other. Toilet paper as we know it today was invented in 1936.

230) Eighteen people have won all four major American entertainment awards (Oscar, Emmy, Tony, Grammy): Richard Rogers, Helen Hayes, Rita Moreno, John Gielgud, Audrey Hepburn, Marvin Hamlisch, Mel Brooks, Whoopi Goldberg, Jonathan Tunick, Mike Nichols, Scott Rudin, Robert

Lopez, John Legend, Tim Rice, Andrew Lloyd Weber, Alan Menken, Jennifer Hudson, and Viola Davis.

231) The border between Texas and Oklahoma is 700 miles long, the longest border between any two states.

232) Red eyes in photographs occur when the camera flash is reflected from the retina and illuminates the rich blood supply of the connective tissue at the back of the eye, producing the red color.

233) There are 42 eyes in a deck of 52 cards. The jack of hearts, jack of spades, and the king of diamonds are in profile with only one eye showing.

234) Due to environmental concerns, Theodore Roosevelt banned Christmas trees from the White House.

235) Bottled water expiration dates are for the bottle, not the water; the plastic will eventually start leaching into the water.

236) The most perfectly-round, natural object known to man in the universe is a star 5,000 light-years away; before this discovery, the sun was the most perfectly-round, natural object known.

237) The Great Basin Desert, covering 200,000 square miles over most of Nevada, and parts of Utah, California, Oregon, and Idaho, is the largest U.S. desert.

238) Four people have served as U.S. president, U.S. vice president, U.S. senator, and U.S. representative: John Tyler, Andrew Johnson, Lyndon B. Johnson, and Richard Nixon.

239) Benjamin Franklin's image is engraved on the Pulitzer Prize gold medals.

240) The cougar has more names than any other animal: puma, mountain lion, panther, catamount, or one of another 40 English, 18 native South American, and 25 native North American names.

241) The hyoid bone in the throat is the only bone in the human body that isn't attached to any other bone.

242) Dr. Seuss wrote *Green Eggs and Ham* after his editor dared him to write a book using fewer than 50 different words.

243) In September 1989, Deion Sanders hit an MLB home run and scored an NFL touchdown in the same week. He is the only person ever to do it.

244) In music, a semihemidemisemiquaver is a 1/128th note.

245) President John Quincy Adams often swam in the Potomac River in the buff; he wrote of waking at about 4 a.m. and taking a nude morning dip.

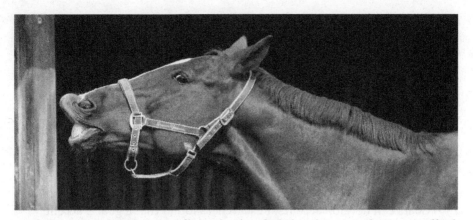

246) Horses curl their upper lip and raise their head to get a better smell of something. The behavior is called the flehmen response and is used to transfer inhaled scent molecules into the vomeronasal organ (VNO), a specialized chemosensory structure found in many mammals.

247) A cricket's ears are located on its front legs.

248) Tomatoes are the most popular crop in U.S. home vegetable gardens.

249) At up to 7 feet tall and 1,500 pounds, the moose is the largest species of deer.

250) The shellac resin used in varnish is a secretion of the lac insect.

251) The device used to measure your foot at a shoe store is called a Brannock Device.

252) Ben & Jerry learned how to make ice cream by taking a $5 correspondence course offered by Penn State University.

253) Millions of Japanese treat themselves to KFC chicken every Christmas. In 1974, KFC created a Japanese marketing campaign called "Kentucky for Christmas"; it became so popular that Christmas KFC sales can be 10 times the normal sales volume. Christmas dinner often requires ordering weeks in advance or waiting in line for hours. Before the original advertising campaign, there was no real Christmas tradition in Japan, so KFC was able to establish its own tradition.

254) Colorado's Pikes Peak was the inspiration for the song "America the Beautiful."

255) At its peak, the Roman Empire was about 2.5 million square miles, only the 19th largest empire by area in history.

256) For humans, the rarest hair and eye color combination is red hair and blue eyes, which account for only about 0.17% of the population. The combination is so rare because both red hair and blue eyes are recessive traits, and both parents must carry the gene for the child to have it.

257) Female Greenland sharks reach sexual maturity at 150 years old. Greenland sharks grow to a similar size as great whites; they live in cold water and can live up to 400 years.

258) In 2009, physicist Stephen Hawking threw a champagne party for time travelers. He didn't put out invitations until after the party; if someone showed up, he hypothesized that it would be proof of time travel. No one came.

259) Goats can develop accents. Researchers found that a goat's accent changes as they age and move in different groups; this disproves the idea that their voices are entirely genetic and suggests that most mammals can develop an accent from their surroundings.

260) Limpet teeth are the strongest natural material known to man. Limpets are small, snail-like creatures; a single spaghetti strand of their teeth material could hold 3,300 pounds.

261) Japan has the shortest national anthem. "Kimigayo" is the title of Japan's four-line national anthem; it is one of the world's oldest anthems and has a total of 32 characters, running a length of eleven measures.

262) Louisa Adams and Melania Trump are the only two U.S. first ladies born outside the United States.

263) If you sneeze while driving at 60 mph, your eyes are closed for about 50 feet.

264) Only three people have died outside the earth's atmosphere; they were aboard *Soyuz 11* in 1971.

265) President John Quincy Adams believed the earth's core was hollow and signed off on an expedition to explore it; the expedition never took place.

266) Four national anthems have no words: Spain, Bosnia and Herzegovina, Kosovo, and San Marino.

267) The giraffe is the only animal born with horns; both male and female giraffes are born with two horn-like structures on their heads called ossicones that consist of hard cartilage.

268) Iguanas have three eyes. They have a third parietal eye on top of their head that can just distinguish light and dark.

269) Only 45% of the London Underground is underground.

270) Platypuses don't have a stomach; their gullet connects directly to their intestines.

271) Abolitionist Frederick Douglass was the most photographed American of the 19th century. He wanted to ensure a more accurate depiction of black Americans and sat for more than 160 portraits.

272) Victoria's Secret was created to be a store where men could feel comfortable buying lingerie for their female partners. The founder was embarrassed years earlier buying lingerie for his wife at a department store, where he felt like an intruder.

273) With a maximum elevation of 19,551 feet, the Saint Elias Mountains that run through southeastern Alaska, southwestern Yukon, and northwestern British Columbia are the world's highest coastal mountain range.

274) In an early form of air conditioning, ancient Romans piped cold aqueduct water through their houses.

275) In 1916 to save energy during WWI, Germany was the first country to implement daylight saving time.

276) Over the last 20,000 years, the size of the average human brain has shrunk by about 10%. There are no clear answers why.

277) The fossa ovalis is the depression in the right atrium of the heart that is a result of our fetal development. An unborn child receives oxygen from its mother, so the blood goes directly from the right to the left atrium through the foramen ovale. After birth, the opening closes, creating the fossa ovalis.

278) In the Middle Ages, most people were illiterate and would sign documents with an x and then kiss it to show their sincerity; this is likely why the letter x became the symbol for a kiss.

279) Flamingos can only eat when their head is upside down.

280) Insecticides were the first product sold in aerosol spray cans.

281) Diarrhea is the second leading cause of death among children under the age of five; it kills more children than AIDS, malaria, and measles combined.

282) Mordhau is a German swordsmanship technique where you hold the sword inverted with both hands gripping the blade and hit the opponent with the pommel or cross-guard. The sword acts as a mace or hammer; the technique was mainly used in armored combat.

283) Texas has more colleges than any other state.

284) Forty-three buildings in New York City are so big that they have their own ZIP Code.

285) Barcelona, Spain, has hundreds of playgrounds for seniors that are designed to promote physical fitness and provide social interaction.

286) Female domestic cats are significantly more likely to be right paw dominant, and male cats typically favor their left paw. Cats don't seem to have an overall preference for right or left, and researchers theorize their preferences are linked to neural differences.

287) President Thomas Jefferson hated public speaking and only made two speeches, which were both inaugural speeches and hardly audible, during his entire eight-year presidency.

288) Sixty-three years before Jackie Robinson's major league debut, Moses Fleetwood Walker became the first African American to play Major League Baseball. He had his major league debut on May 1, 1884, and played 42 games for the Toledo Blue Stockings before suffering an injury and returning to the minor leagues. The Blue Stockings were only in the major league for one season; in 1885, they moved back to the minor leagues for their last season.

289) Movie trailers originally played after the movie; that is why they were called trailers.

290) Eighty percent of the world's lawyers live in the United States.

291) Since 1994, all dogs are banned from Antarctica because they might introduce diseases that could transfer to the native seals.

292) Most Japanese schools don't employ janitors or custodians; they believe that requiring students to clean the school teaches respect and responsibility and promotes equality.

293) Smokey the Bear's original name was Hotfoot Teddy.

294) The word therein contains 10 words without rearranging any letters: the, there, he, in, rein, her, here, ere, therein, and herein.

295) Sergio Leone originally wanted Henry Fonda to play the lead in *A Fistful of Dollars* but couldn't afford his salary. Many actors turned down the role before Clint Eastwood accepted and was paid $15,000 for the role.

296) The dot over the letter "i" is called a tittle.

297) Roman gladiator bouts only resulted in death about 10 to 20% of the time. The bouts were generally not intended to be to the death; gladiators were expensive, and promoters didn't want to see them die needlessly.

298) Vincent Van Gogh only sold one painting while he was alive.

299) The whooping crane is the tallest North American bird; it can be over five feet tall.

300) An orchestra usually tunes up to the oboe; its sound is easy to hear, and its pitch is more stable than strings.

301) The first concept of the atom was developed in the 5th century BC. Greeks Leucippus and Democritus called these particles "atomos," meaning indivisible, and the modern word atom is derived from this term.

302) Your purlicue is the skin connecting your fingers and thumb.

303) The original oranges from Southeast Asia were a tangerine-pomelo hybrid, and they were green. Oranges in warmer regions, such as Vietnam and Thailand, still stay green through maturity.

304) When John Chapman, better known as Johnny Appleseed, planted thousands of apple trees, they weren't intended for eating. The apples on those trees were much more bitter than the ones you would typically eat and were intended to be made into hard apple cider.

305) Firefighters use chemicals to reduce the surface tension of water, so it is easier to spread and soak into objects. It is known as wet water.

306) Adjusted for inflation, *Home Alone* (1990) is the highest-grossing comedy of all time in the United States.

307) The termite queen lives longer than any other insect. They have been known to live for at least 50 years, and some scientists believe they may live to 100.

308) In ancient Greece, a normal jury had 500 people.

309) At 83.7 degrees north latitude, Kaffeklubben Island, also known as Coffee Club Island, is the world's northernmost island and point of land. It is a very small island off the northern tip of Greenland.

310) In 1867, Alaska was purchased from Russia for two cents per acre.

311) Red is the most common color on national flags.

312) Founded about 6000 BC, Plovdiv, Bulgaria, is the oldest city in Europe.

313) Based on land area, Jacksonville, Florida, is the largest city in the 48 contiguous states; it occupies 758 square miles.

314) The most searched tutorial on YouTube is how to kiss.

315) The lungs are the only human organ that can float in water; they contain about 300 million balloon-like structures called alveoli that replace the carbon-dioxide waste in your blood with oxygen.

316) Chinese checkers originated in Germany in 1892.

317) Hexakosioihexekontahexaphobia is the fear of the number 666.

318) Despite her family ruling Egypt for about 270 years before her reign, Cleopatra was the first in her family to learn Egyptian.

319) The manchineel tree, which is native to tropical southern North America and northern South America, is extremely toxic in all forms. Its milky white sap contains skin irritants that can cause blistering, even from standing beneath the tree during rain. Burning the tree can cause eye injuries, and the fruit is potentially fatal, producing internal bleeding.

320) The metal part of a pencil that holds the eraser in place is called the ferrule.

321) George Bernard Shaw and Bob Dylan are the only two people to win both a Nobel Prize and an Oscar. Shaw won the 1925 Nobel Literature Prize and the 1939 Best Adapted Screenplay Oscar for *Pygmalion*; Dylan won the 2001 Best Original Song Oscar for "Things Have Changed" from *Wonder Boys* and the 2016 Nobel Literature Prize.

322) Due to lava flows from the Kilauea volcano, the Big Island of Hawaii is getting 42 acres larger each year.

323) Casu marzu is a traditional Sardinian sheep milk cheese that contains live maggots. The maggots are put into the cheese to promote fermentation

and break down the cheese's fats. The cheese has a very soft texture, and the maggots appear as translucent, white worms. If the maggots in the cheese have died, aficionados consider it unsafe to eat the cheese, so only cheese with living maggots is usually eaten.

324) *Meet the Press* is the longest-running television show of any kind in the United States; it started in 1947.

325) Bulls don't see red. Cows, including bulls, are generally red-green colorblind; they are reacting to the motion of the fabric and not the color.

326) On a section of Route 66 in New Mexico, grooves in the road play "America the Beautiful" if you go over them at the speed limit of 45 mph.

327) Parts of Canada have less gravity than they should. Since gravity is a result of mass, varying densities of the earth at different locations can affect it. However, the Hudson Bay region of Canada has a larger variation; the average resident weighs about a tenth of an ounce less than they would weigh elsewhere. The explanation appears to be the melting of the two-mile-thick Laurentide Ice Sheet, which started melting about 21,000 years ago and is almost gone. The ice sheet left an indent in the earth, which means less mass and less gravity.

328) Adjusted for inflation, *The Exorcist* (1973) is the highest-grossing R-rated movie of all time in the United States.

329) In 1991, the world's first webcam was created to check the status of a coffee pot at Cambridge University.

330) Charlie Chaplin didn't release his first film with sound until 13 years after the first talkie.

331) Wi-Fi doesn't stand for anything. It doesn't mean wireless fidelity or anything else; it is just a branding name.

332) "In God We Trust" didn't become the official U.S. national motto until 1956.

333) Until about 10,000 years ago, all humans had brown eyes. A genetic mutation at about that time produced blue eyes.

334) Traffic roundabouts have 16 points of conflict where there are chances to hit a pedestrian or another car; comparatively, a four-way intersection has 56. That is why roundabouts are safer than regular intersections, and by avoiding excessive stopping, they also speed up travel.

335) Only about 8% of the world's currency exists as physical cash; the rest is in electronic accounts.

336) Alaska has 130 out of the 169 active U.S. volcanoes.

337) Australia has the world's largest feral camel herd, as many as 1 million camels at one point. They were imported in the 19th century, and many were later set free as the automobile took over; they now roam freely with no natural predators.

338) In 18th century England, pineapples were so rare and such a status symbol that a single pineapple could sell for today's equivalent of $8,000, and you could rent a pineapple for the evening to show off to guests.

339) All the gold ever mined in the history of the world would fit in a 67-foot cube.

340) On *The Lucy Show* in 1962, Vivian Bagley was the first regular character on U.S. television that was a divorcee.

341) The toy company Mattel originally sold picture frames and later dollhouse furniture.

342) It wasn't always pink for girls and blue for boys; it was even reversed at one time. Pink for girls and blue for boys didn't take hold until the middle of the 20th century. Earlier, it was common practice for children to wear gender-neutral, mostly-white clothing. When department stores started marketing gender-specific colors, some early advertising suggested pink for boys since it was considered a stronger color and blue for girls since it was more delicate and daintier.

343) While on an African safari in 1954, Ernest Hemingway survived two plane crashes in two days.

344) If you measure from base to summit, Hawaii's Mauna Kea is the world's tallest mountain. Measured from the seafloor where it starts, Mauna Kea is about 33,500 feet tall, almost 4,500 feet taller than Mount Everest, but it only reaches 13,796 feet above sea level.

345) A kangaroo word is a word that contains its own synonym with the letters in the correct order; for example, chocolate contains the synonym cocoa, and masculine contains the synonym male.

346) Cats have fallen from heights as great as 32 stories and survived. The cat that fell 32 stories had a chipped tooth and collapsed lung but went home two days after the fall. Researchers believe that cats instinctively know how to fall; for shorter falls up to about seven stories, cats don't reach terminal velocity and try to land feet first. For higher falls above seven stories where they reach terminal velocity, they splay their limbs out like a parachute and land on their belly, increasing the chance of a collapsed lung or broken rib but greatly reducing the chance of a broken leg.

347) Solitaire is the world's most widely played card game.

348) There are so many possible iterations of a game of chess that no one has been able to calculate it accurately. In the 1950s, mathematician Claude Shannon came up with what is known as the Shannon Number, which estimates the possible iterations between 10^{111} and 10^{123}. In comparison, there are 10^{81} atoms in the known universe.

349) The American television series *Royal Pains* (2009-2016) featured the second-largest private home ever built in the United States. The mansion that the character Boris Kuester von Jurgens-Ratenicz lived in is the 109,000-square-foot Oheka Castle in West Hills, New York, which was built from 1914 to 1919 for Otto Hermann Kahn.

350) Bobby Jones and Tiger Woods are the only golfers that have held all four major championships at the same time.

351) When dissolved in water, small concentrations of Viagra can double the shelf life of cut flowers, making them stand up straight for as long as a week beyond their natural lifespan.

352) The kori bustard is the heaviest bird capable of flight. They are from Africa and can weigh more than 40 pounds.

353) Tokyo, Japan, has more millionaires than any other city.

354) A penny dropped from the 1,250-foot Empire State Building wouldn't kill a bystander below. Due to air resistance, the penny would reach its maximum speed after falling only about 50 feet. When it reached the ground, it would only be moving 25 mph, enough to hurt but nowhere near enough to kill.

355) Scroop is the sound from the rustling of silk or similar cloth.

356) The asshole is the first part of the human body to form in the womb, so every human starts as an asshole; some just stay that way.

357) Ancient Rome had 24 hours in a day, but the hours varied in length based on the time of year. They ensured that there were 12 hours of daylight and 12 hours of darkness, adjusting the length of the hours accordingly.

358) Pepperoni is an American creation of the early 20th century.

359) Less than 1% of dreams contain smell, taste, or pain elements. Most dreams contain visual and movement features, and half of all dreams contain auditory elements.

360) Duncan Hines (1880–1959) was a real person; he was an American pioneer of restaurant ratings for travelers.

361) Despite its western fame, the Pony Express was only in operation for 18 months (April 1860 to October 1861). The route ran from St. Joseph, Missouri, to Sacramento, California, and could transport a letter over 1,800 miles in 10 days.

362) Killer whales are dolphins and not whales; they are the largest member of the dolphin family. The physical similarities with dolphins include teeth, streamlined bodies, rounded heads, and beaks; they also use echolocation, live in pods, and hunt in groups.

363) A rhinoceros horn is made of hair.

364) The praying mantis is the only insect that can turn its head.

365) At the age of 18, President George H. W. Bush was the youngest naval aviator in U.S. history.

366) In old age, human brains shrink by 10-15%; whereas, chimpanzees, our closest primate relatives, show no brain shrinkage with age. Researchers believe it may be due to extended longevity in humans that brain evolution hasn't kept up with.

367) Apples, peaches, and raspberries belong to the rose plant family.

368) Annapolis, Maryland, is the only state capital that was once the national capital.

369) New York City's Wall Street area is named after a barrier built by the Dutch in the 17th century to protect against Indian attacks.

370) An aircraft's black box flight recorder is orange.

371) The average American golf course consumes 312,000 gallons of water per day.

372) Of the world's 25 highest peaks, 10 are in the Himalayas.

373) The word "computer" is referenced as far back as the early 1600s, but it originally meant a person who did arithmetic calculations. It didn't take on its meaning of being a machine until the late 1800s, and it wasn't an electronic device until the mid-1900s.

374) In 1890, Wyoming became the first state to give women the right to vote; as a territory, it had given women the right to vote in 1869.

375) Pablo Picasso's full name was Pablo Diego José Francisco de Paula Juan Nepomuceno María de los Remedios Cipriano de la Santísima Trinidad Ruiz y Picasso.

376) Up until 1954, traffic stop signs in the United States were yellow.

377) While in the White House, Calvin Coolidge had a pet raccoon. The raccoon was a gift and was supposed to be served for Thanksgiving dinner. Coolidge made it a pet and walked it on a leash on the White House grounds.

378) French leader Charles de Gaulle had the nickname "The Great Asparagus"; he got the name in military school because of his looks.

379) Humans have as many hairs per square inch as chimpanzees. Many of our hairs have gotten so fine or are so lightly colored that they are not very visible.

380) The elephant has the longest pregnancy of any mammal, up to 22 months.

381) Bangkok, Thailand, is the world's most visited city; London is second.

382) Agatha Christie is likely the best-selling author in history; she has sold 2 to 4 billion copies.

383) In 1951, *I Love Lucy* was the first U.S. television show to end while it was still at the top of the Nielsen Ratings.

384) The magma chamber of hot and partly molten rock beneath Yellowstone National Park is large enough to fill the 1,000 cubic mile Grand Canyon 11 times over.

385) In the tiny Russian village of Tsovkra-1, every able person can walk a tightrope; the tradition began more than 100 years ago.

386) The meteorologist that first named hurricanes named them after politicians he didn't like, so he could make disparaging comments about them wreaking havoc, etc.

387) Before 1687, clocks didn't have minute hands.

388) *Alice's Adventures in Wonderland* was originally banned in China and other parts of the world because some people objected to the animal characters using human language. They felt it wasn't right to put animals on the same level as humans.

389) The longest English words with no repeating letters are two 15-letter words, uncopyrightable and dermatoglyphics.

390) Lincoln Elementary School is the most popular school name in the United States.

391) In humans, the glabella is the skin between the eyebrows and above the nose.

392) In 1956, Betty Nesmith, the mother of Michael Nesmith of The Monkees pop group, invented Liquid Paper correction fluid in her kitchen. She worked as an executive secretary at a bank and began using white tempera paint to cover up typing mistakes. After perfecting the formula, she named it Liquid Paper and began marketing it herself. In 1979, she sold the rights to the Gillette Corporation for $47.5 million, plus royalties on future sales.

393) The harmonica is the world's best-selling musical instrument.

394) In 1859 in what was labeled the Pig War, the United States and Great Britain nearly went to war over a pig. A few years earlier, the Oregon Treaty had been signed, ending a border dispute between the United States and Britain. Citizens of both countries lived on San Juan Island, off the coast of what is now Washington state, and a pig belonging to the British wandered onto the land of an American farmer and was shot and killed. Tensions spread to the rest of the community, and the governor of British Columbia sent three warships to the area. The two sides continued to escalate over the following month until British Navy Admiral Robert L. Baynes arrived and ended things by saying that he would not go to war over a pig.

395) Due to segregation considerations, the Pentagon's designers included 284 bathrooms, twice the number needed for the anticipated staffing. However, President Franklin Roosevelt issued an executive order banning segregation in federal buildings before the building was open, so it opened as a desegregated facility and was for a time the only desegregated building in Virginia since state laws required segregation.

396) *The Cisco Kid* (1950-1956) was the first television series filmed in color. It was filmed in color from its first season, but its broadcasts were still black and white at the time.

397) Since the origin of humans, the sun has only finished 1/1250th of an orbit around the center of the Milky Way Galaxy.

398) Hippos don't really swim; they walk underwater. If they are submerged, they don't swim back to the surface; they just walk on the bottom until they reach shallower water. They can hold their breath for five minutes or longer.

399) Wisconsin is known as the Badger State because lead miners in the 1830s lived in temporary caves cut into the hillsides that became known as badger dens, and the miners who lived in them were known as badgers.

400) The ant has the highest brain-to-body-weight ratio of any animal. Some species have a ratio of 14-15%; comparatively, human brains are only about 2.5% of body weight.

401) The medical name for the human butt crack is the intergluteal cleft.

402) In ancient Ireland, sucking a king's nipple was a sign of submission.

403) A cockroach can live a week without its head. They are not dependent on their head or mouth to breathe, but they will eventually die without it because they can't drink and die of thirst.

404) If you wanted to dig a hole straight through the center of the earth and end up in China, you would have to start in Argentina.

405) The Argentinosaurus is possibly the largest and heaviest land animal that ever lived. In 1987, their fossils were discovered in Argentina; they were up to 115 feet long and probably weighed 70-85 tons. They existed 92-100 million years ago during the Cretaceous period.

406) September is the most popular birth month in the United States; the time between September 9 and September 20 contains a majority of the 10 most popular birthdates. September is popular due to Christmas holiday conceptions.

407) Future president Theodore Roosevelt delivered an 84-minute campaign speech after being shot just before the event. He was shot as he stood up in an open-air automobile and waved his hat to the crowd; fortunately, the bullet was slowed by his dense overcoat, steel-reinforced eyeglass case, and 50-page speech squeezed into his jacket pocket. X-rays showed the bullet lodged against Roosevelt's fourth right rib on an upward path to his heart.

408) Woolsey Hall auditorium at Yale University still has an extra-wide seat built for William Howard Taft. After his presidency, Taft taught at Yale, and they installed several special chairs with extra-wide seats to accommodate his size, well over 300 pounds. One of the chairs is still in use in Woolsey Hall today; it is balcony seat E-9.

409) In 1950, Diners Club was the first universal credit card that could be used in a variety of places.

410) In 1979, actor Paul Newman finished runner-up in the Le Mans 24-hour auto race.

411) Berlin still hasn't gotten back to its pre-WWII population.

412) To stop dementia residents from leaving, many nursing homes in Germany have fake bus stops.

413) The earliest known reference to a vending machine is in 1st century Egypt. It dispensed holy water; when a coin was deposited, it fell on a pan attached to a lever that opened a valve and let some water flow out. The pan continued to tilt with the weight of the coin until it fell off, and a counterweight snapped the lever up and turned off the valve.

414) Without its mucus lining, your stomach would digest itself. Stomach ulcers are areas where the stomach begins to digest itself.

415) Fireflies are a species of beetle.

416) The terms uppercase and lowercase originated in early print shops. The individual pieces of metal type were kept in boxes called cases; the smaller, more frequently used letters were kept in a lower case that was easier to reach; the less frequently used capital letters were kept in an upper case.

417) At 710 miles long, Borneo's Kapuas River is the longest river located on an island.

418) In 1883, American poet Emma Lazarus wrote the words that are engraved on the Statue of Liberty; it was part of an effort to raise money for the statue's pedestal.

419) In ancient Greece, throwing an apple at someone was a declaration of love.

420) In Germany, you can't name your child Matti because it doesn't indicate gender. Germany has laws regarding the naming of children, such as the name must indicate gender and must not negatively affect the child's well-being.

421) As referenced in the Bible, myrrh is a gum resin from trees.

422) Research has shown that most mammals on average live for about 1.5 billion heartbeats. Larger animals have slower heartbeats, so they live longer. Humans used to fit the pattern, but with health and medical improvements, we last longer than our size predicts. At 60 beats per minute, 1.5 billion heartbeats would be 47.5 years.

423) The Maine state flower isn't a flower; it is the white pinecone and tassel.

424) In case they need to comfort a child during a traumatic experience, every Dutch police car is equipped with a teddy bear.

425) The character of Rudolph the Red-Nosed Reindeer was created as part of a 1939 Montgomery Ward holiday coloring book.

426) President Theodore Roosevelt was the first American to earn a judo brown belt.

427) *Pocahontas* was the first Disney animated film based on the life of a real person.

428) You will be the last person to die in your lifetime.

429) On January 25, 1979, Robert Williams was the first human killed by a robot. He died when he was hit in the head by a mechanical arm at a Ford Motor Company casting plant.

430) The United States has been at war in about 93% of the calendar years it has existed.

431) Dudley Do-Right's horse was named Horse.

432) Statistically, the deadliest job in America is U.S. president; four presidents have been assassinated in office.

433) The longest English word with one syllable has nine letters; there are several words: scratched, screeched, stretched, straights, strengths, etc.

434) Mahatma Gandhi first employed nonviolent civil disobedience to fight for Indian civil rights in South Africa. At age 23, he went to South Africa to work and spent 21 years there before returning to India in 1915.

435) In the 1932 Los Angeles Olympics, the men's steeplechase finalists ran an extra 364 yards because the race official lost track of the laps, and the entire field ran an extra lap.

436) John F. Kennedy was the first president who was a Boy Scout.

437) Gold is so malleable that you could create a wire one micron thick that would stretch around the world with just 20 ounces of gold. One ounce, about the size of a quarter, can be beaten into a continuous sheet of about 100 square feet.

438) Dogs usually use their right ear when listening to other dogs, but they use their left ear when they hear threatening sounds.

439) Humans, killer whales, and short-finned pilot whales are the only animal species known to go through menopause.

440) In 1804, Alexander Hamilton was shot and mortally wounded by Aaron Burr in a duel in the same location where his eldest son was shot and mortally wounded in a duel three years earlier.

441) The blood-red sky in Edvard Munch's famous painting *The Scream* is believed to be due to the 1883 Krakatoa volcanic eruption, rather than the artist's imagination. The dust from the eruption created a red sky in Norway that Munch witnessed.

442) An ultracrepidarian is a person who expresses opinions on matters outside the scope of their knowledge or expertise.

443) Over 80 women worldwide have been elected or appointed head of their country.

444) In 1963, Elizabeth Taylor was the first film star to earn $1 million for a single film for *Cleopatra*.

445) In 1917, Montana's Janette Rankin became the first woman elected to the U.S. Congress.

446) In 2019, Robert Fink received the last Western Union telegram ever delivered; he received it 50 years after it was sent and 13 years after Western Union shut down its telegram business. The telegram congratulated him on his 1969 college graduation and had been lost in old filing cabinets until someone found it and tracked him down to deliver it.

447) The part of a sundial that casts the shadow is called a gnomon, meaning indicator in Greek.

448) President Ulysses S. Grant was arrested and taken into custody for speeding with a horse and buggy in Washington, D.C. The police seized his horse and buggy, and he paid a fine and walked back to the White House.

449) Water polo is the only sport where teams may defend goals of different sizes. The goal at the deep end is smaller than the goal at the shallow end. The inner sides of the goalposts are always 10 feet apart, but when the water depth is 5 feet or more, the crossbar is 3 feet from the water surface, and when the water depth is less than 5 feet, the crossbar is 8 feet from the floor of the pool.

450) South America has more Roman Catholics than any other continent.

451) A polar bear can swim 60 miles without stopping.

452) Patty Duke is the youngest person to have a self-titled U.S. television show. She was 16 years old when *The Patty Duke Show* debuted in 1963.

453) The term "sweat like a pig" comes from the iron smelting process and has nothing to do with pigs sweating. Molten iron was poured into molds with ingots branching off a central channel that reminded people of piglets suckling on a sow, so the iron became known as pig iron. When the pig iron was cool enough to transport, it would sweat from air condensation, giving the term "sweat like a pig."

454) J.R.R. Tolkien coined the word tween in *The Hobbit*; he used it to describe Hobbits in their reckless age period.

455) At up to 19 feet long, the king cobra is the largest venomous snake.

456) On January 23, 1916, Browning, Montana, experienced the greatest temperature variation ever recorded in 24 hours. It had a 100-degree change, from a high of 44 degrees to a low of -56 degrees Fahrenheit.

457) Andrew Johnson is the only U.S. president who made his own clothes; he had been a tailor's apprentice and opened a tailor shop. He made his own clothes for most of his life.

458) In 1957, *Leave It to Beaver* was the first U.S. network primetime television program to show at least part of a toilet. At the time, television standards and practices didn't allow showing a toilet; they could show the toilet tank if they didn't show the bowl.

459) The sound you hear when you hold a seashell to your ear is surrounding environmental noise resonating in the seashell cavity. In a soundproof room, you don't hear anything when you hold a seashell to your ear.

460) Finland has more heavy metal bands per capita than any other country.

461) In WWII, Italy declared war on both Germany and the Allies. One month after surrendering to the allies, Italy declared war on Germany, its former ally.

462) Eleanor of Aquitaine is the only woman who married the kings of both France and England. She married Louis VII of France and Henry II of England.

463) George Washington is the only U.S. president who did not represent a political party when he was elected.

464) A female rat can mate as many as 500 times in six hours and can do that about 15 times per year.

465) If you don't swing your arms while walking, it requires about 12% more effort to walk; in terms of energy expended, it is equivalent to walking about 20% faster.

466) In 2012, scientists discovered a new species of ant that appears to live exclusively in New York City. The ant was discovered in the Broadway medians at 63rd and 76th streets and is called the ManhattAnt. They believe it has evolved to adapt to its warmer, drier, concrete-covered environment.

467) Maine is the only state with a one-syllable name.

468) One of the world's largest living things is Pando, a clonal colony of quaking aspen. It occupies 106 acres and weighs an estimated 6,600 tons, with a single massive root system estimated to be 80,000 years old. A clonal colony is a group of genetically identical individuals that have grown in a given location from a single ancestor; Pando is in the Fishlake National Forest in Utah.

469) Archaeologists have tracked Lewis and Clark's route based on their poop. Mercury-laced laxatives were popular during the Lewis and Clark era, and traces of mercury can be detected for centuries. By testing old latrine sites for mercury, researchers can determine which ones the adventurers visited. They have connected about 600 sites to the expedition.

470) Mexico has the highest annual average hours worked of any country.

471) Under the Articles of Confederation, there were eight U.S. presidents before George Washington; each served a one-year term.

472) In 1942, a German V2 rocket was the first man-made object in space; 62 miles above sea level qualifies as space.

473) The 1883 eruption of Krakatoa is the loudest sound in recorded history; it ruptured people's eardrums 40 miles away and was clearly heard 3,000 miles away.

474) In 1517, Martin Luther didn't likely dramatically nail his 95 Theses to the church door. There is no historical evidence that Luther posted the theses on the church door, and the story didn't appear until 30 years after. He did mail the 95 Theses to the archbishop. Luther was a devout Catholic, and he never intended to start a revolution; he simply wanted the clergy to recognize their corruption.

475) *Marty* (1955) is the only film based on a television show to win the Best Picture Oscar.

476) Turkeys are called Hindi, meaning from India, in the country of Turkey.

477) In the largest free rock concert ever held, Rod Stewart played to 4.2 million people on Copacabana Beach in Rio de Janeiro, Brazil, on New Year's Eve 1994.

478) China's Tibet region has the world's highest elevation asphalt road at 18,258 feet.

479) The letter J is the only letter that doesn't appear in the periodic table of elements.

480) The only two countries where Coca-Cola isn't sold are Cuba and North Korea.

481) At 7,000 feet elevation, Santa Fe, New Mexico, is the highest elevation state capital.

482) Play-Doh was created as a wallpaper cleaning putty to remove coal dust in the 1930s.

483) President Woodrow Wilson holds the record with over 1,000 rounds of golf played while he was in office.

484) In terms of production volume, tomatoes are the world's most popular fruit.

485) Jamais vu is the opposite of déjà vu; it's the feeling you get when you experience something you are already very familiar with, but it feels completely new to you like it is your first time.

486) Marguerite Norris was the first woman to have her name engraved on the Stanley Cup. In 1952, she became the first female chief executive in NHL history after inheriting the Detroit Red Wings presidency from her father, James Norris Sr. In 1954, the Red Wings defeated the Montreal Canadiens in the finals, and she became the first woman to have her name engraved on the Stanley Cup.

487) In 2014 when Queen Elizabeth II visited the *Game of Thrones* set in Belfast, Northern Ireland, she declined an opportunity to sit on the Iron Throne because there is an old tradition that prohibits the reigning English monarch from even sitting on a foreign throne.

488) Good King Wenceslas was king of Bohemia, the current Czech Republic.

489) Established in 1636, Harvard didn't offer calculus classes for the first few years because calculus hadn't been invented yet.

490) The oceans are 71% of the earth's surface but only account for 0.02% of the earth's mass.

491) There is only one species of insect native to Antarctica, the Antarctic midge.

492) The Eiffel Tower is the world's most-visited paid monument.

493) George Burns is regarded as the first television entertainer to step out of character and break the fourth wall by talking directly to the television audience on *The George Burns and Gracie Allen Show* (1950-1958).

494) At 243 Earth days, Venus has the longest day of any planet in our solar system.

495) Austrian psychologist Julius Wagner-Jauregg won the 1927 Nobel Prize for Medicine for curing syphilis by giving people malaria. In the first half of the 20th century, it was found that certain medical conditions could be cured by creating a fever in the patient; this was known as pyrotherapy. Wagner-Jauregg was experimenting with the treatment of mental illness by induced fever; he was working with patients with dementia paralytica caused by syphilis and found that fever could cure syphilis. He used the least aggressive malaria parasite since it produced long, high fevers. The treatment was dangerous, killing up to 15% of patients, but syphilis at the time was a terminal disease, and it was viewed as an acceptable risk since malaria could later be treated with quinine.

496) Penguins and flightless cormorants are the only two birds that can swim but can't fly.

497) Of the earth's total water, 96.5% is in the oceans.

498) In 1891 when electricity was first installed at the White House, President Benjamin Harrison and his wife were so afraid of being electrocuted that they never touched the light switches; they always had staff turn the lights on and off.

499) The only U.S. soil that Japan occupied during WWII were two remote Aleutian Islands; between June 1942 and August 1943, the United States battled Japan to retake the islands.

500) The king of hearts is the only king in a standard card deck that doesn't have a mustache.

Facts 501-1000

501) The slow loris is the only known venomous primate. They are nocturnal and live in southeast Asia, and if they lick a gland under their arms and combine it with their saliva, they have a toxic bite.

502) Napoleon Bonaparte wrote a romance novel called *Clisson et Eugénie*. It was a fictional account of the doomed romance of a soldier and his lover and was based on Bonaparte's relationship with Eugenie Desiree Clary.

503) Spain kept the discovery of chocolate a national secret for nearly a century.

504) The narwhal and walrus are the only two sea creatures with ivory tusks.

505) Actress Hedy Lamarr was also a famous inventor. At the beginning of World War II, she was involved in developing spread spectrum and frequency hopping technology, whose principles are incorporated into today's Bluetooth, CDMA, and Wi-Fi technologies.

506) Tuvalu is the least visited country. At 10 square miles, it is the fourth-smallest country and is located across nine islands in the Pacific Ocean midway between Hawaii and Australia. It has about 2,000 visitors annually.

507) Wombats are marsupials and have a pouch that opens to the rear, rather than towards the head; they dig extensively, so a forward-facing pouch would fill up with dirt.

508) Made from steel wool saturated with soap, the S.O.S Soap Pad stands for "save our saucepans." The inventor's wife came up with the name; the period at the end was left off, so the name wasn't identical to the distress signal and could be trademarked.

509) Since the end of WWII, Canada has had a policy where it has named thousands of its unnamed lakes after fallen soldiers from all three branches of the Canadian armed forces.

510) In 1909, the world's first mile of concrete highway was built in Wayne County, Michigan.

511) The world's first true ATM debuted at a Barclay's Bank branch in London on June 27, 1967; ATMs wouldn't become common until at least 1990.

512) Human babies only blink once or twice per minute; on average, adults blink about 10 times per minute.

513) An adult blue whale's tongue weighs 6,000-8,000 pounds, about the same as a small elephant.

514) Early 18th-century pirate Benjamin Hornigold once attacked a merchant ship just to steal the crew member's hats. His men had gotten drunk the night before and threw their hats overboard.

515) Male horses have more teeth than females. Males typically have 40 teeth; females have 36; the difference is that males usually have four canine teeth located between the front incisors and the cheek teeth. Females don't usually have canine teeth.

516) The mandrill is the largest species of monkey; they are found mostly in tropical rainforests in southern Cameroon, Gabon, Equatorial Guinea, and the Congo and can weigh up to 120 pounds.

517) The world's smallest natural trees are dwarf willows that grow in Greenland and are only about two inches high.

518) Liechtenstein is the world's biggest exporter of false teeth.

519) Florida is the only state on the east coast that falls partly in the Central Time Zone.

520) From 1912 to 1948, the modern Olympics included music, painting, poetry, literature, and architecture.

521) In golf, a score of four-under-par on a single hole is called a condor. There have only been four verified; all were a hole-in-one on a par-five hole.

522) Dry cleaning isn't dry. Clothes are completely immersed in a liquid solvent; it is called dry cleaning because there isn't any water.

523) Of the seven wonders of the ancient world, only the Great Pyramid of Giza still exists. The Lighthouse at Alexandria was the last wonder to disappear; it was toppled by earthquakes in the early 14th century, and its ruined stones were carried off by the late 15th century.

524) Coronated in 1928, King Zog of Albania was Europe's only Muslim king.

525) Detartrated is the longest palindrome word in English; palindromes are the same forward and backward.

526) Pronoia is the opposite of paranoia; it is a feeling that a conspiracy exists to help you.

527) Queen Elizabeth II is the longest-reigning British monarch; she surpassed her great-great-grandmother Victoria's reign in 2015.

528) In the 1956 Melbourne Olympics, the equestrian events took place in Stockholm, Sweden. Australia had a strict six-month quarantine for horses entering the county and would not change it for the Olympics, so Stockholm was selected as the alternate venue for the equestrian events.

529) In Disney's *Snow White and the Seven Dwarfs*, Snow White is 14 years old.

530) When the Mona Lisa was stolen from the Louvre in 1911, Picasso was questioned as a suspect.

531) The Nile crocodile has the greatest bite force of any animal; it can bite down with 5,000 psi.

532) To smell more attractive to females, male goats urinate on their heads.

533) When multiple-story apartments were first built, the rich lived on the ground floor and not on the upper floors. When the Romans first built 9-10 story apartment buildings, wealthier people lived on ground floors since higher floors wouldn't typically have running water or bathrooms and required climbing multiple flights of stairs. It wasn't until the elevator came about in the late 1800s that upper floors became status symbols.

534) At up to 38 pounds, the trumpeter swan is the heaviest North American flying bird.

535) Cockroaches have existed for about 350 million years; they were around 120 million years before dinosaurs.

536) On the animated television show *The Simpsons*, only God and Jesus have five fingers; all other characters have four.

537) Gerald Ford is the only Eagle Scout to become U.S. president.

538) At the 1908 Olympics, dueling was a demonstration sport. Two male competitors fired at each other with dueling pistols loaded with wax bullets. The competitors wore protective equipment for the torso, face, and hands.

539) The brand name WD-40 stands for Water Displacement, 40th formula. The chemist who developed it was trying to create a product to prevent corrosion by displacing water.

540) A jellyfish's mouth also serves as its anus.

541) Jupiter's red spot is a storm that has been shrinking for 150 years; it was once large enough to fit more than three Earths. The spot is growing taller as it gets smaller.

542) Movie theaters make about 85% of their profits from concessions; they must share ticket revenue with movie distributors.

543) James Dean only made three films: *Rebel Without a Cause*, *East of Eden*, and *Giant*.

544) According to legend, Attila the Hun died of a nosebleed on his wedding night.

545) For humans, your blood makes up about 8% of your body weight.

546) The average Major League Baseball game lasts almost 3 hours, but it only has about 18 minutes of action if you include balls in play, stolen base attempts, pitches, running batters, pickoff throws, etc. If you just include balls in play and runner advancement attempts, there are less than 6 minutes of action.

547) In the human body, a limbal dermoid is a cyst in the eye formed in the womb when skin cells get misplaced in the eye. The cyst can grow hair, cartilage, sweat glands, and even teeth.

548) Maryland was the first state to adopt an official sport; in 1962, they named jousting as their official sport.

549) John Quincy Adams was the first president to serve in the U.S. Congress after his presidency.

550) Dogs have 13 blood types; humans only have four.

551) The Macy's Thanksgiving Day Parade used to intentionally release the giant inflatable balloon characters into the sky after the parade. The very first balloons would pop quickly, but in 1929, they added safety valves, so the helium would slowly leak out, allowing the balloons to float for days. They also tagged the balloons with return addresses, so they could be sent back to Macy's, who would reward the finders with gifts. After the 1932 parade when a balloon wrapped around an airplane's wing sending it into a tailspin, they quit releasing the balloons; luckily, there were no fatalities.

552) Besides his moose strength, Bullwinkle Moose's great talent was that he could remember everything he ever ate.

553) Paper cuts hurt more than other cuts for a combination of reasons. They most often occur on the tips of the fingers, which have more pain receptors than almost anywhere else in the body, and paper edges aren't as smooth as they appear and can leave a rough cut. Finally, paper cuts aren't deep enough to trigger some of the body's defense mechanisms like blood clotting and scabbing, so the damaged nerve endings remain exposed.

554) The original jeans had four pockets - the tiny one in front, plus two more on the front, and one in the back. The tiny pocket was designed to hold a pocket watch.

555) President Barack Obama collected Spiderman and Conan the Barbarian comic books.

556) Quasars are the most luminous objects in the known universe. They are highly luminous radio galaxies with a supermassive black hole; the nearest known quasar is 600 million light-years away.

557) In 1908, cellophane was invented as a cloth to repel liquids after the inventor saw wine spilled on a tablecloth.

558) In your lifetime, your long-term memory can hold about 1 quadrillion bits of information.

559) The Titanoboa is the largest snake ever known to have existed; it lived about 60 million years ago and was up to 42 feet long and weighed up to 2,500 pounds.

560) The Canadian province of Alberta is the world's largest rat-free populated area. The government has had very aggressive rat control measures since the 1950s, and only the brown rat is capable of surviving in the prairie region and must still overwinter in buildings.

561) Mississippi is the only state that doesn't have an open bottle law prohibiting drivers or passengers from drinking while driving. If the driver maintains a blood alcohol content below the 0.08% legal limit, it is legal to drink and drive.

562) For a few seconds, a horse can generate about 15 hp; for sustained output over hours, a horse can generate about 1 hp.

563) Elvis Presley memorized every line from *Patton*, his all-time favorite movie.

564) During the American Civil War, Tiffany's supplied the Union army with swords and surgical instruments.

565) Of all the animal species scientists have studied, domestic cats are the only one that shows no outward signs of conciliatory behavior.

566) At the 1976 Summer Olympics, Princess Anne was the only female athlete not given a sex test.

567) The airport in Genoa, Italy, limits liquids to three ounces but makes an exception for pesto sauce, a Genoa specialty. They have a special pesto scanner.

568) The word ukulele means jumping flea, likely after the movements of the player's fingers.

569) A human fart travels about 7 mph.

570) Flyting was a poetic exchange of insults practiced between the 5th and 16th centuries. The exchange of insults could get quite rude, including accusations of cowardice or sexual perversion.

571) In Finland, the amount you are fined for a speeding ticket is based on your annual income; fines as high as 112,000 euros have been assessed for speeding with a multi-million-euro income.

572) When a flea jumps, its acceleration is so intense that it must withstand 100 times the force of gravity. Humans pass out at about 5 times the force of gravity.

573) CarRentals.com, CheapTickets, Expedia.com, HomeAway, Hotels.com, Hotwire.com, Orbitz, Travelocity, and Trivago are all owned by the same company, Expedia Group.

574) Stephen Girard was one of the wealthiest men in American history, and he saved the United States from financial collapse during the War of 1812. He placed most of his assets at the disposal of the government and underwrote about 95% of the war loans.

575) Sweat doesn't smell. The smell is caused by bacteria on your skin that break the sweat down into acids. Deodorants work by killing the bacteria on your skin that does this; antiperspirants work by temporarily plugging the sweat glands, reducing the amount of sweat.

576) Brunch was invented in 1895 by English writer Frank Beringer. He wrote that waking up early was no fun for those who had been out late on Saturday nights, and brunch around noon was the best place for these people to gather and share their experiences.

577) Time passes faster for your face than it does for your feet. The difference is much too small for humans to perceive, but technically, time passes faster at higher elevations because the pull of the earth's gravitational field is weaker. Researchers have proven the effect with height differences of less than one meter.

578) North Dakota is the geographic center of North America.

579) Christopher Columbus' three ships weren't likely called the Nina, Pinta, and Santa Maria. In the 15th century, most sailing ships were named after saints, so Santa Maria is likely the real name, but Nina and Pinta were probably sailor nicknames. Nina's real name was most likely Santa Clara; Pinta's real name is unknown.

580) Scarlett O'Hara's real first name in *Gone with the Wind* is Katie; Scarlett is her middle name.

581) The United States doesn't have an official language.

582) The United States borders three oceans: the Atlantic, Pacific, and Arctic. Alaska's northern border is on the Arctic Ocean.

583) Under the 5th amendment to the U.S. Constitution, you can't be forced by police to unlock a phone with a password, but you can be forced to unlock it with a fingerprint. A fingerprint isn't protected under the amendment since it is something you have rather than something you know.

584) About 95% of Americans are sleeping at 3:00 a.m., more than at any other hour.

585) *The Simpsons* has been the longest-running primetime scripted show on U.S. television longer than any other show in history; it has been the longest-running show since July 1998.

586) Owls can't move or roll their eyes because their eyes aren't round; they are elongated and held in place by a bony structure in the skull.

587) If you have a buccula, you have a double chin.

588) The Mona Lisa is painted on wood, a thin poplar panel.

589) The sun orbits around the center of the Milky Way Galaxy at a speed of 536,865 mph.

590) Octopus blood is blue. It contains a copper-rich protein that carries oxygen instead of the iron-rich protein in other animals.

591) Up until 800 years ago, New Zealand was undiscovered and devoid of humans.

592) In 1978, Czech Vladimir Remek was the first person in space who wasn't American or Russian.

593) Almost 100% of kangaroos are left-handed.

594) Five presidents regularly wore beards while in office: Abraham Lincoln, Ulysses S. Grant, Rutherford B. Hayes, James A. Garfield, and Benjamin Harrison.

595) Until 2018, "Don't be evil" was the unofficial corporate motto of Google.

596) Depending on the type of impulse, nerve signals in the human body travel at different speeds. Muscle position impulses travel at speeds up to 266 mph; pain signals travel much slower at only 1.4 mph; touch signals travel at 170 mph. You feel the touch that produces the pain 2-3 seconds before you feel the associated pain.

597) More country names begin with "A" than any other letter; there are 11 countries: Afghanistan, Albania, Algeria, Andorra, Angola, Antigua and Barbuda, Argentina, Armenia, Australia, Austria, and Azerbaijan.

598) The caribou (or reindeer) is the only animal species where females have antlers.

599) Deion Sanders is the only person to ever play in the Super Bowl and World Series.

600) Canada has a larger inland water area than any other country.

601) Between 1838 and 1960, most of all photos taken were of babies.

602) The television sitcom *Happy Days* originated the term "jumped the shark" for when a show takes a sharp drop in quality or has inserted desperate attempts for ratings. During the season five opening episode, Fonzie jumped a shark while water skiing, marking the beginning of a sharp decline in the show's quality.

603) Lucille Ball was the first woman to run a major television studio. Starting in 1962, she ran Desilu Studio, which produced many popular shows, including *Mission Impossible* and *Star Trek*.

604) Agatha Christie called her character Hercule Poirot "a detestable, bombastic, tiresome, egocentric little creep."

605) The color of an egg has nothing to do with nutrition, quality, or flavor. In general, white-feathered chickens with white earlobes lay white eggs, and reddish-brown-feathered chickens with red earlobes lay brown eggs.

606) Australian Barry J. Marshall couldn't convince the scientific community that the H. pylori bacteria caused gastritis and stomach ulcers, so he drank the bacteria himself and developed gastritis within two weeks, proving his theory. He went on to win the 2005 Nobel Prize in Physiology or Medicine for his work.

607) Ronald Reagan's pet name for Nancy was mommy poo pants.

608) Horseshoe crabs have 10 eyes spread all over their body; they have eyes on top of their shell, on their tail, and near their mouth.

609) While floating in lunar orbit, astronaut Al Worden became the most isolated human ever. While in the *Apollo 15* command module, he was 2,235 miles from the nearest human.

610) Pocahontas was the first woman to appear on U.S. paper currency; in 1865, she appeared on the back of the $20 bill.

611) Your right ear is better at receiving sounds from speech, and your left ear is more sensitive to sounds of music.

612) Cleopatra spoke as many as a dozen languages and was educated in mathematics, philosophy, oratory, and astronomy. She is often portrayed as being an incomparable beauty and little else, but there is also evidence that she wasn't as physically striking as once believed.

613) Bookkeeper and bookkeeping are the only two English words with three consecutive double letters.

614) Twelve American prisoners of war were killed in the Hiroshima atomic bomb blast.

615) When accused of being two-faced, Abraham Lincoln said, "If I had two faces, would I be wearing this one?"

616) If you drilled a hole straight through the center of the earth to the other side and jumped in, it would take 42 minutes to get to the other side. You would accelerate until you got to the center and then decelerate until you got to the other side, where your speed would be zero again.

617) Russia has 36 rivers over 600 miles long; more than any other country.

618) In some circumstances, female dragonflies fake death to avoid mating. The process is called sexual death feigning; a female dragonfly will drop to the ground, as if dead, to avoid an overly aggressive male. Scientists found that it worked about 60% of the time.

619) Oregon has the only two-sided (different designs on each side) state flag.

620) U.S. First Lady Eleanor Roosevelt refused secret service coverage and was given her own gun.

621) Since 1993, tear gas has been banned in warfare, but it is still used in U.S. domestic law enforcement.

622) Each year, 15,000 to 18,000 new animal species are discovered; about half are insects.

623) Cleopatra was Greek.

624) Some snakes, Komodo dragons, sharks, and turkeys are capable of virgin births.

625) In 1880, Wabash, Indiana, was the world's first electrically lighted city.

626) A Munchausen number, also known as a perfect digit-to-digit invariant, is a natural number that is equal to the sum of its digits each raised to the power of itself. For example, 3,435 is a Munchausen number because $3{,}435 = 3^3 + 4^4 + 3^3 + 5^5$. In base 10 numbers, there are only four Munchausen numbers: 0, 1, 3435, and 438579088.

627) If not limited to the major parties, over 200 women have run for U.S. president.

628) In 1957, bubble wrap was invented by sealing two shower curtains together with some air pockets between them; it was originally intended to be used as wallpaper.

629) Spices come from every part of a plant other than the leaf; herbs are the leaf itself.

630) The night Abraham Lincoln was assassinated he had a bodyguard, but he had left his post to have a drink at the Star Saloon next to Ford's Theatre. John Frederick Parker was the police officer assigned to guard Lincoln and was initially seated outside the president's box. To be able to see the play, he moved to the first gallery, and at intermission, he joined Lincoln's footman and coachman for drinks next door. It isn't clear if he returned to the theater at all, but he wasn't at his post outside the president's box when Lincoln was shot by John Wilkes Booth. Ironically, Booth had been at the same saloon working up his courage. In November 1864, the Washington police force created the first permanent detail to protect the president; it was made up of four officers. The Secret Service did not begin protecting the president until 1901 after the assassination of President William McKinley.

631) Rhinotillexomania is excessive nose picking.

632) In 1938, *Snow White and the Seven Dwarfs* was the first movie ever to release a soundtrack recording.

633) President Warren G. Harding was known for his gambling and once lost a set of priceless White House china on a bet.

634) The flute is the oldest surviving musical instrument; 43,000-year-old flutes have been found.

635) By volume, the world's largest pyramid is in Mexico; the Great Pyramid of Cholula has a base of 450 meters on each side and a height of 66 meters.

636) The term blockbuster has meanings going back to large bombs in WWII, but as it is used to describe films, it was first used for *Jaws* (1975).

637) Between 1853 and 1859, New York spent $7.4 million buying the 843 acres for Central Park; comparatively, in 1867, the United States spent $7.2 million to buy Alaska, which is 424 million acres.

638) The United Kingdom has the longest official name of any country; its official name is the United Kingdom of Great Britain and Northern Ireland.

639) Borborygmus is the sound of a stomach growling, gurgling, or rumbling caused by gas moving through the intestines.

640) Overmorrow is the day after tomorrow.

641) In 1893, Thomas Edison built the world's first film studio.

642) Functional buttons with buttonholes for fastening or closing clothes first appeared in the 13th century.

643) Manon Rheaume was the first woman to appear in an NHL game. In September 1992, she goaltended for the Tampa Bay Lightning in a pre-season game against the St. Louis Blues.

644) Canada eats the most donuts per capita of any country; the presence of 3,000 Tim Hortons restaurants is a major factor.

645) Alaska has the largest water area of any state; it has 94,743 square miles of water.

646) At a maximum depth of 25,217, the Caribbean is the deepest sea.

647) Janis Joplin, Jimi Hendrix, and Kurt Cobain all died at age 27.

648) Cows, sheep, and goats don't have upper front teeth; they have a thick layer of tissue called a dental pad where you would expect incisors. They use it along with their bottom teeth to pull out grass.

649) The U.S. film industry relocated from New York to Los Angeles largely because of Thomas Edison, who held many patents on the production and showing of movies and controlled the industry. To get away from his control, filmmakers escaped to Los Angeles.

650) Originating in Missouri in 1811 and 1812, a series of earthquakes raised the soil beneath the Mississippi River and temporarily changed its course, causing it to flow backward.

651) For sedation, natural redheads require about 20% more anesthesia. They also require more topical anesthetics, but they need lower doses of pain killers and seem to be less sensitive to electric shock, needle pricks, and stinging pain. Both parents must pass along a recessive trait for their child to have red hair; the trait is also responsible for skin color and for midbrain function that determines pain response.

652) Catfish have more taste buds than any other animal. They have over 100,000 taste buds, both in their mouth and all over their body; humans have about 10,000.

653) In psychology, the tendency for people to believe they are above average is called the Lake Wobegon effect from Garrison Keillor's *A Prairie Home Companion*.

654) Adolf Hitler was a Roman Catholic.

655) In 1987, Aretha Franklin was the first woman inducted into the Rock and Roll Hall of Fame.

656) Only one time in NHL history has a goalie been credited with scoring a goal against an opposing goalie (not an empty-net goal). On March 21, 2013, in a game between the New Jersey Devils and Carolina Hurricanes, a delayed penalty was called against New Jersey, and Carolina goalie Dan Ellis headed for the bench for an extra attacker. After he left the crease, the Hurricanes accidentally sent the puck the length of the ice back toward their empty net; Ellis tried to race back but was too late. Because Devils goalie Martin Brodeur had been the last Devils player to touch the puck, he was given credit for the goal, and because Ellis was on the ice when the puck went in, the goal went on his record.

657) Badminton is the fastest racquet sport; the shuttlecock can travel over 200 mph.

658) Antarctica is the windiest continent.

659) President George H. W. Bush played in the first two College World Series baseball tournaments.

660) By slowing their heart rate, sloths can hold their breath for 40 minutes.

661) Planck time is the smallest named time interval; it is the length of time required for light to travel a Planck length, about 5.39×10^{-44} seconds.

662) The Maldives is the lowest elevation country; it is composed of 1,200 mostly uninhabited islands in the Indian Ocean with a maximum elevation of six feet.

663) *It's a Wonderful Life* (1946), *Miracle on 34th Street* (1947), and *The Bishop's Wife* (1947) are the only three Christmas movies ever nominated for the Best Picture Oscar.

664) Lucy, a star in the constellation Centaurus 50 light-years away, is about 90% crystallized carbon, making it a 10-sextillion-carat diamond.

665) Morocco has the world's oldest continuously operating university; it has existed since 859 AD.

666) In the original book *The Wonderful Wizard of Oz*, Dorothy's slippers are silver, not ruby.

667) Studies have shown that the shape of an animal's eye pupil are evolutionary adaptations based on whether it's a predator or prey and how low to the ground the animal is. Circular pupils tend to belong to predators; rectangular pupils belong to grazing prey and provide a wider field of vision to see predators. Rectangular pupils also allow more light in without absorbing too much light from above the head, so grazing animals can see the grass and their surroundings better. For predators, the proximity to the ground seems to dictate whether an animal has round or vertical pupils. Vertical pupils, like snakes and small cats, can expand much more than round pupils and provide more light for nocturnal activity and greater depth perception, but the advantages diminish as the animal gets further away from the ground. This may be why larger cats and humans have round pupils.

668) Presidents John Tyler, Millard Fillmore, Andrew Johnson, Chester A. Arthur, and Gerald Ford never had a public inauguration and address. All five ascended to the presidency after the death or resignation of a president; they weren't elected president.

669) Snickers is the world's best-selling candy bar.

670) A baby blue whale gains about 200 pounds of weight each day.

671) Studies have shown that people over age 60 have a 14% higher chance of dying on their birthday than on any other day. Due to increased stress on birthdays, heart attacks, strokes, falls, and suicides are all more likely.

672) According to research by Johns Hopkins, medical errors rank as the third-leading cause of death in the United States, behind heart disease and cancer.

673) The average person spends about six years of their life dreaming.

674) The term sniper originates from how hard it is to shoot the snipe bird.

675) *Gone with the Wind* has sold more tickets than any other movie in the United States. About 208 million tickets have been sold; in 1939 when it was released, the U.S. population was 131 million.

676) The goose was the first bird domesticated by man more than 4,000 years ago in Egypt.

677) Mary Edwards Walker is the only woman ever awarded the U.S. medal of honor; she received it for her service in the American Civil War. She was a surgeon at a temporary Washington, D.C., hospital and was captured and arrested as a spy after crossing enemy lines to treat wounded civilians.

678) The word muscle comes from the Latin musculus, meaning little mouse; a flexed muscle was thought to resemble a mouse.

679) Most members of the nightshade family, such as tomatoes, potatoes, eggplants, and green peppers, contain small quantities of nicotine.

680) In 1968, the United States adopted the 911 emergency phone number; the first call was made in Haleyville, Alabama.

681) The whale shark is the largest current-day shark; they are up to 41 feet long and 47,000 pounds.

682) In 1881, the United States had three presidents. Rutherford B. Hayes started the year as president and was succeeded by James A. Garfield in March after his election. Chester A. Arthur, Garfield's vice president, became president in September after Garfield's assassination.

683) At 22,595 feet elevation, Ojos Del Salado, on the Chile and Argentina border, is the world's highest active volcano.

684) William Howard Taft was the heaviest U.S. president; when he left office, he weighed about 340 pounds.

685) The ancient Romans used human urine as a mouthwash. It was supposed to purge bacteria, and physicians claimed it whitened teeth and made them stronger. Upper-class women paid for bottled Portuguese urine since it was supposed to be the strongest on the continent.

686) Ted Kaczynski was called the Unabomber because his early targets were universities (un) and airlines (a).

687) At the first modern Olympics, silver medals were awarded to the winners; second place received bronze medals.

688) With speeds up to 188 mph, jai-alai has the fastest moving ball of any sport.

689) Historians estimate that Genghis Kahn may have been responsible for as many as 40 million deaths. During his lifetime, the population of China fell by tens of millions, and he may have reduced the entire world population by up to 11%.

690) President Rutherford B. Hayes was the first American to own a Siamese cat. The cat was a gift to the president and first lady from the American consul in Bangkok.

691) Pork is the world's most widely-eaten meat; poultry is second; beef is third.

692) The McMurdo Dry Valleys of Antarctica are the driest place on Earth; they are a row of snow-free valleys that haven't seen water in millions of years.

693) In the 18th century, a footman or valet was also sometimes called a fart catcher because they always walked behind their master or mistress.

694) Ironically, dentists helped popularize cotton candy. In 1897, machine-spun cotton candy was invented by John C. Wharton, a candy maker, and William Morrison, a dentist. They called it fairy floss and sold thousands of servings at the 1904 St. Louis World's Fair. In 1921, Joseph Lascaux, a dentist, patented another machine and was the first to use the name cotton candy.

695) The coldest temperature ever recorded on Earth was -128.56 degrees Fahrenheit on July 21, 1983; it was at Antarctica's Vostok station.

696) Most streets in Japan don't have a name. Instead, blocks are given a number, and buildings or houses within the block have a number. The house or building number is typically assigned by the order they were built, so building number 1 might be right next to building number 13.

697) The bison is the U.S. national animal.

698) A group of owls is called a parliament.

699) In 1982, the movie *TRON* was not considered for a visual effects Oscar because they felt the filmmakers had cheated by using computers.

700) At age 29, Adrien Brody is the youngest Best Actor Oscar winner for *The Pianist* (2002).

701) The pope can't be an organ donor. According to the Vatican, his body belongs to the Catholic Church and must be buried intact.

702) Alligators are only naturally found in the United States and China.

703) Originally, people bowed to the U.S. president; Thomas Jefferson was the first president to shake hands rather than bow.

704) Before electricity and gas lamps, it was common for people to wake in the middle of the night, splitting their sleep into two periods. When they woke, people would engage in different activities and then go back to sleep. People went to bed much earlier, and there was no prestige or value placed on staying up late by candlelight; even the wealthy, who could afford candlelight, felt there were better ways to spend their money.

705) Since at least the 1500s, chocolate has been used as medicine. The Aztecs brewed a drink from cacao and tree bark to treat infections. Children with diarrhea received a drink made from the grounds of cacao beans and other roots. A 1552 text lists a host of ailments cacao could treat including angina, fatigue, dysentery, gout, hemorrhoids, and dental problems.

706) Romania has the world's heaviest building. Bucharest's Palace of Parliament is 276 feet high, covers an area of 1.41 square miles, has a volume of 2.55 million cubic meters, and weighs about 9 billion pounds. After the Pentagon, it is the world's second-largest building by surface area.

707) Of cities of 5 million or more population, Singapore is closest to the equator; it is 85 miles north of the equator.

708) Instead of soap, the ancient Greeks used olive oil to clean themselves; they rubbed it into their skin and then scraped it off along with dirt and dead skin.

709) Of cities of 1 million or more population, Quito, Ecuador, is closest to the equator; it is 15.9 miles south of the equator.

710) About 7% of all the people that have ever lived are alive today. The total human population historically is estimated at over 108 billion.

711) Fish yawn, cough, and burp.

712) Monaco's orchestra is bigger than its army.

713) Tristan da Cunha Island, a British overseas territory in the South Atlantic Ocean, is the world's most remote inhabited island. It is approximately 1,511 miles off the coast of Cape Town, South Africa. The island is 38 square miles and is only accessible via a six-day boat trip from South Africa.

714) Eigengrau is the name for the dark-gray color the eyes see in perfect darkness as a result of optic nerve signals.

715) The ostrich is the only animal with two kneecaps on each knee.

716) Australia has about 965,000 square miles of desert, more than any other country.

717) The first patented work uniform in the United States was the Playboy Bunny outfit.

718) Jumping beans jump because there is a moth grub moving around inside the bean.

719) In 1799 when he died, George Washington's distillery produced nearly 11,000 gallons of whiskey, making it one of the largest whiskey distilleries in America at the time.

720) Due to the U.S. Electoral College, you could theoretically win the presidential election with only 23% of the popular vote. This requires winning the required 270 electoral votes in the smallest electoral vote states by one vote in each state and not getting any votes in the largest electoral vote states.

721) John Cazale is the only actor to appear in multiple films and have every one nominated for the Best Picture Oscar; he appeared in *The Godfather*, *The Conversation*, *The Godfather Part II*, *Dog Day Afternoon*, and *The Deer Hunter*.

722) Roger Maris' 61 home runs in 1961 are still the American League record for most home runs in a season; the seasons that have surpassed his record have all been in the National League.

723) John B. Kelly Sr. won 1920 Antwerp Olympic gold medals in the single and double sculls and a 1924 Paris Olympic gold medal in the double sculls; he was also the father of actress Grace Kelly, who became Princess of Monaco in 1956.

724) Based on oxygen usage, the jellyfish is the most efficient swimmer of any animal. Jellyfish use 48% less oxygen than any other known animal; they never stop moving.

725) The story of Cinderella originated in China.

726) In the original script for the movie *Back to the Future*, the time machine wasn't a DeLorean; it was a refrigerator.

727) Via the world's longest continuous train route, you can travel from Portugal to Vietnam, covering over 10,700 miles and 17 countries in 13 days.

728) Owls have three eyelids; they have one for blinking, one for sleeping, and one for keeping their eyes clean.

729) In 1925, Nellie Tayloe Ross became the first female U.S. state governor; she won a special election after her husband, Wyoming Governor William Ross, died.

730) Ice hockey originated in the United Kingdom. There are references to similar games being played on ice in England, Scotland, and Ireland 200 years before the first documented game in Canada.

731) Human testicles hang outside the body because sperm dies at body temperature.

732) Almost 1% of the world's population eats at McDonald's each day.

733) To allow turtles to cross safely and avoid railway delays, Japanese railways have started installing shallow tunnels under the rail tracks.

734) Along with being a world-famous escape artist, Harry Houdini was an aviation pioneer; in 1910, he made the first controlled powered flight of an airplane in Australia.

735) Canada has more than 2 million lakes, more than the rest of the world combined.

736) The border between the United States and Mexico is the world's most frequently crossed international border.

737) The Faroe Islands have the most Nobel Prize winners per capita of any country. Located halfway between Norway and Iceland, it has one Nobel Prize winner out of a population of about 50,000.

738) Pantheism is the belief that the universe as a whole is God.

739) At up to 10 feet long and 250 pounds, the Komodo dragon is the world's largest lizard.

740) The average person spends three months of their life sitting on the toilet.

741) About 40% of the world's cultures engage in romantic kissing.

742) Ethiopia uses a calendar that has 13 months. Twelve months have 30 days each; the 13th month has five days in a normal year and six days in a leap year. They also celebrate Christmas on January 7.

743) In 1797, John Hetherington, who is often credited with inventing the top hat, caused a riot when he first wore it in public. He was charged with breaching the king's peace and ordered to pay a 50-pound fine. People had never seen a top hat before and were scared and started rioting.

744) In 1979, Sweden was the first country to ban corporal or physical punishment in all forms, including parental spanking.

745) While the first usage of the word "selfie" didn't occur until 2002, the world's first known selfie was taken in 1839. Robert Cornelius took the first

selfie inside his family's store in Philadelphia; he had to remove the camera's lens cap, run into frame, and hold his pose for a full minute.

746) Southern Florida is the only place in the world where alligators and crocodiles exist together naturally in the wild.

747) The Pacific Ocean side entrance to the Panama Canal is further east than the Atlantic Ocean side entrance.

748) Three countries are completely surrounded by one other country; Lesotho is surrounded by South Africa, and Vatican City and San Marino are both surrounded by Italy.

749) Almost 96% of passengers involved in aviation accidents survive.

750) In 1964 at age 62, Louis Armstrong was the oldest artist to have a number one hit on Billboard's Hot 100 with "Hello Dolly."

751) Both rubies and sapphires come from corundum, a very hard mineral composed of aluminum oxide. If it is red, it is a ruby; if it is any other color, it is a sapphire, although the most popular and valued sapphire color is blue.

752) Glass is neither a liquid nor a solid; it is an amorphous solid, a state somewhere between those two states of matter.

753) Africa has more French speakers than any other continent; it has about 120 million French speakers.

754) All the water on Earth would create a ball 860 miles wide.

755) The 1920 Antwerp Olympics was the only Olympics where a single event was held in two countries. The 12-foot dinghy sailing event's early races were held in Belgium, but the final two races were held in the Netherlands since the only two remaining competitors were Dutch.

756) Someone with oniomania is obsessed with shopping.

757) In 1897, Pearl B. Wait, a cough syrup manufacturer from Le Roy, New York, invented Jell-O by adding fruit syrup to gelatin, which was first created in 1682.

758) Time is the most used noun in the English language.

759) Facebook has a blue color scheme because its founder, Mark Zuckerberg, has red-green color blindness, and blue is the color he sees best.

760) About 5,500 WWII bombs are still discovered in Germany each year.

761) Early in his career, Picasso was so poor that he burned most of his early work to keep his apartment warm.

762) The word "set" has the most definitions of any English word. It has 464 definitions in the Oxford English Dictionary; the word "run" is second with 396 definitions.

763) Nearly half the world's population are lifetime abstainers of alcohol.

764) The movie *Ben-Hur* is based on a novel by Lew Wallace, an American Civil War general and governor of the New Mexico Territory. *Ben-Hur: A Tale of the Christ* was published in 1880 and was the all-time best-selling novel in the United States until the publication of *Gone with the Wind* in 1936.

765) The earth weighs about 13,170,000,000,000,000,000,000,000 pounds.

766) Bananas have a curved shape because they grow against gravity towards the sun; the process is called negative geotropism.

767) Fish odor syndrome is a genetic disease characterized by an offensive body odor and the smell of rotting fish due to the excessive excretion of trimethylaminuria (TMA) in the urine, sweat, and breath.

768) A pair of brown rats can produce 2,000 descendants in a year and up to 500 million descendants in three years.

769) Action-movie star Jackie Chan is also a pop star in his native China. In his youth, he attended the China Drama Academy, where he learned his acrobatic style of martial arts as well as singing and acting. He has produced over 20 different albums, including over 100 songs in five languages, and he won the 1984 Best Foreign Singer Award in Japan.

770) Jellyfish are the world's oldest multi-organ animals. They evolved 550 million years ago and have no brain or nervous system.

771) Horse racing's Triple Crown has only been won once in consecutive years; Seattle Slew and Affirmed won in 1977 and 1978.

772) In Elizabethan times, beards were taxed.

773) The heat of a bolt of lightning is about five times hotter than the surface of the sun.

774) Donald Trump was the inspiration for the character Biff Tannen, the bully in the movie *Back to the Future*.

775) Adult domestic cats only meow to communicate with humans. They don't meow to each other; it is thought to be a post-domestication extension of kittens mewing.

776) Humans have about 5 million olfactory receptors; dogs have about 220 million.

777) Sharks existed 200 million years before the dinosaurs and have changed relatively little.

778) Lake Malawi, located between Malawi, Mozambique, and Tanzania, has more fish species than any other freshwater lake. By volume, it is the world's fourth-largest freshwater lake and has at least 700 species of cichlid fish alone.

779) At some point in their life, about 1 in 8 American workers have worked at McDonald's.

780) Ulysses S. Grant was the first president to run against a woman candidate; in 1872, Virginia Woodhull was a nominee of the Equal Rights Party.

781) In Sanskrit, the word Himalayas means "house of snow."

782) The original name for Los Angeles was El Pueblo de Nuestra Señora la Reina de los Ángeles del Río Porciúncula.

783) The Danube River flows through more countries than any other river; it flows through 10 countries: Germany, Austria, Slovakia, Hungary, Croatia, Serbia and Montenegro, Romania, Bulgaria, Moldova, and Ukraine.

784) In 1781 under the Articles of Confederation, John Hanson became the first U.S. president. He was chosen by Congress and was in office for one year; the Articles of Confederation limited the president to a one-year term during any three years.

785) The Eskimo kiss of rubbing noses isn't really a kiss; it is called a kunik and is typically used as an expression of affection between an adult and a child. The Inuit kiss on the lips like many other cultures.

786) Table tennis balls were originally made from wine bottle corks.

787) At any given time, there are about 1,800 thunderstorms in progress around the world. About 18 million thunderstorms occur annually worldwide, with about 100,000 to 125,000 in the United States.

788) Seahorses are very bad swimmers. They propel themselves using a dorsal fin that beats 30-70 times per second. The tiny fin and awkward body shape make it difficult to get around, and they can easily die of exhaustion navigating in stormy water.

789) The Who is the only band to play at both Woodstock and Live Aid.

790) For racing purposes, the birthday of all horses in the Northern Hemisphere is January 1. A horse born on December 31 is one year old on January 1.

791) At up to 46 feet long, colossal squid are the largest invertebrate (no backbone) animal.

792) At 23.9 degrees south latitude, Sao Paulo, Brazil, is the world's southernmost urban area with a population of over 20 million.

793) Due to the television series *MacGyver*, the word MacGyver was added to the Oxford English Dictionary in 2015. As a verb, it means to make or repair an object in an improvised or inventive way, making use of whatever items are at hand.

794) Studies have shown that male rhesus macaque monkeys will pay to look at pictures of a female monkey's bottom. The male monkeys were willing to give up their juice rewards to look at the pictures, so it is akin to paying to look at images. They would also pay to look at images of high-ranking or powerful monkeys, just like people look at famous or powerful people.

795) Giraffes need the least sleep of any mammal; on average, they only sleep 30 minutes a day, just a few minutes at a time.

796) A susurration is a whisper or murmur.

797) Ancient Romans had a sewer goddess (Cloacina), a toilet god (Crepitus), and an excrement god (Stercutius).

798) In 1893, Grover Cleveland was the first president to have a child born in the White House.

799) Pandiculating is stretching and stiffening your trunk and extremities when fatigued, drowsy, or waking.

800) Virtually all barramundi fish are born male, and after two years, they turn into females.

801) India has more people living in rural areas than any other country.

802) The surface area of your lungs is about the same size as a tennis court.

803) Billiards, the forerunner to pool, was played on lawns, like croquet; that is why pool table felt is commonly green.

804) Due to the loss of players to military service in WWII, the NFL Pittsburgh Steelers and Philadelphia Eagles were forced to merge for the 1943 season. They formed the Steagles; official record books list the combined team as the Phil-Pitt Combine.

805) Abraham Lincoln was the first Republican president.

806) Even though the human sense of smell is not near as sophisticated as some animals, research estimates that the human nose can detect at least 1 trillion different scents.

807) At age 26, Edward Rutledge, a lawyer from South Carolina, was the youngest signer of the U.S. Declaration of Independence. Benjamin Franklin was the oldest signer at 70.

808) In 1925, the world's first motel opened in San Luis Obispo, California; the original room charge was $1.25 per night.

809) Horses can't breathe through their mouths. Except when swallowing, a soft palate blocks off the pharynx from the mouth.

810) Hans Island, in the middle of the Arctic, is claimed by both Canada and Denmark. The two countries periodically send a military mission to dismantle the other's flagpole and erect their own; they leave a bottle of Canadian whiskey or Danish schnapps for the other.

811) On the shores of Lake Huron, Canada's Wasaga Beach is the world's longest freshwater beach; it is 14 miles long.

812) Ophiophagy is the act of feeding on snakes; there are ophiophagous mammals, birds, lizards, and even other snakes.

813) England and Portugal are part of the world's oldest alliance that is still in effect, the 1373 Anglo-Portuguese Alliance.

814) Michelangelo hated painting the ceiling of the Sistine Chapel so much that he wrote a poem about it in 1509 that includes the following, "I've already grown a goiter from this torture, hunched up here like a cat in Lombardy (or anywhere else where the stagnant water's poison). My stomach's squashed under my chin, my beard's pointing at heaven, my brain's crushed in a casket, my breast twists like a harpy's. My brush, above me all the time, dribbles paint so my face makes a fine floor for droppings!"

815) Texas has 254 counties, the most of any state.

816) Fraser Clarke Heston, Charlton Heston's real son, played the infant Moses in *The Ten Commandments*.

817) Grawlix is a string of typographical symbols (e.g. %@$&*!) used in place of an obscenity.

818) The human ears and nose never stop growing.

819) McDonald's is by far the world's largest toy distributor; about 20% of its meals are Happy Meals with a toy.

820) Hummingbirds have the biggest brain relative to their body size of any bird. Their brain is over 4% of their body weight.

821) The letter j was the last letter added to the English alphabet. The letters i and j were treated the same for a long time until Italian Gian Giorgio Trissino made the distinction between them in 1525; j finally entered the alphabet in the 19th century.

822) Approximately 470 million years ago, Mount Everest was seafloor; it didn't become a mountain until about 70 million years ago when it was pushed up by plate tectonics.

823) The modern hula hoop came from bamboo hoops used for exercise by Australian children. The Wham-O founders noticed the popularity of the Australian product and began making plastic hoops.

824) In Mozambique, human honey hunters work with wild birds known as honeyguides. The hunters use calls to bring out the honeyguides, which find the beehives in the cavities of baobabs and other tall trees. The humans break open the hives, remove the honey, and leave behind the wax and larvae for the honeyguides, one of the few birds who can digest wax.

825) In 2018, researchers discovered a new human organ, the interstitium, that accounts for about 20% of your body weight. It is a network of fluid-filled spaces in connective tissues all over the body that hadn't been seen before.

826) First awarded in 1893, the Stanley Cup is the oldest championship in North American professional sports.

827) San Francisco's cable cars and the New Orleans Saint Charles streetcar line are the only two mobile U.S. national monuments.

828) By area, Michigan is 41.5% water, the highest percentage of any state.

829) President John Tyler had 15 children, the most of any U.S. president.

830) Over the last two centuries, each year has added about three months to average human life expectancy.

831) The device that would evolve into the chainsaw was developed as a childbirth aid. Around 1780, two doctors were trying to create something to help remove bone and cartilage from the birth canal to widen it during problematic childbirths. At the time, this method was preferred to caesarian sections and was done with a saw and knife. The early chainsaw developed for this purpose looked like a regular knife with a small chain around it that was operated by a hand crank.

832) Until the 1770s, de-crusted, moistened, and balled up bread was used to erase lead pencil marks.

833) In high enough doses, nutmeg is toxic and can induce hallucinations, convulsions, pain, nausea, and paranoia that can last several days. It typically takes two teaspoons or more to see toxic symptoms. Nutmeg comes from the seed of a tropical evergreen.

834) The fax machine is older than the telephone and was patented the same year the first wagon train crossed the Oregon Trail. In 1843, Scottish inventor Alexander Bain patented the Electric Printing Telegraph (fax), and the first commercial use of the machine was in France in 1865, 11 years before the telephone was invented and the year the American Civil War ended.

835) Worldwide, there are about 6,900 living languages. Just 6% of the languages account for 94% of the world's population. About half of the languages have fewer than 10,000 speakers, and one-quarter have fewer than 1,000 speakers.

836) Agatha Christie is the world's most widely translated author.

837) About 25% of Americans with two-car garages don't have room to park cars inside them.

838) Amen means "So be it" in Hebrew.

839) La Rinconada, Peru, a mining town at 16,700 feet in the Andes, is the world's highest elevation city and has about 30,000 residents.

840) Regardless of the job, Cuba has a maximum wage law of $20 per month.

841) Using a thin, flexible sheet of plastic, scientists have created a device that can collect electricity from snowfall. Snow is positively charged and gives up electrons; silicone is negatively charged and accepts the electrons. As snow lands on the silicone, a charge is produced and captured.

842) The television series *South Park* has a Guinness World Record for the most swearing in an animated television series.

843) The first U.S. car race ever was on Thanksgiving Day, November 27, 1895. The *Chicago-Times Herald* sponsored a 54-mile race from downtown Chicago to Evanston and back. The top speed of the winning car was 7 mph

844) The main reason for the character layout of the qwerty keyboard we use today is to prevent typewriter jams by placing often used keys further apart.

845) William Shakespeare is the only person to have their own Dewey Decimal classification.

846) Toilet paper traces its origins to at least 6th century China when it was first referenced in writings. Most people didn't use toilet paper until at least 1857 when American inventor Joseph Gayetty commercialized the product, much as we know it today.

847) Facebook is cited in one-third of American divorce filings.

848) Napoleon Bonaparte has been portrayed more often in films than any other real person.

849) Dogs aren't colorblind, but compared to humans, they only have 20% of the cone photoreceptor cells that control color perception. Dogs see in shades of yellow and blue and cannot see the range of colors from green to red, so dogs see the colors of the world as basically yellow, blue, and gray.

850) The Andes pass through seven countries, more than any other mountain range; they pass through Venezuela, Colombia, Ecuador, Peru, Bolivia, Chile, and Argentina.

851) When you die, some companies will put your ashes in fireworks, so you can go out with a bang.

852) Through nuclear fusion, the sun loses about 4.3 million tons of mass per second as it is transformed into energy.

853) The U.S. icon Uncle Sam was based on Samuel Wilson, a meatpacker during the War of 1812. He supplied barrels of beef to the army stamped with "U.S." for the United States, but soldiers started referring to it as Uncle Sam's.

854) Before modern shoes, people walked toe first, which allows you to test the surface in front of you and puts less stress on your knees. Modern shoes allow you to step harder heel first.

855) Ronald Reagan was the first U.S. president to have been divorced.

856) W is the shortest three-syllable word in English. The letters of the alphabet are generally also considered words since they are nouns referring to the letter.

857) Until 2011, Russia legally defined any beverage containing less than 10% alcohol as a foodstuff, so beer was considered a soft drink.

858) Since 1863, Norway has published all personal tax returns for everyone to see; you can see total income and total taxes for anyone. In 2014, they added the restriction that the person whose information is being requested will be notified of who is looking; this has resulted in far fewer inquiries.

859) The baobab tree can store up to 32,000 gallons of water in its trunk. Various species are native to Africa, Australia, and India; they can grow to almost 100 feet tall with a trunk diameter of up to 36 feet and can live for thousands of years. Because it stores such large volumes of water in its trunk, elephants, eland, and other animals chew the bark during dry seasons.

860) King Nebuchadnezzar, who built the Hanging Gardens of Babylon, is the best-known historical sufferer of the psychological disorder boanthropy, where the sufferer believes they are a cow or ox. In the Book of Daniel, Nebuchadnezzar "was driven from men and did eat grass as oxen."

861) In 1930, Louis Armstrong was one of the very first celebrities arrested for drug possession. He described marijuana as "a thousand times better than whiskey," and in 1930, he and his drummer were arrested after police caught them smoking marijuana outside the Cotton Club in California. He served nine days in jail but continued using marijuana regularly for the rest of his life.

862) The NFL Green Bay Packers get their name from the Indian Packing Company. Curly Lambeau, the team founder, got his employer to sponsor the team on the condition that he named them the Packers.

863) President James Buchanan was morally opposed to slavery but believed it was protected by the constitution, so he bought slaves with his own money and freed them.

864) In 16th century France, women could sue their husbands for erectile dysfunction. The trials could involve examinations of the genitals to prove that the man could achieve an erection or even evidence that the couple could consummate their marriage by forcing a husband and wife to have sex in front of witnesses. Divorce was largely forbidden, but producing children was viewed as a marital responsibility, so if a man could not, it was viewed as an act against religion and a reason to re-evaluate the marriage.

865) If you fly directly south from Detroit, Michigan, you will hit Canada. You will fly over Windsor, Ontario, before re-entering the United States.

866) Chinese prostitute Ching Shih (1775-1844) is widely regarded as the greatest pirate ever. At the height of her power, she controlled more than 1,500 ships and 80,000 sailors, one of the largest naval forces in world history. She robbed and taxed towns and plundered ships along the South China Sea coast.

867) In 1989, *Spy Magazine* sent out small checks to some of the wealthiest and most famous people to see who would cash them. They first sent out checks for $1.11 to 58 people; 26 people cashed them. They sent a second check for $0.64 to the 26 people who cashed the first check; 13 people cashed the second check. They sent a third check for $0.13 to the 13 people who cashed the second check; only 2 people, a Saudi Arabian arms dealer and Donald Trump, cashed the third check.

868) In the movie *Jaws*, Quint describes the WWII sinking of the *USS Indianapolis*. After four days in the water, only 317 of the original 1,196-man crew were rescued. Estimates of how many died due to shark attacks range from a few dozen to 150; it is the U.S. Navy's single worst loss at sea and the worst shark attack in recorded history.

869) Queen Alexandra's birdwing is the largest butterfly. Females can have a wingspan over 11 inches and weigh over an ounce; they are native to Papua New Guinea.

870) Since 1869, over a million people have been buried on Hart Island, which has served as the burial place for New York City's unclaimed bodies. The island is at the western end of Long Island Sound and is one mile long by one-third mile wide.

871) A blue whale's pulse is 8-10 beats per minute.

872) The primary difference between our current Gregorian calendar and the prior Julian calendar is that years evenly divisible by 100 are not leap years unless they are also evenly divisible by 400. This corrects for the Julian calendar's length of the year inaccuracy.

873) When mating, flatworms compete to see which one can inject sperm into the other; the winner becomes the father; the loser becomes the mother. Flatworms are hermaphroditic, having both male and female reproductive organs.

874) Due to behavioral differences, men are five times more likely than women to be hit by lightning.

875) Famed WWII General George S. Patton placed fifth in the 1912 Olympics pentathlon.

876) Eleven states have land farther south than the most northern part of Mexico: Alabama, Arizona, California, Florida, Georgia, Hawaii, Louisiana, Mississippi, New Mexico, South Carolina, and Texas.

877) In 868 AD, the earliest woodblock-printed paper book was the Chinese book *Diamond Sutra*, which was created almost 600 years before the Gutenberg Bible. It was the first book printed on a mechanical press.

878) Mercury and Venus are the only two planets in our solar system that don't have moons.

879) Wombats are the world's only animal with cube-shaped poop. It appears to be due to the irregular shape and elasticity of their intestines.

880) The first published use of the word hello was in 1827. Hello is a relatively recent word and was initially used to attract attention or express surprise; it didn't get its current meaning until the telephone arrived.

881) Russia's Trans-Siberian Railway has 3,901 bridges along its 5,772 miles.

882) The national animal of Scotland is the unicorn.

883) Leonardo da Vinci first proposed the concept of contact lenses.

884) Alfred Nobel made his money to establish the Nobel Prizes through his invention of dynamite; he wanted to make up for all the destruction his invention had caused.

885) William Henry Harrison's term as U.S. president was just 31 days, the shortest of any president. On inauguration day, he caught a cold that turned into a fatal case of pneumonia. His grandson, Benjamin, would later also be president.

886) Theodore Roosevelt was the first president to leave the United States while in office; he went to Panama to inspect the canal construction.

887) The Yukon River is the third-longest river in the United States; it starts in British Columbia, Canada, and runs 1,979 miles, flowing through Alaska.

888) In 1920, Polish businessman, beautician, entrepreneur, and inventor Max Factor coined the word makeup.

889) Since the late 1990s, Oscar-winning actor J.K. Simmons has been the voice of the Yellow Peanut M&M.

890) The cheerleader effect is a bias that causes people to think that individuals are more attractive when they are in a group, likely due to the averaging out of unattractive idiosyncrasies.

891) One million people live under the streets of Beijing, China, in bomb shelters built during the Cold War. When tensions eased, the government leased the bunkers to landlords.

892) In 1869, Rutgers and Princeton played the first college football game. There were 25 players on each side and one-point touchdowns; the first team to reach six points was declared the winner. Rutgers beat Princeton 6-4.

893) Just before he sold the script for *Rocky*, Sylvester Stallone was so poor that he sold his dog for $50; one week later, he bought it back for $3,000.

894) The largest named bottle of wine is Melchizedek; it has a volume of 30 liters, equivalent to 40 standard 750 ml wine bottles.

895) From the Late Cretaceous period, the Quetzalcoatlus is the largest known flying animal ever. It had a wingspan up to 36 feet and may have weighed as much as 500 pounds.

896) Matthias was the apostle that replaced Judas Iscariot.

897) The megalodon shark is thought to be the largest shark ever. It became extinct about 2.6 million years ago and was up to 59 feet long and 65 tons.

898) On average, a U.S. dollar bill only lasts about 18 months before it needs to be taken out of circulation and replaced.

899) Less than a year before Abraham Lincoln was assassinated, his oldest son, Robert, was saved from being hit by a train by Edwin Booth, the brother of John Wilkes Booth.

900) Elvis Presley's only three Grammy awards were for gospel music. Most of his main work was before the Grammys existed.

901) Bears have the best sense of smell of any land animal. Black bears have been observed traveling 18 miles in a straight line to a food source; grizzlies can find an elk carcass underwater, and polar bears can smell a seal through three feet of ice.

902) The United States has the most domestic cats of any country; China has the second most.

903) By volume, Russia's Lake Baikal is the world's largest freshwater lake. It has a maximum depth of 5,387 feet and contains about 20% of the world's total unfrozen surface fresh water.

904) Chuck Berry's only number-one hit was "My Ding-a-ling."

905) Papua New Guinea has the largest number of languages spoken of any country; it has about 850 languages, one for every 8,000 citizens.

906) The longest English words with their letters in alphabetical order have six letters, such as abhors, almost, begins, biopsy, chimps, and chintz.

907) Of any non-microscopic animal, the blanket octopus has the largest size difference between males and females. Females are 10,000 to 40,000 times larger than males; females can be 6.5 feet in length; males are 1 inch.

908) The English language is not native to Britain; it is a Germanic language and was brought to Britain by Anglo-Saxon settlers in the mid-5th to 7th centuries.

909) Human life expectancy has increased more in the last 50 years than it has in the prior 200,000 years.

910) If the salt in the oceans was removed and spread evenly over the earth's land surface, it would form a layer more than 500 feet thick.

911) The project that would become the Statue of Liberty was originally conceived of as a peasant Muslim woman in traditional dress. The statue was originally intended for Egypt before they turned the project down and it was redesigned for the United States.

912) The human body is bioluminescent; it is just too faint for our eyes to see. A 2009 study found that human bioluminescence in visible light exists; the human body glimmers, but the intensity of the light emitted is 1,000 times lower than the sensitivity of our eyes.

913) Victoria Island, in the Canadian territory of Nunavut, has the world's largest island-in-a-lake-on-an-island-in-a-lake-on-an-island. Victoria Island is the world's eighth-largest island; the final, smallest island has an area of four acres.

914) Published in 1852, *Uncle Tom's Cabin* was the first American novel to sell 1 million copies.

915) Australia has over 860 different reptile species, more than any other country. They include lizards, crocodiles, turtles, and snakes. North America only has 280 reptile species.

916) Deja reve is the feeling of having already dreamed something that you are now experiencing.

917) Killing or attempting to kill a U.S. president wasn't a federal offense until 1965, two years after John F. Kennedy's death.

918) *The French Connection* (1971) was the first R-rated movie to win the Best Picture Oscar.

919) Albert Einstein called income taxes "the hardest thing in the world to understand."

920) Ronald Reagan is the only president who was the leader of a union; he was president of the Screen Actors Guild.

921) Michael Jackson wanted to buy *Marvel Comics,* so he could play Spider Man in his own movie.

922) Richard Nixon was an accomplished musician and regularly played five different instruments: piano, saxophone, clarinet, accordion, and violin.

923) Belgium invented French fried potatoes in the late 17th century.

924) Adjusted for inflation, *Snow White and the Seven Dwarfs* (1937) is the highest-grossing animated movie of all time in the United States.

925) The original television series *Lost in Space* was set in 1997.

926) Sixty thousand years ago, Neanderthals mass-produced thousands of flint tools in a huge workshop. Archaeologists in Poland recovered 17,000 stone products at the site.

927) The Statue of Liberty gets hit by lightning about 600 times per year.

928) The Italian word vermicelli means little worms.

929) In addition to being able to see the universe via light, you can "hear" the universe through gravitational waves. In 2017, researchers heard gravitational waves that resulted from two neutron stars colliding, something never before witnessed

930) Q is the least used letter in the English alphabet.

931) A group of flamingos is called a flamboyance.

932) Nishiyama Onsen Keiunkan hotel in Yamanashi, Japan, is the world's oldest hotel; it has been in operation since 705 and has been run by the same family for 52 generations. It has six natural hot springs baths and is on the edge of the Southern Japan Alps.

933) Denver, Colorado, is named after James William Denver, the great-grandfather of actor Bob Denver, Gilligan on *Gilligan's Island*.

934) Gerald Ford had the shortest time in office of any U.S. president who didn't die in office; he was in office 895 days.

935) American Bob Mathias is the youngest male track and field Olympic gold medalist ever; he was 17 years old when he won the 1948 decathlon.

936) Most of the wasabi served outside of Japan is a mixture of horseradish, mustard, and food coloring. Real wasabi is very expensive and is often not used even in Japan.

937) Cleopatra was the last Pharaoh of Egypt.

938) In 1952, Albert Einstein was offered the presidency of Israel but turned it down.

939) Bob Dylan is the only person ever to win a Nobel Prize, Pulitzer, Oscar, and Grammy.

940) The red kangaroo is the largest marsupial. It can be over 6 feet tall standing with a tail up to 44 inches long and weigh up to 200 pounds.

941) Although it hasn't been fully proven, the consensus among scientists is that déjà vu results from a very small delay in transferring information from one side of the brain to the other, so your brain gets the information twice and processes the event as if it had happened before.

942) There were active volcanoes on the moon. Most of the volcanoes probably stopped one billion years ago, but there might still have been active lava flow 100 million years ago.

943) Bill Clinton is the only U.S. president who was a Rhodes Scholar.

944) Barack Obama was the first sitting U.S. president to visit Hiroshima.

945) In the 1960s, the CIA spent $20 million training cats to spy on the Soviet Union; it didn't work.

946) Abstemious and facetious are the only two words in the English language that have all five vowels in order.

947) Linus Pauling is the only person to win two unshared Nobel Prizes.

948) *Snow White and the Seven Dwarfs* (1937) was the first full-length, color, cartoon, talking picture.

949) Bhutan is the only carbon negative (produces less carbon dioxide than it absorbs) country; 72% of the country is still forested.

950) Scientists believe that human fingers and toes prune in water due to an evolutionary adaptation where the wrinkles in the skin improve your grip on wet or submerged objects by channeling away water, like rain treads on car tires.

951) King Sobhuza II of Swaziland ruled for 82 years and 254 days, the longest verifiable reign of any monarch in recorded history. Sobhuza reigned from 1899 until 1982.

952) Wyoming has only two escalators in the entire state.

953) Washington is the most common place name in the United States.

954) Bananas are the most widely eaten fruit in the United States; apples are second.

955) Eye floaters are those spots, specks, or cobwebs that drift around in your field of vision. Most eye floaters are caused by age-related changes that occur as the jelly-like substance inside your eyes becomes more liquid. Microscopic fibers within the eye clump and can cast tiny shadows on your retina; what you see are the shadows and not the floaters themselves.

956) Famous Italian painter Caravaggio (1571-1610) spent the last four years of his life on the run from murder charges.

957) Stockholm, Sweden, is built on 14 islands.

958) Samuel Morse, the inventor of the telegraph, was an accomplished painter and didn't dedicate himself to improving long-distance communications until it took so long to get notified of his wife's illness that she was already dead and buried by the time he got home. Morse was working in Washington, D.C., on a painting commission when he received a letter from his father that his wife was gravely ill. He left immediately for his Connecticut home, but by the time he arrived, his wife had died and was already buried.

959) IKEA uses almost 1% of the world's commercial wood supply.

960) Philosopher Plato was a double winner at the ancient Olympics. He won in pankration, a submission sport combining elements of wrestling and boxing but with very few rules; only eye-gouging and biting were banned.

961) The burnt part of a candlewick is called the snaste.

962) The Volkswagen Beetle debuted in 1938. Its concept and functional objectives were formulated by Adolf Hitler, and it was designed by Ferdinand Porsche.

963) British mathematician Charles Lutwidge Dodgson is better known as Lewis Carroll, author of *Alice's Adventures in Wonderland*.

964) The opossum has more teeth, 50, than any other land mammal.

965) In the game Monopoly, Rich Uncle Pennybags is the mascot depicted as a portly older man with a mustache, suit, bowtie, and top hat. He was inspired by tycoon J.P. Morgan. The character in jail is named Jake the Jailbird, and the police officer who sent him there is Officer Mallory.

966) The superstition of walking under a ladder dates back 5,000 years to the ancient Egyptians. A ladder leaning against a wall forms a triangle that represented the trinity of the gods to the Egyptians, and it was a desecration to pass through a triangle.

967) Herbert Hoover was the first president born west of the Mississippi River; he was born in Iowa.

968) The sperm whale produces the loudest sound of any animal. It can reach 230 decibels; a loud rock concert is 120 decibels.

969) Australia is the only continent without glaciers.

970) Dental drilling dates back at least 9,000 years. Ancient dentists drilled nearly perfect holes as early as 7000 BC.

971) As originally written, Aladdin is Chinese.

972) Liechtenstein has a very low crime rate and only has a single prison with about 10 inmates; any criminal requiring a sentence of more than two years is sent to Austria.

973) President James A. Garfield lived for 80 days after being shot.

974) In 1977, newly inaugurated President Jimmy Carter pardoned draft dodgers, but only about half came back to the United States.

975) Instead of 212 degrees Fahrenheit, the boiling point of water at the top of Mount Everest is about 160 degrees.

976) The loudest land animal is the howler monkey; it can reach 140 decibels and can be heard 3 miles away.

977) Rascette lines are the creases on your inner wrist.

978) For more than 150 million years, tiny mammals lived alongside dinosaurs. They were small nocturnal animals, and they remained relatively small until the demise of the dinosaurs 65 million years ago left more niches for them to fill.

979) Saying "God bless you" when someone sneezes can be traced to a 6th-century order by Pope Gregory I. A pandemic was spreading across the eastern Roman Empire, and the first symptom was severe, chronic sneezing followed quickly by death. Pope Gregory urged people to pray for the sick and ordered that responses to sneezes should be "God bless you."

980) Mozart wrote a six-piece canon titled *Leck mich im Arsch*, which translates as *Kiss My Ass*.

981) In 1906, Australia made the world's first feature film.

982) A human can live unprotected in space for about 30 seconds provided they don't hold their breath. You would be unconscious in about 15 seconds; if you hold your breath, your lungs explode.

983) The word girl used to refer to any young child regardless of sex. In the 1300s, the word "gyrle," which later became "girl," was used for any young child.

984) If your mind believes that an object is further away based on visual clues, it assumes it is larger even if it is the same size as an object that appears to be nearer. This is known as the Ponzo illusion and was first demonstrated in 1911 by the Italian psychologist Mario Ponzo, who suggested that the human mind judges an object's size based on its background.

985) Shark skin was once used commercially as sandpaper.

986) French mime Marcel Marceau spoke the only word in Mel Brooks' film *Silent Movie* (1976).

987) Floccinaucinihilipilification is one of the longer words in the English language and means the action of estimating something as worthless.

988) Of all the world's people who have ever lived to 65 years old, about two-thirds are alive today.

989) *Bambi* was the first Disney film without human characters.

990) Armadillos are good swimmers, but they also walk underwater to cross bodies of water. They can hold their breath for six to eight minutes.

991) When you peel a banana, the strings that come off are called phloem bundles; the strings distribute nutrients up and down the banana as it grows.

992) Nauru, in the central Pacific Ocean, is the only country without an official capital. It is the third-smallest country and has less than 10,000 people.

993) Peppermint was the first Lifesaver flavor.

994) Michelangelo was struck in the face by a rival with a mallet and disfigured for life.

995) Bumblebees have been found at altitudes as high as 18,000 feet, and tests have shown that they can fly at over 29,000 feet.

996) The earliest evidence of tattooing in the United States is a 2,000-year-old prickly pear cactus spine needle with a handle carved from lemonade sumac and bound with yucca fiber.

997) Humans aren't either left-brained or right-brained as once thought; most behaviors and abilities require the right and left sides of the brain to work together. You have characteristics and abilities that define who you are, but they have nothing to do with what side of the brain you use more.

998) Rhythms is the longest common English word without any of the five main vowels.

999) Halley's Comet appeared the day Mark Twain was born and the day he died.

1000) At 5,000 years old, the bristlecone pine species is the oldest living individual tree.

Facts 1001-1500

1001) A kangaroo can hop at 40 mph.

1002) In the Middle Ages, men who wanted a boy sometimes had their left testicle removed because people believed that the right testicle made boy sperm and the left made girl sperm.

1003) A fire rainbow looks like a rainbow in the clouds, but it is technically called a circumhorizontal arc. It occurs when the sun is higher than 58 degrees above the horizon and its light passes through high-altitude cirrus clouds made up of hexagonal plate ice crystals. When aligned properly, the ice crystals act as a prism, resulting in refraction that looks like a rainbow in the clouds.

1004) The duffel bag gets its name from Duffel, Belgium, where the thick cloth used to make the bag originated.

1005) A dog's DNA is 99.9% the same as a gray wolf.

1006) Gibbons are the smallest species of apes; they are up to 3 feet tall when standing upright and weigh 12-20 pounds.

1007) Benjamin Franklin wrote a collection of essays titled *Fart Proudly*.

1008) Twenty-seven U.S. states are at least partly north of the southernmost point of Canada. Middle Island in Lake Erie is the most southern point of Canada; it is approximately the latitude of Chicago, so Alaska, California, Connecticut, Idaho, Illinois, Indiana, Iowa, Maine, Massachusetts, Michigan, Minnesota, Montana, Nebraska, Nevada, New

Hampshire, New York, North Dakota, Ohio, Oregon, Pennsylvania, Rhode Island, South Dakota, Utah, Vermont, Washington, Wisconsin, and Wyoming are all at least partly north of Canada.

1009) The tallest mountain in the known universe is 69,459-foot Olympus Mons on Mars.

1010) In 1980, the world's first one-gigabyte disk drive took up the space of a refrigerator, weighed 1,000 pounds, and cost $81,000.

1011) A googolplexian is the largest named number. A googol is one followed by 100 zeroes; a googolplex is one followed by a googol of zeroes; a googolplexian is one followed by a googolplex of zeroes.

1012) Circus Maximus, the ancient Roman venue for chariot racing, could seat 250,000 spectators. The track was 540 meters long by 80 meters wide and had 12 chariot starting gates. It was constructed in the 6th century BC, and the last chariot races were held there in the 6th century AD.

1013) Chinese astronauts are called taikonauts.

1014) The Centennial Light is the world's longest-lasting light bulb. It has burned since 1901 in Livermore, California.

1015) The smallest thing ever photographed is the shadow of a single atom. In 2012, scientists were able to take a picture of the shadow produced by a single atom. Using an electrical field, they suspended the atom in a vacuum chamber and shot a laser beam at it to produce the shadow.

1016) Australia is the only country with all 10 of the world's deadliest snakes.

1017) If you pay a kidnapping ransom in the United States, you can deduct it on your taxes.

1018) By area, Great Salt Lake is the largest lake entirely within one state.

1019) Besides the United States and its territories, only the Bahamas, Palau, Belize, the Cayman Islands, the Federated States of Micronesia, and the Marshall Islands use the Fahrenheit temperature scale.

1020) Worldwide, there are about 107 human deaths per minute, about 1.78 deaths per second.

1021) Wrigley's gum was the first product with a barcode.

1022) Of all countries that aren't landlocked, Monaco has the shortest coastline, 2.4 miles.

1023) To allow greater flexibility running, a dog's shoulder blades are somewhat unattached to the rest of its skeleton. They have floating shoulders that aren't attached to any bones at the top but do have muscle and ligament attachments.

1024) "Yo Mama" jokes date back to a Babylonian tablet from about 1500 BC; William Shakespeare also told several "Yo Mama" type jokes in his plays.

1025) Like other mammals and all air-breathing vertebrates studied to date, adult humans have a diving reflex. The diving reflex is triggered when the nostrils become chilled and wet while holding your breath. The body reacts with slowed heart rate, redirection of blood to the vital organs to conserve oxygen, and a release of red blood cells stored in the spleen, enabling the body to survive submersion for a longer time.

1026) Most East Asians and almost all Korean people don't have underarm odor. A genetic mutation called ABCC11 determines whether people produce underarm odor; people who have the ABCC11 mutation still produce sweat, but they lack a chemical that creates the smell when sweat is broken down by bacteria. While only 2% of Europeans have the mutation, over 99% of Koreans have it.

1027) The first accurate eyewitness report of the Wright brothers' first flight appeared in the magazine *Gleanings in Bee Culture*.

1028) In 1902, Enrico Caruso had the first record to sell over a million copies.

1029) To preserve freshness, prevent combustion, and create cushioning during shipping, chip bags are filled with nitrogen. Oxygen would make the chips go stale.

1030) The average garden snail has over 14,000 teeth arranged in rows on its tongue. The typical snail tongue might have 120 rows of 100 teeth; some species have more than 20,000 teeth.

1031) If uncoiled, the DNA in all cells of the human body would stretch about 10 billion miles.

1032) Tibet's Yarlung Tsangpo Canyon is the world's largest canyon. It is 314 miles long and has an average depth of 7,440 feet.

1033) Franklin D. Roosevelt was the first president to name a woman to his cabinet; in 1933, he named Frances Perkins as secretary of labor.

1034) Gorillas are several times stronger than humans; a male silverback gorilla can lift 1,800 pounds.

1035) The band Led Zeppelin got their name because another musician said their band would go down like a lead balloon.

1036) The United States is collectively overweight by about 4 billion pounds.

1037) Calvin Coolidge is the only U.S. president born on the 4th of July.

1038) Rutherfordium has the longest name of any periodic table element.

1039) The Fitzroy River turtle, a species that can only be found in the Fitzroy River in Australia, can breathe through its anus. They are constantly pumping water in and out of their anus, collecting as much as 70% of all the oxygen they need to survive. Consequently, they can stay underwater for up to three weeks at a time. They are not the only turtle species that can breathe through their anus, but they can use the function to a greater extent.

1040) In 1959, the U.S. Navy submarine *USS Barbero* assisted the U.S. Post Office Department in a test to deliver mail via a cruise missile. The submarine launched a cruise missile with 3,000 pieces of mail from Norfolk, Virginia, and it landed at its target in Mayport, Florida, 22 minutes later. While the success of the test was lauded at the time, it never went any further since the cost could not be justified.

1041) In 1935, Krueger's Finest beer became the first canned beer to go on sale in the United States.

1042) *Pocahontas* was the first animated Disney film to have an interracial romance.

1043) At age 52 in 1999, Cher is the oldest female artist to have a number-one hit on Billboard's Hot 100.

1044) By area, Belarus is the largest country without any mountains (greater than 2,000 feet elevation); it is 80,155 square miles, and its highest point is 1,130 feet.

1045) King Tut's tomb had already been robbed several times before it was discovered by Howard Carter in 1922.

1046) Butterflies taste with their feet.

1047) Because of the speed the sun moves, the maximum possible length for a solar eclipse is 7 minutes and 58 seconds.

1048) At 37.8 degrees south latitude, Melbourne, Australia, is the world's southernmost city with a population of over 1 million.

1049) Like other equines, such as zebras and donkeys, horses have a single toe. Their ancient ancestors that lived 55 million years ago were dog-like in size and had 14 toes, four toes on their front feet and three on their back.

1050) In 1960, Sri Lanka was the first nation with a female prime minister.

1051) In polo, you are banned from playing left-handed. If a left-handed player and a right-handed player went for the ball, they would collide.

1052) Christopher Cross and Billie Eilish are the only artists to win the best new artist, record, album, and song of the year Grammys in the same year. Adele is the only other artist to win all four awards, but she didn't win them in the same year.

1053) Equestrian and sailing are the only Olympic sports where men and women compete against each other.

1054) Indian chief Geronimo rode in Theodore Roosevelt's inaugural parade.

1055) Venus has a longer day than its year. It takes 243 days for one rotation (one day) and 225 days for one orbit around the sun (one year).

1056) In June 1944, a German V2 rocket was the first man-made object to achieve sub-orbital space flight.

1057) Switzerland last went to war with another country in 1515.

1058) Famed writers Miguel de Cervantes and William Shakespeare died on the same day, April 23, 1616.

1059) At 41 degrees south latitude, Wellington, New Zealand, is the world's most southern national capital.

1060) Canada has a longer coastline than the rest of the world combined. At 125,567 miles, Canada's coastline is 3.5 times longer than any other country.

1061) In ancient Greece, prostitution was common, accepted, and regulated. Prostitutes wore sandals that left the words "follow me" imprinted on the ground as they walked.

1062) According to his wife, Abraham Lincoln's hobby was cats. He loved them and could play with them for hours; he once allowed a cat to eat from the table at a formal White House dinner.

1063) During WWII in Australia, Gunner, an Australian shepherd dog with extremely acute hearing, was able to warn air force personnel of incoming Japanese planes 20 minutes before they arrived. He could also differentiate between allied and enemy aircraft.

1064) Cats can drink salt water and stay hydrated. Their kidneys are efficient enough to filter out the salt and use the water.

1065) The world's most spoken word is OK.

1066) Episcopalian is the most common religious affiliation for U.S. presidents.

1067) Beyonce has won more Grammy Awards than any other artist.

1068) The loop on a belt that keeps the end in place after it has passed through the buckle is called the keeper.

1069) In the Humpty Dumpty nursery rhyme, there is no indication that he is an egg. Early illustrations portrayed him as a young boy.

1070) Manatees are tropical animals and can suffer from cold stress if water temperatures fall below 68 degrees Fahrenheit.

1071) At its peak in 1270, Genghis Khan's Mongol Empire spanned 9.27 million square miles in one mass, the largest contiguous land area empire in history. At its peak in 1920, the British Empire was larger but scattered around the world.

1072) Lightning strikes the earth's surface about 100 times per second.

1073) Before unifying Italy, Giuseppe Garibaldi was a spaghetti salesman in Uruguay.

1074) Saturn is the only planet in our solar system less dense than water.

1075) Cornicione is the name for the outer part of a pizza crust.

1076) Jimmy Carter was the first president to attend Monday night football.

1077) Composer Vivaldi was also a priest.

1078) Cats can't taste sweet. They don't have taste receptors for sweet; this applies to all cats, domestic and wild.

1079) At 78.2 degrees north latitude, Svalbard Airport, Longyear in Svalbard, Norway, is the world's northernmost airport with scheduled flights.

1080) With 836 deaths, *The Lord of the Rings: The Return of the King* has the highest number of on-screen deaths of any movie.

1081) Strengths is the longest word in the English language with only one vowel.

1082) Delaware has three counties, the fewest of any state.

1083) John Tyler was the first U.S. vice president to succeed a president upon death. He succeeded William Henry Harrison, who died of pneumonia 31 days into his presidency.

1084) About 100 billion people have died in all of human history.

1085) Scientists believe that herrings use farts to communicate. Herrings have excellent hearing, and their farts produce a high-pitched sound. The farts are from gulping air at the surface and storing it in their swim bladder.

1086) In 1977, the USSR started a televised song contest that allowed viewers to vote by turning on their light switches. The show was called *Intervision* and was like *Eurovision* but designed for the Eastern Bloc countries. Since phones were rare in USSR at the time, people voted by turning their light switches on for their favorites. Mail was too slow, and people didn't trust paper ballots, so they arranged with the state power authorities to measure the power spikes and report them to determine points for each contestant.

1087) The practice of using BC and AD for years wasn't established until the 6th century.

1088) UY Scuti, a bright red supergiant star in the Scutum constellation about 9,500 light-years away, is believed to be the largest star in the Milky Way Galaxy. Its volume is about 27.3 quadrillion times larger than the earth, and its radius is about 1,700 times larger than the sun.

1089) William Shakespeare has more films based on his work than any other author.

1090) The video game company Nintendo was founded in 1889; it originally produced handmade playing cards.

1091) Acmegenesis is better known as an orgasm.

1092) Baron Pierre de Coubertin, the founder of the modern Olympics, won a gold medal at the 1912 Olympic games in mixed literature. Art competition was introduced in 1912 and continued in the Olympics through 1948; Coubertin won for a poem.

1093) Of the first five U.S. presidents, three died on July 4. John Adams and Thomas Jefferson both died on July 4, 1826; James Monroe died five years later on July 4, 1831.

1094) Great Smoky Mountains is the most visited U.S. National Park.

1095) China has more individual deserts than any other country. It has 13 deserts: Gobi Desert, Badain Jaran Desert, Dzungaria, Gobi Desert, Gurbantunggut Desert, Hami Desert, Kumtag Desert, Lop Desert, Mu Us Sandyland, Ordos Desert, Shapotou District, Taklamakan Desert, and Tengger Desert.

1096) The average chocolate bar has eight insect parts.

1097) In medieval times, a moment was a unit of time equal to 1/40th of an hour. An hour was defined as 1/12th of the time between sunrise and sunset, so the length of an hour depended on the time of year. Therefore, the length of a moment wasn't fixed either, but on average, it corresponded to 90 seconds.

1098) A month beginning on a Sunday always has a Friday the 13th.

1099) Sloths are good swimmers; using a version of a dog paddle, they can swim up to three times as fast as they move on land.

1100) According to legend, Pheidippides ran the first marathon in 490 BC. He ran 140 miles round trip from Athens to Sparta over mountain terrain to ask for military aid, marched 26 miles from Athens to Marathon, fought all morning, and then ran 26 miles to Athens with the victory news and died of exhaustion.

1101) In 1939, Earl Wild was the first pianist to give a recital on U.S. television; in 1997, he was also the first person to stream a piano performance over the internet.

1102) Kiribati, an island nation in the central Pacific, is the only country that falls in all four hemispheres.

1103) Delaware has an average elevation of 60 feet, the lowest of any state.

1104) Churches in Malta have two clocks to confuse the devil; one clock has the right time, and one has the wrong time.

1105) Israel has the highest number of museums per capita of any country.

1106) Ancient Rome had a four-story shopping mall called Trajan's Market with 150 shops and offices. It was built around 110 AD, and its ruins can still be visited today.

1107) Barns are traditionally red because of rust. Hundreds of years ago, choices for paints, sealers, and other building materials were very limited, and farmers had to find ways of making a paint that would protect and seal the wood on their barns. Many farmers would seal their barns with linseed oil, which is orange-colored, and they would add things such as milk, lime, and rust (ferrous oxide). Rust was plentiful, and because it killed fungi and mosses that might grow on barns, it was very effective as a sealant and turned the mixture red in color. Over time, it became a tradition to paint barns red, even as more paint options became available.

1108) According to Wurlitzer, the most popular jukebox song of all time is "Hound Dog" by Elvis Presley.

1109) Brazil's Santa Rita do Sapucai prison allows prisoners to reduce their sentences by riding stationary bicycles to generate power for a nearby city. If they pedal for 16 hours, a prisoner's sentence is reduced by one day. The energy from the bikes charges batteries that are taken to the closest city.

1110) Humans are the most populous large mammal (average of 10 pounds or more).

1111) When you die, hearing is the last sense to go.

1112) Italy has won the Best Foreign Language Film Oscar more times than any other country.

1113) Before Facebook, Mark Zuckerberg initially created a website called FaceMash to rate the attractiveness of female Harvard students; he received a six-month academic probation for it.

1114) From the late 1920s until the 1960s, Omero C. Catan became known as "Mr. First" in New York City because he made it his mission to participate in major firsts. He was the first person to board five different subway lines, first to dive into New York City's first public swimming pool, first ticket holder to enter two World Fairs, first to skate at the Rockefeller Center ice rink, first to use the Brooklyn-Battery Tunnel, first to use the Lincoln Tunnel, first to feed a dime into the city's first parking meter, and many more. Catan went to great lengths to obtain his firsts, waiting up to four days to gain a position or spending money to charter planes. In total, he achieved 537 major firsts.

1115) In 1849, Elizabeth Blackwell was the first American woman to earn a medical degree. She graduated first in her class at New York's Geneva College.

1116) In its natural form, aspirin comes from the bark of the white willow tree.

1117) About 70% of the atmospheric oxygen we breathe is produced by ocean plants, mainly by phytoplankton.

1118) Oscar Hammerstein II is the only person named Oscar to win an Oscar.

1119) Hannibal Hamlin was the first Republican U.S. vice president; he was Abraham Lincoln's first vice president.

1120) The word mortgage comes from a French word that means death contract.

1121) Manatees control their buoyancy by farting. They can regulate the distribution of their intestinal gases, holding them in when they want to approach the surface and letting them loose when it is time to sink.

1122) At age 42, Theodore Roosevelt was the youngest U.S. president; at age 43, John F. Kennedy was the youngest elected president.

1123) With 22 competitive and 4 honorary awards, Walt Disney won more Oscars than any other individual.

1124) Neil Armstrong was the first non-military American astronaut in space; he had been a Navy fighter pilot but was a civilian when he joined NASA.

1125) Hydrogen is the most abundant element in the universe; it accounts for about 75% of the universe's mass.

1126) Recent research has shown that the phrase "bloodcurdling" is physically accurate. The phrase can be traced back to medieval times when people believed that being scared could make your blood run cold or congeal. Studies have now shown that watching a horror film produces a significant increase in a blood-clotting protein. If you are frightened, the body seems to prepare itself for the possibility of blood loss.

1127) The world's oldest snack food is the pretzel, dating back to the 6th century.

1128) Political cartoonist Thomas Nast popularized the use of the elephant and donkey as symbols of the two main U.S. political parties; he also created the modern Santa Claus image.

1129) The poodle didn't originate in France; it is German. The name poodle came from the German "pudel," meaning "to splash about."

1130) Worldwide, more than 10% of marriages are between first or second cousins.

1131) The white dashed lines that divide lanes on U.S. roads are 10 feet long. Federal guidelines specify that the length is standard for all roads.

1132) The human eye can differentiate more shades of green than any other color; that is why night vision goggles are green.

1133) Liza Minnelli is the only Oscar winner whose parents, Vincent Minnelli and Judy Garland, were both Oscar winners.

1134) The term "guys" originated with Guy Fawkes, who is famous for the plot to explode 36 barrels of gunpowder under the London House of Lords on November 5, 1605. When he was caught, Fawkes was in the basement under the House of Lords ready to light the fuse; that led to a Fifth of November Act for giving thanks. The new holiday featured special religious services during the day and bonfires at night, lighting fires to mock the man who hadn't succeeded. They burned effigies of the Pope, Guy Fawkes, and other archenemies and referred to the effigies of Fawkes as "guys." Early in the 18th century, some people began to use "guys" to refer to real people, men of the lowest kind. Gradually, speakers and writers began to view "guys" more positively. Guys shifted meaning to become a term for working-class men and then all men.

1135) On Saturn's moon Titan, humans could fly under their own power with artificial wings. Titan has a very high ratio of atmospheric density to surface gravity.

1136) Dogs were the first domesticated animal; they were domesticated up to 40,000 years ago.

1137) Over 25% of the world's hazelnuts are used to make Nutella.

1138) *Gone with the Wind* and *All the King's Men* are the only two Pulitzer Prize-winning novels made into Best Picture Oscar winners.

1139) At up to 90 mph, the horsefly is the fastest known flying insect.

1140) A snail's reproductive organs are in its head.

1141) In 1917, Germany invited Mexico to join WWI by attacking the United States to recover lost territories.

1142) Artist Salvador Dali loved money, and in his later years, he developed a method to avoid paying at restaurants. He would have a party out with a group and write a check for the whole meal. He would then make a drawing on the back of the check, knowing that the restaurant owner would rather keep the check because of the value of the drawing rather than cash it.

1143) Based on land area, Yakutat, Alaska, is the largest city in the United States; it is 9,459 square miles, is larger than New Hampshire.

1144) Genghis Khan once had a feast with his army while seated on top of Russian army generals and nobility. In 1223 in Russia, the Mongol army had just won the Battle of the Kalka River; the Russian army surrendered, and the Mongols decided to have a celebration feast. The Russian army generals and nobility were forced to lie on the ground, and a heavy wooden gate was thrown on top of them. Chairs and tables were set on top of the gate, and the Mongols sat down for a feast on top of the still-living bodies of their enemies.

1145) North Korea has the highest percentage of its population in the military. Between active, reserves, and paramilitary, 30.8% of the entire population is in the military. Comparatively, 0.7% of the U.S. population is in the military.

1146) Mount Augustus, in the Australian Outback, is the world's largest rock. It is about 2,350 feet high and 5 miles long, occupying an area of about 18.5 square miles. It is about 2.5 times larger than Ayers Rock.

1147) Due to inflation since 1970, Argentina has changed the value of its currency by a factor of 10 trillion.

1148) Great Britain is the only country to win a gold medal at every Summer Olympics. Due to boycotts, only Great Britain, France, Australia, Greece, and Switzerland have participated in every Summer Olympics.

1149) Sunglasses were invented in China to hide the eyes of judges.

1150) "Mark twain" means two fathoms or twelve feet. It was used to call out the water depth on riverboats; Samuel Clemens worked as a steamboat pilot and took his pen name from it.

1151) The Amazon rainforest is home to 10% of the world's known species.

1152) In the original, 1740 version of *Beauty and the Beast* story by French novelist Gabrielle-Suzanne Barbot de Villeneuve, the beast was a hideous combination of an elephant and fish, and the story was written to encourage girls to accept arranged marriages.

1153) Pure water isn't a good conductor of electricity; the impurities in water make it a good conductor.

1154) Eleven of the twelve men who walked on the moon were Boy Scouts.

1155) Khone Falls, in the Champasak Province of Laos on the Mekong River, is the world's widest waterfall. It is 35,376 feet wide.

1156) Britain's Graham Hill is the first driver to ever complete the Motorsport Triple Crown, consisting of winning the Indianapolis 500, 24 Hours of Le Mans, and the Monaco Grand Prix over a career. He won the 1963 Monaco Grand Prix, 1966 Indianapolis 500, and 1972 24 Hours of Le Mans.

1157) A crocodile can't stick its tongue out. It is attached to the roof of its mouth. Their tongue helps keep their throat closed underwater, so they can open their mouth to hunt prey.

1158) Saffron is made from crocus flowers; only the stigma part of the flower is used. It takes 70,000 to 250,000 flowers to make one pound of saffron, which is why it is so expensive.

1159) James is the most common first name of U.S. presidents; six presidents have shared the name: Madison, Monroe, Polk, Buchanan, Garfield, and Carter.

1160) The world's largest waterfall is underwater. The Denmark Strait cataract, located between Greenland and Iceland, is 100 miles long and drops 11,500 feet from the Greenland Sea into the Irminger Sea. It is three times taller than Venezuela's Angel Falls and has 2,000 times more water volume than Niagara Falls. The cataract is formed by the difference in temperature between the cold Arctic waters of the Greenland Sea and the slightly warmer Irminger Sea. When the waters meet, the colder Greenland Sea water falls to the bottom.

1161) Four presidential candidates have won the popular vote but lost the election: Andrew Jackson against John Quincy Adams, Samuel Tilden against Rutherford B. Hayes, Al Gore against George W. Bush, and Hilary Clinton against Donald Trump.

1162) St. Lucia is the smallest population country with two or more Nobel Prize winners; it is in the Caribbean and has 185,000 people and two Nobel Prize winners.

1163) Russia has 11 time zones; it spans over 5,700 miles east to west.

1164) During 10 days in 2001, Argentina had five presidents; it was during an economic crash combined with defaulting on foreign debt.

1165) Tooth enamel is the hardest substance in the human body.

1166) Switzerland and Vatican City are the only two countries with square flags.

1167) The very first internet search engine was created in 1990 and was called Archie. The name stood for archive without the letter v and was created by a group of computer science students at Montreal's McGill University.

1168) Ulysses S. Grant was the first president known to have died of cancer; he died of throat cancer after smoking 20 cigars a day most of his adult life.

1169) Max Baer Jr., who played Jethro on television's *The Beverly Hillbillies*, is the son of Max Baer Sr., a world heavyweight boxing champion in the 1930s.

1170) The Czech Republic drinks the most beer per person of any country, 235 liters per person annually.

1171) Buddha, Confucius, and Socrates all lived about the same time. Buddha is believed to have died in 483 BC; Confucius died in 479 BC, and Socrates was born in 469 BC.

1172) In 1997, Pope John Paul II decided that Saint Isidore of Seville would be the patron saint of the internet.

1173) Astronauts in space are exposed to radiation that is the equivalent of up to 6,000 chest x-rays.

1174) Oklahoma City and Indianapolis are the only two state capitals that include the name of the state.

1175) George Washington and Benjamin Franklin appeared on the first U.S. postage stamps issued in 1847.

1176) *The Howdy Doody Show* (1947-1960) was the first U.S. television show to broadcast 1,000 episodes.

1177) Denmark's flag has lasted longer without change than any other country; it has been the same since at least 1370.

1178) A newborn human baby has about one cup of blood in their body.

1179) The black kite, whistling kite, and brown falcon are Australian birds of prey that intentionally spread fires. Aborigines have known this for centuries, and scientists have now confirmed it. These birds hang out around the edges of fires looking for escaping prey, and they will also pick up smoldering debris and fly up to a kilometer away and drop it to spread the fire. The act appears to be very intentional to create a new area where they can wait for prey escaping the fire.

1180) George Washington, Thomas Jefferson, Andrew Jackson, Martin Van Buren, and Dwight Eisenhower were all redheads.

1181) Estivation is the summer equivalent to hibernation. During estivation, animals slow their activity for the hot, dry summer months.

1182) The sword-billed hummingbird is the only bird with a bill longer than its body.

1183) It would take about 150 ruby-throated hummingbirds to weigh one pound.

1184) The chameleon has the longest tongue relative to its size of any animal.

1185) Cicadas are the world's loudest insects; they can reach about 120 decibels, equivalent to sitting in the front row of a loud rock concert.

1186) Grant Wood's *American Gothic* painting depicts his sister and his dentist.

1187) The mangrove is the only tree that grows in saltwater.

1188) The Congo is the world's deepest river, up to 750 feet deep.

1189) The male honeybee's testicles explode on mating, and then he dies.

1190) Both men and women have Adam's Apples. It is thyroid cartilage surrounding the larynx; it is just more prominent in males because their larynx is larger.

1191) At 71.1 degrees north latitude, Beerenberg volcano, on the Norwegian island of Jan Mayen in the Arctic Ocean, is the world's northernmost active volcano.

1192) The average person will spend about six months of their life waiting for red lights to turn.

1193) Alcohol changes the receptors in your body, making it think it is being burned. The vanilloid receptor-1 (VR1) normally activates at temperatures of 107 degrees Fahrenheit or higher to let you know that you're getting burned. Alcohol lowers the VR1 activation temperature to about 93 degrees. That is why open wounds sting when you pour alcohol over them and why you can get a burning in your throat when you drink potent alcohol.

1194) Educated people have believed the earth was round for about 2,500 years. Pythagoras postulated the earth was round in the 6th century BC; Aristotle agreed it was round in the 4th century BC.

1195) Hollywood star Clark Gable was the inspiration for Bugs Bunny.

1196) The D-Day invasion password was Mickey Mouse.

1197) Washington, D.C., has a smaller percentage of the country's population than any other national capital; it has just 0.2% of the U.S. population.

1198) During the 18th century, you could pay for your admission to the London Zoo by bringing a cat or dog to feed the lions.

1199) Venus rotates so slowly that you could watch a sunset forever just by walking towards it. At the equator, Venus rotates 4 mph; the Earth rotates 1,038 mph at the equator.

1200) The stage before frostbite is called frostnip. There is skin irritation causing redness and a cold feeling followed by numbness, but there is no permanent damage.

1201) Bangkok, Thailand's full official name is Krung Thep Mahanakhon Amon Rattanakosin Mahinthara Yuthaya Mahadilok Phop Noppharat Ratchathani Burirom. Udomratchaniwet Mahasathan Amon Piman Awatan Sathit Sakkathattiya Witsanukam Prasit.

1202) Throughout history, about 5-6 billion Bibles have been printed.

1203) In space, blood flow doesn't work the same without gravity. Blood can flow up towards the head instead of pulling down toward the feet. Astronaut's faces typically look puffy from extra blood flow for the first few days until their bodies adapt.

1204) The Sahara is the world's largest non-polar desert; it is 3.3 million square miles.

1205) In ancient China, only the aristocracy could have a Pekingese dog.

1206) The United States, Liberia, and Myanmar are the only three countries that don't use the metric system.

1207) *Mary Poppins* (1964) was the only film personally produced by Walt Disney nominated for the Best Picture Oscar.

1208) Even though Froot Loops cereal has a variety of colors, all colors have the same flavor, a fruit blend.

1209) The Camellia sinensis evergreen shrub produces tea.

1210) A second is called a second because it was the second division of the hour; the original term was second minute.

1211) With 55 appearances, Richard Nixon has been on the cover of *Time* magazine more times than any other person.

1212) You will never actually see yourself; you only see representations of yourself or a flipped image in a mirror.

1213) Although he was 73 years old at the time, Frank Sinatra had to be first offered the role of John McClane in *Die Hard*. The movie is based on the book *Nothing Lasts Forever*, a sequel to *The Detective* that had been made into a movie in 1968 starring Sinatra, so contractually, he had to be offered the role first.

1214) Husband and wife Emil and Dana Zatopek both won gold medals at the 1952 Helsinki Summer Olympics. Emil won the 5,000 meters, 10,000 meters, and marathon, despite never running a marathon before; Dana won the javelin.

1215) During U.S. prohibition from 1920 to 1933, doctors were still allowed to prescribe alcohol to their patients for medicinal purposes.

1216) In 1841, Oberlin College was the first U.S. college to confer degrees on women.

1217) When you shuffle a deck of 52 cards, there are so many possible sequences that it is statistically likely that a well-shuffled deck is in a sequence that has never occurred before and will never occur again. There are 8.07×10^{67} possible sequences for a deck of 52 cards; there are only about 10^{24} stars in the observable universe.

1218) By area, Vatican City is the smallest country; it is so small that there are 5.9 popes per square mile with just the current pope.

1219) Lettuce is a member of the sunflower family.

1220) In 1958, a B-47 carrying an atomic bomb, larger than the one dropped on Nagasaki, accidentally dropped it on Mars Bluff, South Carolina. The core of the bomb was still on the plane, so there wasn't a nuclear explosion, but the 6,000 pounds of conventional high explosives detonated. The bomb fell on a garden in a rural area and created a 35-foot-deep by 75-foot-wide crater and destroyed the nearby house and outbuildings. Fortunately, no one was killed, and there were only minor injuries.

1221) President Thomas Jefferson wasn't fond of formal events, and he often greeted foreign dignitaries in his pajamas.

1222) Natural vanilla flavoring comes from orchids.

1223) Search engines can access about 0.03% of the internet. About 99.96% of the internet is the deep web, which is anything that is password protected or requires filling out a form, such as email, social media profiles, databases, etc. The tiny remaining portion is the dark web, which is a subset of the deep web and is encrypted for illegal or secretive purposes.

1224) The only WWII U.S. mainland combat deaths occurred on May 5, 1945, when a Japanese balloon bomb exploded and killed a woman and five children in Oregon. The balloon bombs had a 33-foot diameter balloon with 35 pounds of explosives and were designed to rise to 30,000 feet and ride the jet stream east, making it from Japan to the United States in about three days. An altimeter would trigger a reaction that would jettison the bombs. Japan released about 9,000 of the bombs. A Sunday school teacher and five students happened upon an unexploded balloon bomb on the ground; it exploded while they were investigating it.

1225) When you blush, your stomach lining also turns red due to increased blood flow throughout the body from the release of adrenaline.

1226) The geographic center of the contiguous United States is two miles northwest of the town of Lebanon, Kansas, on a pig farm.

1227) According to research, cannibalism for certain fish, reptiles, and amphibians may be a way to help their offspring survive when overcrowding becomes a problem.

1228) The moon is moving away from the earth by about 1.5 inches per year.

1229) The last man on the moon was in 1972.

1230) In the interests of her own rule or her son's future rule, Cleopatra likely had a hand in the deaths of both of her sibling husbands and the execution of her sister.

1231) Due to a global surge in jellyfish populations, nuclear power plants around the world are experiencing an increasing number of outages caused by jellyfish clogging cooling water intakes. Outages have occurred in Japan, Israel, Scotland, and the United States. The surging populations are likely due to overfishing reducing predation and the jellyfish's ability to withstand increasing ocean acidity levels.

1232) 111,111,111 multiplied by 111,111,111 equals 12,345,678,987,654,321.

1233) The closest living relative to the Tyrannosaurus Rex is the chicken.

1234) On average, men say 12,500 words per day; women say 22,000.

1235) Sandy Island, an island about the size of Manhattan off the coast of Australia, was supposedly discovered by Captain James Cook in 1876 and appeared on maps from 1908 until 2012 when it was discovered that it didn't exist. There is speculation that Cook may have seen a raft of floating pumice ejected by underwater volcanos and mistaken it for an island, but no one is sure.

1236) Phosphenes are the rings or spots of light you see when you rub your eyes.

1237) *Dumbo* was the first Disney animated feature film set in America.

1238) At 69.7 degrees north latitude, the University of Tromsø in Tromsø, Norway, is the world's northernmost university.

1239) The Amazon River has the world's largest drainage basin area, 2.7 million square miles.

1240) The loudest instrument in a standard orchestra is the trombone; it peaks at about 115 decibels.

1241) Armadillos always give birth to four identical offspring. As part of their normal reproduction, a single embryo splits into four.

1242) London didn't get back to its pre-WWII population until 2015.

1243) Blood donors in Sweden receive a text each time their blood is used.

1244) George Washington wanted to call himself chief magistrate rather than president.

1245) Leprosy is probably the oldest known infectious disease in humans. Its roots may stretch back millions of years.

1246) In early Greece and Rome, it was essentially impossible to understand a text on a first reading. There was no punctuation or spacing and no distinction between uppercase and lowercase letters; text was just a run-on string of letters.

1247) Uncopyrightable and dermatoglyphics are the longest English words with no repeated letters.

1248) The opossum has an average gestation period of just 12 days, the shortest of any mammal.

1249) Detroit is the only U.S. city to win three of the four major professional sports championships in the same year; in 1935, it won the NFL, NBA, and NHL championships.

1250) Human stomach acid is about as strong as battery acid and can destroy metal. Gastric acid consists of potassium chloride, sodium chloride, and hydrochloric acid, and on a PH scale of 0-14, with 0 being the most acidic and 7 being neutral, it typically measures between 1 and 3.

1251) If you complete courses in archery, pistol shooting, sailing, and fencing at the Massachusetts Institute of Technology, you can be recognized as a certified pirate.

1252) From the 1920s until the 1970s before the risk of x-rays was well understood, shoe shops used x-ray machines for shoe fittings in the United States, Canada, United Kingdom, South Africa, Germany, and Switzerland. The device had an opening where the customer would place their feet, and while standing, they would look through a viewing window at the top to see the x-ray view of their feet and shoes. There were typically two other viewing windows on either side to allow a parent and sales assistant to look at the fit. The bones of the feet, the outline of the shoe, and the stitching around the edges were clearly visible.

1253) Insects only have one blood vessel. They have a single tube, with the heart at one end and the aorta at the other, that pumps blood to the brain. The blood flows back and fills all the spaces in the insect's body, so all the internal organs are floating in blood.

1254) In the film *The Bridge on the River Kwai*, the prisoners whistle the "Colonel Bogey March"; it was written in 1914 by a British army bandmaster.

1255) The singular forms of spaghetti, confetti, and graffiti are spaghetto, confetto, and graffito.

1256) The movie *Seven Samurai* (1954) is often credited as the first modern action film, using elements such as slow motion for dramatic effect.

1257) Wheeled luggage was first sold in 1970 at Macy's department stores in the United States.

1258) Alabama's state constitution is the world's longest constitution; it has 310,000 words.

1259) Before *The Artist* (2011), *The Apartment* (1960) was the last entirely black and white movie to win the Best Picture Oscar. *Schindler's List* (1993) had color in some scenes.

1260) Bamboo Harvester was the real name of television's Mister Ed.

1261) A zarf is the piece of cardboard that goes around your hot cup of coffee.

1262) Harry S. Truman was the last U.S. president without a college degree.

1263) By looking at a variety of animal species, a study found that yawns get longer as brains get bigger.

1264) Chess has more books written about it than any other game.

1265) The sweaters children's television star Mr. Rogers wore on his show were all hand-knitted by his mother.

1266) Chameleons don't change their colors for camouflage purposes. They change color by stretching and relaxing cells that contain crystals, affecting how light is reflected. Their primary purposes for changing color are to communicate with other chameleons (dark colors signal aggression) and to regulate their temperature (lighter colors reflect the heat).

1267) The Maillard reaction is the process where food browns during cooking.

1268) The heat index is a measure of the discomfort the average person experiences because of the combined effects of air temperature and humidity. The world's highest recorded heat index was 178 at Dhahran, Saudi Arabia, on July 8, 2003, with a temperature of 108 and a dew point of 95.

1269) William Howard Taft was the last U.S. president with facial hair.

1270) Prince Charles was the first member of the British royal family to ever graduate from university.

1271) The Bible doesn't say how many wise men there were. It says wise men and mentions the gifts; there is no indication of how many wise men.

1272) In 1992, *Malcolm X* was the first non-documentary film permitted to film in Mecca.

1273) At Coney Island in 1884, LaMarcus Thompson created the first roller coaster in America. He wanted to provide a family-friendly, sin-free way to have fun, compared to the saloons and brothels popular in New York in the late 1800s.

1274) Nebraska is the only triply landlocked state; it is at least three states or provinces away from the ocean in all directions.

1275) Abraham Lincoln's first choice to lead the Union army was Robert E. Lee.

1276) Panama hats were originally made in Peru.

1277) During WWI, the British tried to train seagulls to poop on the periscopes of enemy submarines.

1278) A nurdle is the wave-like gob of toothpaste you put on your toothbrush.

1279) Robins can eat up to 14 feet of earthworms in a day.

1280) Fred Flintstone's "yabba-dabba-doo" was inspired by Brylcreem's "A little dab'll do you." The mother of the actor who voiced Fred Flintstone liked to say the Brylcreem slogan, so he suggested it to the show's creators.

1281) Mark Twain is generally credited with first saying "When in doubt, tell the truth."

1282) The greyhound is the only dog breed specifically mentioned in the Bible.

1283) The word fizzle originally meant "to break wind quietly."

1284) Nevada is 81% federal land, the highest percentage of any state.

1285) Saudi Arabia imports camels and sand from Australia. Camels are a large part of the Muslim diet and are in short supply in Saudi Arabia, so they import camels from Australia, which has the world's largest wild camel population. Saudi Arabia also imports Australia's garnet sand because its unique properties make it ideal for sandblasting.

1286) Australia's first police force was composed entirely of criminals; the best-behaved convicts were selected.

1287) Lipsticks, nail polishes, and cosmetic products made with pearl essence contain fish scales. It is a silvery substance added for its shimmer effect and is primarily sourced from herring.

1288) About 50% of human DNA is the same as a banana.

1289) At 76 degrees north latitude, Northeast Greenland National Park is the world's northernmost national park.

1290) As they lose oxygen, bruises change color. Bruises are due to bleeding under the skin; the trapped blood initially looks red because the blood is still oxygen rich. As the blood loses oxygen, it turns purple and then green, yellow, or gray. Biliverdin and bilirubin compounds break down the hemoglobin to absorb vitamins and minerals for the body to use.

1291) Because of its very high salt content, it is almost impossible for a human to drown in the Dead Sea. A human body can't sink, but drownings have occurred when someone gets stuck on their stomach and can't get turned over. Experts recommend spending no more than 20 minutes at a time in the water to avoid dehydration and electrolyte imbalance from the high salt content.

1292) Monowi, Nebraska, is the only incorporated town in the United States with a population of one. Elsie Eiler, its lone resident, used to live there with her husband until he died in 2004. She is the mayor, bartender, and librarian and is responsible for paying herself taxes and granting herself a liquor license.

1293) The world's first television sitcom was *Pinwright's Progress*, which debuted on the BBC on November 29, 1946. it featured the adventures of the world's smallest store and included the store proprietor, his pretty daughter, a nemesis, and helpful staff, who end up making things worse.

1294) Avocados don't ripen on the tree. They only ripen once they are off the tree, so the trees can be used as storage and will keep avocados fresh for up to seven months.

1295) While a queen ant can live for up to 30 years, male ants typically only live for a few weeks, and workers live for several months.

1296) Foreign accent syndrome is extremely rare and typically caused by stroke or brain injury. It affects the way a person forms words, giving the perception they are speaking with a foreign accent.

1297) Mary Shelley came up with the idea for *Frankenstein* in the summer of 1816 while she was staying on Lake Geneva with her future husband, Percy Bysshe Shelley, and writers Lord Byron and John Polidori. Byron challenged them all to write a ghost story, and *Frankenstein* was published two years later when Shelley was 20 years old.

1298) Before it was stolen from the Louvre in 1911, the *Mona Lisa* was not widely known outside the art world. Leonardo da Vinci painted it in 1507, but it wasn't until the 1860s that critics noticed it as a masterpiece. It wasn't even the most famous painting in its gallery at the Louvre, let alone the entire Louvre.

1299) A photon of light takes about 8 minutes to get from the sun to the earth, but it can take a photon 100,000 years to get from the core of the sun to the surface.

1300) Walter Johnson has the highest season batting average ever for an MLB starting pitcher; in 1925, he batted .433.

1301) Fish skin can be used to treat burns. In Brazil, medical professionals sometimes use tilapia skin to bandage and treat burns; the fish skin cuts down on healing time and scarring and reduces the need for pain medication.

1302) In Roman times, men held their testicles as a sign of truthfulness when bearing witness in public.

1303) Tuna need to swim continuously to breathe. They can't pump water through their gills without swimming.

1304) You need 14 calendars, seven for January 1 falling on each day of the week without a leap year and seven for January 1 falling on each day of the week with a leap year, for a perpetual calendar.

1305) The term fired, as in "get fired" or "you're fired," comes from the historical practice of burning down the dwelling place of unwanted members of a community, who had no choice but to leave and would potentially not survive.

1306) The Hundred Years War lasted 116 years, from 1337 to 1453.

1307) At 55.8 degrees north latitude, Moscow is the world's northernmost city with a population of over 10 million.

1308) By area, Ukraine is the largest country entirely in Europe; it is 223,000 square miles.

1309) The 1960 Squaw Valley Winter Olympics were the first Olympics televised in the United States.

1310) An average adult English speaker has a vocabulary of 20,000 words.

1311) Vito Corleone is the only movie character that has won Oscars for two different actors; Marlon Brando won for *The Godfather*, and Robert de Niro won for *The Godfather Part II*.

1312) In bowling, three strikes in a row are called a turkey because late 18th and early 19th-century bowling tournaments gave out food items as tournament prizes. At some point, getting three strikes in a row became associated with winning a turkey, and the name spread and stuck. Due to the much cruder equipment and lanes of long ago, getting three strikes in a row was a very difficult feat.

1313) The goliath frog, which lives in Cameroon and Equatorial Guinea, is the largest frog. It can be more than a foot long and weigh more than seven pounds.

1314) The giant armadillo has up to 100 teeth, the most of any land animal.

1315) The world's largest single living organism is a honey mushroom in Malheur National Forest in Oregon. It covers more than three square miles, weighs at least 7,500 tons, and is at least 2,000 years old. For most of the year, the honey mushroom is a thin white layer of fungus that spreads up under a tree's bark and rots its roots, eventually killing the tree over possibly decades. DNA testing has confirmed it is the same organism that has spread from a single location thousands of years ago.

1316) In 1967, *The Fugitive* was the first U.S. television series to feature a final episode where all plot lines were resolved and all questions were answered.

1317) Of the 48 contiguous states, Austin, Texas, is the southernmost state capital.

1318) A contronym is a word with two opposite meanings; for example, clip can mean fasten or detach.

1319) Sleep seems to clean the brain of harmful toxins. During sleep, the flow of cerebrospinal fluid in the brain increases dramatically, washing away harmful waste proteins that build up in the brain during waking hours.

1320) Through the LRP5 gene mutation, some people may have bones that are up to eight times denser than average.

1321) To mourn the deaths of their cats, ancient Egyptians shaved off their own eyebrows.

1322) Zugzwang is a situation in chess and other games where a player must move, but all moves are bad or put them at a disadvantage.

1323) In 1784, Benjamin Franklin first suggested the idea of daylight saving time.

1324) President Gerald Ford was born as Leslie Lynch King Jr.; after his mother remarried, he was adopted by his stepfather.

1325) Cappuccino gets its name from the similarity of its color to the robes of the Capuchin monks.

1326) After dropping out 34 years earlier, Steven Spielberg got his Bachelor of Arts degree from Cal State Long Beach; for his final project in advanced film making, he submitted *Schindler's List*.

1327) The GPS service used around the world is paid for by American taxpayers, mainly through the Department of Defense, which has primary responsibility for developing and operating the system. The operational cost of the system is over $2 million per day. GPS is not the only space-based radio navigation system; Russia has GLONASS; the European Union has Galileo, and China has BeiDou.

1328) Sound travels over four times faster in water than it does in air.

1329) Worldwide, Subway has the most fast food locations.

1330) Leo Fender, inventor of the Stratocaster and Telecaster guitars, couldn't play guitar.

1331) The number zero, with its own unique value and properties, did not exist until the 7th century. Before that, early counting systems only saw zero as a placeholder, not a true number.

1332) To minimize the risk of drowning, dolphins are usually born tail first.

1333) In 1958, Bob Richards was the first athlete to appear on the front of the Wheaties box; he was the 1952 and 1956 Olympic pole vault gold medalist.

1334) Johnny Vander Meer is the only pitcher in MLB history to throw consecutive no-hitters. He did it for the 1938 Cincinnati Reds.

1335) Writer T.S. Eliot wore green makeup; no one is quite sure why he dusted his face with green powder, but some speculate he was just trying to look more interesting.

1336) After discovering at the 1936 Summer Olympics that their flag was identical to Haiti, Liechtenstein added a crown to their flag.

1337) A bog body is a human body that has been preserved in a bog; the preservation can be extremely effective. In 1952, researchers discovered a man who lived around 300 BC who was so well-preserved they could determine his cause of death, a slit throat.

1338) At the population density of New York City, the entire population of the world would fit in an area 9% larger than the state of Texas.

1339) The June 28, 1914, assassination of Austria's Archduke Franz Ferdinand, considered the event that initiated WWI, could have been avoided if the archduke's driver hadn't made a wrong turn. Ferdinand was visiting Sarajevo, where seven potential assassins in favor of Bosnia and Herzegovina's freedom from Austria-Hungary were scattered along his car route. One of the assassins threw a hand grenade at the archduke's open car, but it only wounded members of the archduke's entourage, and the remaining assassins didn't get a chance. Later the same day, the archduke decided to visit the hospital to see the men wounded in the grenade attack. His driver took a wrong turn on the way to the hospital, and while turning around, they came to a stop in front of a sidewalk cafe where one of the assassins, 19-year-old Gavrilo Princip, happened to be. From only about five feet away, Princip fired two shots, killing the archduke and his wife.

1340) Crayola means oily chalk. It combines the French word "craie," meaning chalk, with "ola," shortened from the French word "oléagineux," meaning oily.

1341) In 2014 in an attempt to encourage children to eat healthier, McDonald's tested bubblegum-flavored broccoli. The flavor proved confusing to children and was never introduced.

1342) Captain Crunch's full name is Captain Horatio Magellan Crunch.

1343) The word "barbarian" originated in ancient Greece and was used for all non-Greek speaking people. It derives from the Greek word "bárbaros," which meant babbler since the Greeks thought speakers of foreign tongues made unintelligible sounds.

1344) Contrary to what we see today, ancient Greek sculptures were painted in bold primary colors. Between the use of special ultraviolet lamps and passages in Greek literature referring to colored statues, it is clear that statues were originally colored, and they only look the way they do today because the color has worn off.

1345) Based on passenger traffic, Atlanta, Georgia, is the world's busiest airport.

1346) Of the ten largest U.S. private homes ever built, nine were built in 1932 or earlier, and four were built in the 1880s and 1890s.

1347) *Bambi* holds the record for the longest time between an original film and its sequel; *Bambi II* was released in 2006, 64 years after the original.

1348) Platypuses sweat milk. They secrete milk from mammary glands like other mammals, but they don't have nipples, so the milk oozes from the surface of their skin, more like sweat. Because the delivery system is less hygienic, platypus milk contains antibacterial proteins to protect the babies.

1349) The sun accounts for 99.8% of our solar system's total mass.

1350) When Tic Tacs debuted in 1969, they were called Refreshing Mints; in 1970, the name was changed to Tic Tac because of the sound the mints made rattling in their container.

1351) When the queen of a bee colony becomes too old or unproductive, the worker bees dispose of her by clustering around her in a tight ball until she overheats and dies. The process is known as "cuddle death" or "balling."

1352) Despite having by far the longest coastline of any country, Canada's navy only has about 36 ships.

1353) In 18th century England, black teeth from eating too much sugar were considered a sign of wealth. Sugar was very expensive, and only the wealthy could afford it.

1354) Marilyn Monroe was the first Playboy centerfold.

1355) The largest private home ever built in the United States is the Biltmore Estate in Asheville, North Carolina. It was built for George Washington Vanderbilt II and was completed in 1895; it is 175,856 square feet.

1356) In 1965 at the age of 59, Satchell Paige pitched three innings for the Kansas City Athletics against the Boston Red Sox.

1357) The earth's core has enough gold to coat the entire surface of the earth to a depth of 1.5 feet.

1358) In a study, the smell of Crayola crayons was among the top 20 most frequently identified smells. The unique smell is largely due to stearic acid, a derivative of beef fat used to create the waxy consistency.

1359) Influenza killed an estimated 43,000 U.S. servicemen mobilized for WWI; it accounted for about half of all U.S. military deaths in Europe.

1360) There is a difference between coffins and caskets; coffins are typically tapered and six-sided; caskets are rectangular.

1361) From the age of 12 until just before his death, President John Quincy Adams kept a journal; it totaled 51 volumes and 14,000 pages.

1362) In 1908, U.S. Attorney General Charles Bonaparte, French Emperor Napoleon's great-nephew, founded the FBI. He created the Bureau of Investigation; in 1935, it was renamed the Federal Bureau of Investigation.

1363) Kangaroos continue to grow until they die.

1364) What we ate historically may have altered how we speak. The rise of agriculture thousands of years ago introduced softer foods into human diets that altered how human teeth and jaws wore down with age and made softer sounds like "f" and "v" slightly easier to produce.

1365) The greatest distance any human has ever been from the earth is 248,655 miles aboard *Apollo 13*.

1366) Abel Tasman discovered Tasmania, New Zealand, and Fiji on his first voyage, but he completely missed Australia.

1367) Koala bear fingerprints are virtually indistinguishable from human fingerprints, even with careful analysis under a microscope. They have the same loopy, whirling ridges as humans.

1368) Five countries have effectively 100% literacy rates: Andorra, Finland, Liechtenstein, Luxembourg, and Norway.

1369) Eleven countries are in the Nile River's drainage basin: Tanzania, Uganda, Rwanda, Burundi, the Democratic Republic of the Congo, Kenya, Ethiopia, Eritrea, South Sudan, Republic of Sudan, and Egypt.

1370) Until 1917, the NHL didn't allow goalies to drop to the ice to make saves. Before this, goaltenders were required to remain standing.

1371) With four miles to go in the 2004 Olympic men's marathon, Brazilian Vanderlei de Lima, who was leading by almost 30 seconds, was tackled to the ground by a spectator. Officials arrived and pulled the spectator off, and he continued the race, but he was subsequently caught and passed and ended up winning the bronze medal. He filed a protest that was not upheld.

1372) You can tell the age of a whale by counting the rings in its earwax.

1373) The initials "B.B." in B.B. King's name stand for Blues Boy.

1374) Because you can't tell if your bladder is full in space, astronauts are trained to go to the bathroom every two hours.

1375) An obligate carnivore is an animal that must eat meat as a biological necessity, such as cats.

1376) At 100 pounds, James Madison was the lightest U.S. president.

1377) The term genuine leather means that the product is made of real leather, but it also means it is the lowest quality of all products made from real leather.

1378) Aluminum is the most abundant metal in the earth's crust.

1379) The most common job in the United States is a retail salesperson.

1380) On average, most people have fewer friends than their friends have; this is known as the friendship paradox. You are more likely to be friends with someone who has more friends than someone who has fewer friends.

1381) Coffee originated in Ethiopia in the 11th century.

1382) Based on land area, Hulunbuir, China, is the world's largest city; it is 102,000 square miles, about the size of Colorado.

1383) Petrichor is the word for the pleasant odor after a rain. Streptomyces bacteria in the soil produce a molecule called geosmin that is released into the air when rain hits the ground, creating the smell. Humans are extremely sensitive to the smell.

1384) In the United States, there are 96 mountains at least 14,000 feet high.

1385) The longest tennis rally (a single point) ever recorded in professional tennis lasted 643 shots. It was in a 1984 women's tournament and lasted 29 minutes.

1386) Since space is defined as 100 kilometers or 62 miles above the earth, it would only take one hour to drive to space if you could.

1387) There is enough stone in the Great Pyramid of Giza to build a two-foot-tall by four-inch-wide wall around the entire earth.

1388) Warren G. Harding had size 14 feet, the largest of any U.S. president.

1389) Extirpation is local extinction; the species is extinct locally but still exists elsewhere.

1390) If the original Barbie doll was a real woman, she would be 5'9" tall, weigh 110 pounds, have measurements of 39-18-33, and wear a size 3 shoe. She would have a body mass index of 16.2, which would make her anorexic, and she wouldn't be able to menstruate.

1391) Founded in 1919, A&W is the oldest restaurant chain in the United States.

1392) The United Kingdom has more tornadoes per square mile than any other country.

1393) The elephant is the only animal with four forward-facing knees.

1394) In 1861, the *Times of London* carried the world's first weather forecast.

1395) Abraham Lincoln was the first president born outside the original 13 states.

1396) Jason Robards is the only actor or actress to win consecutive supporting acting Oscars; he won for *All the President's Men* (1977) and *Julia* (1978).

1397) Florida is the flattest state; there are only 345 feet between its highest and lowest points.

1398) Zebras are black with white stripes. Zebra embryos are completely black; the white stripes appear during the last embryonic stage.

1399) Bob Fitzsimmons was the lightest world heavyweight boxing champion ever; when he won the title in 1897, he was 167 pounds.

1400) Over the entire *Bonanza* television series, the Cartwrights proposed marriage 22 times: Little Joe (11), Hoss (6), Ben (3), and Adam (2). A lot of the engagements ended in death.

1401) The U.S. $10,000 bill was last printed in 1945 and is the largest denomination ever in public circulation; it had a portrait of Secretary of the Treasury Salmon P. Chase.

1402) Martha Washington was the first woman to appear on the front of U.S. paper currency. In 1886, she appeared on the $1 silver certificate.

1403) Morton's toe is when your second toe is longer than your big toe; it occurs in 10-20% of the population.

1404) The longest English word in any major dictionary is the 45-letter pneumonoultramicroscopicsilicovolcanoconiosis, a lung disease caused by inhalation of silicate or quartz dust.

1405) In the James Bond films, the acronym SPECTRE stands for Special Executive for Counterintelligence, Terror, Revenge, and Extortion.

1406) At 21,331 square miles, Devon Island, in Nunavut Territory, Canada, is the world's largest uninhabited island. It is at 75.2 degrees north latitude and is the world's 27th largest island.

1407) In 1776, Margaret Corbin became the first woman recognized as a soldier in the American Revolutionary War; she was also the first woman to receive a U.S. military pension.

1408) A googleganger is a person with the same name who shows up in results when you Google yourself.

1409) The moon and the sun fit together so perfectly in a solar eclipse because the sun is about 400 times larger than the moon, and it is also about 400 times further away from the earth, so the two appear to be the same size in the sky.

1410) Ravens can learn to talk better than some parrots, and they also mimic other noises, including other animals and birds. They have even been known to imitate wolves or foxes to attract them to a carcass to break it open, so the raven can get at it when they are done.

1411) Approximately 88% of the world's population lives in the Northern Hemisphere. About half of the world's population lives north of 27 degrees north latitude.

1412) In 1995, astronomers found a gas cloud 10,000 light-years away in the constellation Aquila that contains enough alcohol to make 400 septillion pints of beer.

1413) The X in airport code names is usually just a filler. Airports typically used the two-letter codes that the National Weather Service used for cities; when the three-letter code was made standard, some airports simply added the X to comply, thus LAX, PDX, etc.

1414) In the 1st century, the Romans had polar bears fight seals in amphitheaters they flooded with water.

1415) Unlike most other snakes, Anacondas deliver live babies instead of laying eggs; they give birth to up to 40 young at a time, each around two feet long.

1416) The "no animals were harmed" statement in movies only applies when the film is recording.

1417) In 1916, four years before women were given the right to vote, the first woman was elected to the U.S. Congress.

1418) The term Nazi existed before Hitler and was associated with backward peasants. The term was popularized by Hitler's opponents, and it was disliked and rarely used by the Nazis.

1419) In their lifetime, the average person produces 25,000 quarts of saliva.

1420) A group of giraffes is called a tower.

1421) Excluding insects and crustaceans, rabbits and parrots are the only two animals that can see completely behind themselves without turning their heads.

1422) A semordnilap is a word that makes a completely different word spelled backward, such as stressed and desserts. The word semordnilap is palindromes spelled backward.

1423) In 1898, heroin was introduced by Bayer and marketed as a non-addicting alternative to morphine and a treatment for cough-inducing illnesses like bronchitis. In 1906, the AMA approved it for general use and recommended it as a morphine replacement; soon, there were 200,000 heroin addicts in New York City alone.

1424) Saint John was the only apostle of Jesus to die a natural death.

1425) The Atlantic Ocean is the saltiest ocean.

1426) Baby carrots are regular carrots that have been chopped up and rounded by a machine. They were created in 1986 by a farmer who had too many misshapen carrots that he couldn't sell.

1427) Reindeer can see ultraviolet light. The human eye blocks UV light from reaching the retina, and in situations with a lot of reflected UV light like snow, it can damage the eye causing snow blindness. For reindeer, who must deal with reflected UV light from arctic snow most of the year, it makes sense they would develop a way of seeing into the UV light to protect themselves from snow blindness, but it also helps them in their survival. Important things like urine from predators or competitors, fur from predators, and lichen, one of their main food sources in the winter, absorb UV light and appear black against the snow, making them easy to see.

1428) Before 1824, no one knew that dinosaurs had existed. Although the name dinosaur wasn't applied until 1842, William Buckland, a geology professor at Oxford, was the first person to recognize dinosaurs when he used the name Megalosaurus to describe an extinct carnivorous lizard fossil.

1429) Thomas Edison is credited with suggesting the word hello be used when answering a telephone; Alexander Graham Bell thought ahoy was better.

1430) In 1956, the first enclosed, climate-controlled mall in the United States was opened in Edina, Minnesota.

1431) After man, the longest living land mammal is the elephant; the oldest known lived to 86.

1432) One regular 12-ounce can of Coca-Cola contains 10 teaspoons of sugar, about the recommended amount of sugar for an adult for an entire day.

1433) Griffonage is careless handwriting, a crude or illegible scrawl.

1434) When he first appeared in 1938, the original comics Superman couldn't fly; he could only jump the very specific distance of one-eighth of a mile. His flying ability first appeared in cartoons and radio plays; it wouldn't appear in comics until 1941.

1435) Albert Einstein co-invented a refrigerator. The coolants used in the original refrigerators were toxic and could leak; Einstein got involved when he read about a Berlin family killed in their sleep by leaking coolant. In 1926, he worked with one of his former students, Leo Szilardtor, to develop a refrigerator with no moving parts, so there were no seals to potentially leak. It operated at constant pressure and only required a heat source and was patented in the United States in 1930.

1436) Queen Victoria was prescribed marijuana for her menstrual cramps.

1437) In 1903, the first eight packs of Crayola crayons were sold door-to-door for a nickel. Due to their poor paper adhesion, the creators felt they wouldn't appeal to artists, so they decided to market to children and educators.

1438) Kevin Smith's comedy movie *Clerks* is loosely based on Dante's *The Divine Comedy*, which was written in the 14th century. The main protagonist, Dante Hicks, gets his name from this, and there are nine breaks in the film, representing the nine rings of hell.

1439) Peter Sellers was the first man to appear on the cover of *Playboy*.

1440) During WWII when Hitler visited Paris, the French cut the Eiffel Tower lift cables, so Hitler would have to climb the steps if he wanted to go to the top.

1441) When feeding, a hummingbird can lick 10-15 times per second.

1442) Alaska has 6,640 miles of coastline, more than the rest of the United States combined.

1443) The United States and the Soviet Union were in talks to go to the moon together; Nikita Khrushchev was about to accept the plan proposed by John F. Kennedy when Kennedy was assassinated. Khrushchev had built up a relationship with Kennedy and was suspicious of the new Johnson administration, so he rejected the plan.

1444) At 19,341 feet, Mount Kilimanjaro is the world's highest mountain that isn't part of a range.

1445) In 1934 on Thanksgiving Day, the first nationally televised football game was broadcast; Detroit played Chicago.

1446) In 1999, Albert Einstein was named *Time* magazine's Man of the Century.

1447) Checkers originated in Egypt as early as 200 BC.

1448) The average cumulus cloud weighs 1.1 million pounds.

1449) George Washington, John Adams, and Thomas Jefferson were all avid marble collectors and players.

1450) Corn, rice, and wheat account for about 51% of the world's calorie intake.

1451) Seahorses don't have teeth or stomachs and must eat constantly, so they don't starve.

1452) In 1932, the first NFL indoor game took place. With temperatures of 30 below in Chicago, the Bears played a game indoors against the Portsmouth Spartans in the Chicago Stadium, which was used mainly for horse shows; they played on a modified 80-yard field.

1453) The only land mammal native to New Zealand is the bat.

1454) Park is the most popular street name in the United States.

1455) The average adult human heart pumps about 2,000 gallons of blood each day.

1456) Charlton Heston has the longest screen time performance to ever win the Best Actor Oscar; he was on screen for 2 hours 1 minute and 23 seconds for *Ben-Hur* (1959).

1457) In 1938, the first U.S. minimum wage was instituted. It was $0.25 per hour, the equivalent of about $4.13 today.

1458) The brain is the highest percentage fat human organ. It is up to 60% fat, so everyone is a fathead.

1459) On May 23, 2012, the U.S. nuclear submarine *USS Miami* was damaged beyond repair by a fire set by an employee to get out of work early. While it was docked in a navy shipyard for overhaul, civilian employee Casey J. Fury started the fire by igniting some rags; he was sentenced to 17 years in federal prison and ordered to pay $400 million.

1460) If war is defined as an active conflict that has claimed more than 1,000 lives; humans have been entirely at peace for about 268 of the past 3,400 years, just 7.9% of the time.

1461) Cheetahs can't roar; they can purr, meow, hiss, bark, and growl.

1462) In 1930, the movie *Ingagi* was marketed as a documentary of a 1926 expedition led by British explorers Sir Hubert Winstead and Captain Daniel Swayne, who found a Congo tribe that worshipped a giant gorilla. It turned out to be fake, with Hollywood actors and Los Angeles children playing pygmies, but it was still the 11th highest-grossing film of the 1930s.

1463) Mountain Dew was originally developed in the 1940s as a mixer for whiskey.

1464) Worldwide, about 86% of adults are literate.

1465) A tornado can be nearly invisible. Since a tornado is just made up of wind, you don't see the tornado; what you see are the water droplets, dust, and debris that it picks up.

1466) While Kodak didn't introduce color film to the masses until 1935, the first color photograph was taken in 1861. Thomas Sutton and James Clerk Maxwell created a picture of a Scottish tartan ribbon of red, white, and green. They created the photo by taking three separate photos, using three different filters (red, green, and blue-violet) and superimposing them together. This is the basic three-color method that is used in all color imaging to this day.

1467) Blind people still dream. People who were born blind or lost their sight at four to five years old or younger don't have visual imagery in their dreams, but people who lost their sight later in life continue to dream with visual imagery as if they could still see.

1468) Singer Johnny Mathis was a world-class athlete in the high jump. He was invited to the Olympic trials but didn't go when he was also offered a recording contract. His major high jump competitor in the San Francisco Bay area, where he grew up, was future NBA Hall of Fame star Bill Russell.

1469) Jiffy is an actual measured unit of time. It has been used for different time values in different fields; in computer science, a jiffy defines the duration of one tick of a timer interrupt, usually 1-10 milliseconds. It also was defined as the time between electrical alternating current cycles. Today, it typically means 0.01 seconds.

1470) Since the formation of eggshells relies on a protein found only in a chicken's ovaries, scientists have concluded that the chicken came first.

1471) The blue whale has the longest tongue of any animal; it is about 18 feet long.

1472) When you snap your finger, the sound is from the finger hitting the palm; it doesn't come from the finger rubbing the thumb.

1473) The farthest object visible to the naked human eye is the Andromeda Galaxy, 2.6 million light-years away. It is visible as a dim, large, gray cloud almost directly overhead in a clear night sky.

1474) At 34.6 degrees south latitude, Buenos Aires, Argentina, is the world's southernmost city with a population of over 10 million.

1475) During WWII, Queen Elizabeth II served as a mechanic and driver.

1476) In 1903, Thomas Edison electrocuted an elephant. Edison was in a battle with Nikola Tesla over whether direct or alternating current would be implemented for the electric grid. Edison backed direct current, and to prove the dangers of alternating current, he went around the country electrocuting animals with alternating current. Edison lost the battle, and alternating current was implemented.

1477) In 1931, female pitcher Jackie Mitchell struck out Babe Ruth and Lou Gehrig. In an exhibition game between the New York Yankees and the Chattanooga Lookouts, a Class AA minor league team, she struck out Ruth and Gehrig in succession; she was 17 years old at the time. Baseball commissioner Kenesaw Mountain Landis banned women from the sport later that year.

1478) In 1975, the first McDonald's drive-thru was created in Sierra Vista, Arizona, near the Fort Huachuca military base. It was designed to serve military personnel who weren't permitted to get out of their cars off base while wearing fatigues.

1479) About 97.5% of Americans are awake at 6:00 p.m., the highest percentage of any hour.

1480) Because there isn't gravity for tears to flow downward, you can't really cry in space. The liquid builds up in a ball in the eye until it is large enough to break free of the eye and float around.

1481) Four planets in our solar system have rings: Jupiter, Saturn, Uranus, and Neptune. Galileo discovered Saturn's rings in 1610; the rings on the other planets weren't discovered until the 1970s.

1482) Because of the severe damage caused by rabbits in Australia, it is illegal to own a pet rabbit for private purposes in Queensland, Australia. You can only have a rabbit for public entertainment or science and research.

1483) Cats have 32 muscles in each ear and can move each ear independently. To locate sounds, they can swivel and rotate their ears 180 degrees. Humans have 6 muscles in each ear.

1484) It takes about 1,000 years for any cubic meter of ocean water to circulate around the world.

1485) With 50 stars, the U.S. flag has the most stars of any national flag.

1486) The clavicle (collar bone) is the most frequently broken bone in the human body.

1487) Kopi Luwak, known as civet coffee, is a very expensive type of coffee; it is made from partially digested coffee cherries eaten and defecated by civet cats.

1488) Dolphins call each other by name. Scientists have found evidence that dolphins use a unique whistle to identify each other.

1489) In 1693, *The Ladies' Mercury* was the world's first periodical designed and published for women.

1490) Even though it is the third most common element in the earth's crust, aluminum was more valuable than gold in the 1800s because it was so rare. Aluminum is seldom found in its pure form, and it is difficult to extract from ores, so before more efficient processes were developed to extract it, aluminum was quite rare. In the 1850s, aluminum was priced at $1,200 per kilogram, and gold was priced at $664 per kilogram.

1491) Feeding on krill, blue whales can consume 500,000 calories in a single mouthful.

1492) At 5,525 miles long, the United States and Canada share the world's longest land border.

1493) Benjamin Franklin earned an honorary induction into the International Swimming Hall of Fame. He had a lifelong love of swimming and invented some swim fins.

1494) At 5.6 mph, the Australian tiger beetle is the fastest known running insect.

1495) Despite what you see in the movies, Roman warships were not rowed by slaves. Only free Roman citizens had a duty to fight for the state; in exceptional times if they needed more men, they would admit slaves to the military, but they were either freed before enlisting or promised freedom if they fought well.

1496) At 60.0 degrees north latitude in Yekaterinburg, Russia, Vysotsky Business Center is the world's northernmost skyscraper (at least 150 meters tall).

1497) If you wrapped a rope around the earth's equator tightly hugging the ground, you would only need to add about 6.3 feet of rope for it to hover one foot above the ground around the earth.

1498) Baby elephants suck their trunk for comfort, just like human babies suck their thumbs.

1499) There are about 10 times more bacterial cells in the human body than there are body cells.

1500) Michelin restaurant stars are given out by the Michelin Tire Company, the same company whose mascot is the marshmallow-like Michelin Man.

Facts 1501-2000

1501) Abraham Lincoln established the Secret Service on the day he was assassinated, but it was originally only focused on counterfeiting and didn't protect the president until 1902 after William McKinley's assassination.

1502) For a human, a lethal dose of chocolate would be about 22 pounds. Theobromine is a powerful stimulant in chocolate and can cause death in high enough doses.

1503) In 1971 after a drilling rig collapsed into a crater in Darvaza, Turkmenistan, engineers set the gases on fire to prevent the spread of methane; they thought it would burn for a few weeks, but it has been burning ever since. The crater is about 230 feet in diameter and 100 feet deep and has become one of the most popular tourist attractions in the country.

1504) Edith Head won more Oscars than any other woman; she won eight for costume design.

1505) China has about half of the world's pigs.

1506) In *Gilligan's Island*, the *S.S. Minnow* was named after Newton Minow, head of the Federal Communications Commission (FCC). Sherwood Schwartz, the show's creator, did not care for Minow, who had called television "America's vast wasteland," so he named the soon-to-be shipwrecked ship after him.

1507) The competition between dogs and cats goes back millions of years. About 20 million years ago in North America, it appears that early cats led to the extinction of most of the ancient dogs.

1508) Whales, dolphins, orcas, and porpoises have an unusual form of sleep called unihemispheric slow-wave sleep. They shut down one hemisphere of their brain and close the opposite eye. During this time, the other half of the brain monitors what is happening in their environment and controls breathing functions. Dolphins will sometimes hang motionless at the surface of the water during sleep, or they may swim slowly.

1509) Rodents have more species than any other mammal.

1510) Gillis Grafstrom won a gold medal in the same event in both the Summer and Winter Olympics. He won a figure skating gold medal in the 1920 Antwerp Summer games; in 1924 when figure skating was moved to the Winter Olympics, he won gold again. He also repeated as the 1928 gold medalist.

1511) Research indicates that everyone dreams, whether they remember doing so or not.

1512) The zombie ant fungi can hijack an ant's central nervous and force the ant to do what it wants. When an ant contacts the fungal spores, the fungus infects the ant and quickly spreads throughout its body. Fungal cells in the ant's head release chemicals that hijack the ant's central nervous system. The fungus forces the ant to climb up vegetation and clamp down on a leaf or twig before killing it. After the ant is dead, the fungus grows a spore releasing stalk out of the back of the ant's head that infects more ants on the ground below.

1513) The largest currency denomination ever printed in the United States is the 1934 $100,000 bill, featuring a picture of Woodrow Wilson. It was only printed for three weeks in December 1934 and January 1935, and they were only used for official transactions between Federal Reserve Banks.

1514) The busiest muscles in the human body are in the eyes; it is estimated that they move 100,000 times a day.

1515) If you weigh 150 pounds on the earth, you would weigh 4,200 pounds on the sun.

1516) The character of Frasier Crane, played by Kelsey Grammar, was on U.S. television for more consecutive years than any other live-action sitcom character; between *Cheers* and *Frasier*, Grammer played Crane for 20 consecutive years.

1517) Iceland's phone book is alphabetized by first name. Everyone is referenced by their first name, and they don't have surnames in the traditional sense. Their surname is their father's first name suffixed with either son or daughter.

1518) The average human body has 30-40 trillion cells, and over 80% of them are red blood cells.

1519) The primary reason dog noses are wet is because dogs secrete mucus that aids their sense of smell.

1520) The Great Pyramid of Giza has eight sides; each of the four sides is split from base to tip by slight concave indentations, creating eight sides. The indentations were first noticed in 1940 by a pilot flying over.

1521) Orson Welles was only 25 years old when he co-wrote, produced, directed, and starred in *Citizen Kane*, which is still widely regarded as the greatest movie ever made.

1522) The Big Dipper isn't a constellation; it is an asterism. There are 88 official constellations in the night sky; any other grouping of stars that isn't one of the 88 is an asterism. In the Big Dipper's case, it is part of the Ursa Major (Great Bear) constellation.

1523) In 1879, Liege, Belgium, attempted to use 37 cats as mail carriers. Messages were placed in waterproof bags the cats carried around their necks. Not surprisingly, the cats proved to be unreliable and slow, taking many hours or a day to deliver the mail, and the service didn't last long.

1524) To make their urine smell sweet like roses, women in ancient Rome drank turpentine.

1525) If you smoothed out all the wrinkles in your brain, it would lie flat about the size of a pillowcase.

1526) The most common time to wake up in the middle of the night is 3:44 a.m.

1527) At the age of 13, Leann Rimes is the youngest solo singer ever to win a Grammy.

1528) In a short spurt, a domestic cat can run up to 30 mph; the fastest speed a human has ever run is about 28 mph.

1529) When the American Civil War started, Robert E. Lee didn't own any slaves, but Ulysses S. Grant did.

1530) Stephenie Meyer, the author of the *Twilight* books, chose the real town of Forks, Washington, as the setting for the books because it is the wettest town in the contiguous 48 states, and it is small, out of the way, and surrounded by forest. She had never been there.

1531) Since 2016, it has been illegal in France for supermarkets to throw away edible food; they must donate it to charities.

1532) In 1870, the first African American was elected to serve in the U.S. Congress; he was a senator from Mississippi.

1533) Desynchronosis is the technical term for jet lag.

1534) In about 1000 AD, Norse explorer Leif Erikson arrived in continental North America, approximately 500 years before Christopher Columbus.

1535) Pepsi was the first U.S. consumer product sold in the former Soviet Union.

1536) The giant and colossal squid's eye is up to 11 inches in diameter, the largest of any animal.

1537) Some expensive perfumes still contain whale poop. Ambergris, a waxy substance produced in the intestines of sperm whales, has been incorporated in perfumes for a long time as a binding agent; it helps the fragrance linger on the skin and intensifies the scent of the perfume. It has been mostly replaced by synthetic alternatives.

1538) Worldwide, there are about 3 trillion trees.

1539) Australia has the largest population of poisonous snakes of any country.

1540) The Barbie doll's full name is Barbara Millicent Roberts.

1541) Wendy's hamburgers are square because founder Dave Thomas took the phrase "not cutting corners" seriously, and he wanted the burgers to be square, so the patties stick out of the bun in a way that showcases the meat's quality.

1542) The pronghorn antelope is the second-fastest land animal; pronghorns can achieve speeds of 55 mph.

1543) Mead is the oldest, widely-popular, alcoholic beverage. It is made from honey and was popular as far back as 2000 BC.

1544) Hitler, Stalin, and Mussolini were all nominated for the Nobel Peace Prize.

1545) Typewriter is the longest English word that can be made using the letters on only one row of a standard keyboard.

1546) Psychologist William Marston was one of the inventors of the polygraph and created the comic character Wonder Woman and her Lasso of Truth.

1547) During WWII due to a lack of anti-tank weapons, the Soviet Union used dogs strapped with explosives against German tanks. The machine guns on German tanks were too high to reach the low-running suicide dogs, and the Germans couldn't easily emerge from their tanks and shoot them. The dogs were trained to go under the tanks and helped destroy over 300 tanks.

1548) Snapping shrimp can snap their specialized claw shut producing a cavitation bubble that releases a sound as loud as 218 decibels, louder than a rocket launch. When the bubble collapses, it can reach temperatures of 4,700 degrees Celsius, almost as hot as the surface of the sun.

1549) Except for sloths and manatees, all mammals have seven neck vertebrae.

1550) To make money off people that didn't like his client, Colonel Tom Parker, Elvis Presley's manager, sold "I Hate Elvis" and other anti-Elvis buttons.

1551) Eight presidents have been left-handed: Garfield, Hoover, Truman, Ford, Reagan, G.W. Bush, Clinton, and Obama.

1552) The locust is the only insect considered kosher.

1553) Squirrels cause about 10-20% of all power outages in the United States. Squirrel outages tend to be more localized and more quickly fixed than those caused by storms.

1554) At 16.5 million acres, southeastern Alaska's Tongass National Forest is the largest forest in the United States.

1555) The division sign (short horizontal line with a dot above and below) in math is called an obelus.

1556) The word tragedy comes from the Greek word "tragōidia," which means "goat song." There are several theories about what the word referred to, including that a goat was awarded as a prize to the winning play in early competitions and that performers wore goat skins.

1557) Koalas are one of the world's sleepiest animals; they sleep 22 hours per day.

1558) When Lord Byron became a student at Cambridge, dogs were prohibited, so he got a bear as a pet. The bear stayed in his lodgings, and Byron would take him for walks around the grounds.

1559) Depending on conditions, the lifespan of a housefly is 15-30 days.

1560) As soon as sand tiger shark embryos develop teeth while still in the womb, the largest of the embryos in each of the two uteruses attacks and eats its siblings, leaving just two pups to be born.

1561) Four-time Oscar-winning actress Katharine Hepburn was the Connecticut state golf champion at age 16.

1562) Canada is the only host country not to win a gold medal at its own Summer Olympics, the 1976 Montreal games.

1563) David is the most frequently mentioned name in the bible; Jesus is second.

1564) Without your pinky finger, you would lose 50% of your hand strength.

1565) Abraham Lincoln's son Robert is the only person known to have witnessed the assassination of three U.S. presidents; he witnessed the assassinations of his father, James A. Garfield, and William McKinley.

1566) Due to the Mpemba Effect, hot water may freeze faster than cold water. It still isn't clearly understood why.

1567) Mosquitos are by far the world's deadliest animal, killing over 700,000 people annually worldwide, primarily from malaria. Snakes are the second-most deadly animal, killing about 50,000 people; dogs are third, killing about 25,000 people, mainly through rabies. Crocodiles are the deadliest of the large animals, killing about 1,000 people. The hippopotamus is the deadliest large land mammal, killing an estimated 500 people annually.

1568) At 59.9 degrees north latitude, St. Petersburg, Russia, is the world's northernmost city with a population of over 1 million.

1569) Until 1953, New York City had a pneumatic tube mail network that spanned 27 miles and connected 23 post offices. At its peak, the system moved 95,000 letters a day at speeds of 30-35 mph.

1570) In 1973 in its first attempt at original programming, HBO put on a polka festival.

1571) Horses can't vomit. They have very strong lower esophageal sphincters that make it impossible for the valve to open under backward pressure from the stomach.

1572) About 1 in 2,000 human babies are born with a tooth, known as a natal tooth.

1573) Gold is the most malleable naturally occurring metal.

1574) When you read to yourself, your tongue and vocal cords still get movement signals from the brain. The process is known as subvocal speech and is characterized by minuscule movements in the larynx and other muscles involved in the articulation of speech; the movements are undetectable without the aid of machines.

1575) Interracial marriage wasn't fully legal in all U.S. states until 1967, so it was banned in some form for 191 years.

1576) President Dwight D. Eisenhower played football at West Point and was injured trying to tackle future Olympic and NFL star Jim Thorpe.

1577) Today's British accent first appeared among the British upper class about the time of the American Revolution. Before that, the British sounded like Americans.

1578) If they are swimming near each other, alligators will always give manatees the right of way.

1579) Neil Armstrong didn't say, "one small step for man" when he set foot on the moon. He said, "one small step for a man"; that is what Armstrong claims he said, and audio analysis confirms it. The famous line has been misquoted all these years.

1580) Since the start of the Winter Olympics, five athletes have won medals at both the winter and summer games: Eddie Eagan (U.S.), Jacob Tullin Thams (Norway), Christa Luding-Rothenburger (East Germany), Clara Hughes (Canada), and Lauryn Williams (U.S.).

1581) Laurence Olivier for *Hamlet* (1948) and Roberto Benigni for *Life Is Beautiful* (1997) are the only two people to direct themselves to the best actor or best actress Oscar.

1582) The Antarctic ice sheet has 90% of the earth's fresh water; it is equivalent to about 230 feet of water in the world's oceans.

1583) *Tom Jones* was the last film John F. Kennedy saw before his assassination.

1584) A mouse's sperm is bigger than an elephant's sperm. Large animals tend to have high numbers of smaller sperm.

1585) The most used letter in the English alphabet is e.

1586) Leatherback sea turtles have a third eye on the top of their head that allows them to detect night-day and seasonal cycles. The pink spot on their heads has very thin layers of bone and cartilage that allow light to pass through to the pineal gland in their brain. It acts as a biological clock regulating night-day and seasonal cycles, letting the turtles detect the subtle changes in sunlight from changing seasons.

1587) Alfred Hitchcock appeared in more than 30 Alfred Hitchcock films.

1588) Three-digit emergency phone numbers were first introduced in London in 1937. After a fire killed five people and the person calling for the fire brigade was kept waiting by the operator, they implemented the original 999 number.

1589) Written out in English (one, two, three, etc.), eight is the first number alphabetically, no matter how high you go.

1590) Wells Fargo has an ATM in McMurdo Station, Antarctica. A maintenance person shows up to service it every two years.

1591) In 1932, Mildred "Babe" Didrikson won the team championship single-handedly at the AAU national track and field meet. She competed in

8 out of 10 events; she won five and tied for first in a sixth event. She won the team championship, despite being the only member of her team.

1592) The television Emmy awards get their name from a tube used in early cameras. Image orthicon tubes were called immys, and the name was feminized to Emmy to match the female statuette.

1593) Producer Julia Phillips was the first woman to win a Best Picture Oscar; she won for *The Sting* (1973).

1594) New Zealand has the world's steepest drivable street; it has a 35-degree grade.

1595) Roman charioteer Gaius Appuleius Diocles, who lived in the 2nd century, was one of the most celebrated ancient athletes and might be the best-paid athlete of all time. He raced four-horse chariots, and records show he won 1,462 out of the 4,257 races he competed in. He also seemed to be a showman, making many of his victories come from behind last-second victories that made him even more popular. He raced for 24 years and retired at age 42. His winnings amounted to the equivalent of 2,600 kilograms of gold; considering the buying power at the time, that would make him a multi-billionaire in today's dollars.

1596) The Fahrenheit and Celsius temperature scales are the same at 40 degrees below zero.

1597) The longest earthworm is South African Microchaetus rappi; they can grow as long as 22 feet and average about 6 feet.

1598) Melania Trump is the only first lady not born a citizen of the United States. Louisa Adams was also born outside the United States, but her father was American, so she was still a citizen by birth.

1599) The hippopotamus is responsible for the most human deaths of any of the large African animals.

1600) At President Andrew Jackson's funeral in 1845, his pet parrot was removed for swearing.

1601) When the Gregorian calendar replaced the Julian calendar, 10 days were skipped; October 4, 1582, was followed by October 15, 1582, to get the calendar back on track with the position of the sun.

1602) Hawaiian pizza is Canadian; it was invented in 1962 in Ontario, Canada.

1603) The oldest surviving photograph was taken in 1826 by French photography pioneer Joseph Nicéphore Niépce. It is the view from the window of an estate in Burgundy, France; it was taken with an eight-hour exposure and was made on a pewter plate.

1604) The Pilgrims didn't first land at Plymouth Rock; they first landed in what is now Provincetown, Massachusetts, and signed the Mayflower Compact there. They arrived at Plymouth Rock five weeks later.

1605) China is the largest country with only one time zone; geographically, it has five time zones, but it chooses to use one standard time.

1606) With two exceptions, China owns all the world's giant pandas. Any panda in a foreign zoo is on loan from China with the agreement that China owns the panda and any offspring and that all offspring must also be returned to China before they are four years old. The only exceptions are two pandas China gave to Mexico before implementing the current policy.

1607) With an annual average temperature of 85.8 degrees Fahrenheit, Khartoum, Sudan, is the world's hottest national capital city.

1608) In 1891, Whitcomb Judson invented the zipper; it was originally for fastening shoes.

1609) Women spend about one year of their lives deciding what to wear.

1610) A gross is equal to 144 units; a great gross is 1,728 units (12 gross).

1611) Unwinding a roll of Scotch tape can produce enough x-rays to image a finger. As the tape is unpeeled and its adhesive snaps free of the surface, flows of electrons are released. The electrical currents generate strong, short bursts of x-rays, each about one billionth of a second long containing about 300,000 x-ray photons. Scientists were able to use the x-rays to image a finger. However, the phenomenon has been observed only when the tape is unpeeled in a vacuum.

1612) *Sesame Street's* Mr. Snuffleupagus has a first name, Aloysius.

1613) The male antechinus, a small mouse-like mammal in Australia, essentially kills itself mating. During their first mating season, males mate as much as 14 hours straight with as many females as they can over three weeks. Physically, males rapidly deteriorate during the mating period, and very few survive.

1614) Most of the world's supply of cork comes from cork oak trees, predominantly in Portugal and Spain.

1615) Squidgers are the larger discs used to shoot the winks in tiddlywinks.

1616) The frisbee was originally called the Pluto Platter.

1617) Pumice is the only rock that floats in water.

1618) In Victorian times, photography subjects were encouraged to say prunes instead of cheese. Among other reasons, Victorians thought it was classless to show a big toothy smile.

1619) The spire on the Empire State building was meant to be used as an airship dock.

1620) The United Kingdom and Great Britain are not the same. Great Britain includes England, Scotland, and Wales; the United Kingdom also includes Northern Ireland.

1621) At 0.05 millimeters thick, the eyelid is the thinnest skin on the human body; the palms and soles of the feet are the thickest, about 30 times thicker.

1622) Niddick is the term for the nape of the neck.

1623) Treason is the only crime defined in the U.S. Constitution (Article III, Section 3).

1624) The boa constrictor is the only living animal that has the same common and scientific name.

1625) A group of rhinoceros is called a crash.

1626) At an elevation of 13,615 feet, El Alto, Bolivia, is the world's highest elevation city with a population of over 1 million.

1627) As is often the case, the Disney film *Pinocchio* was a much lighter take on the original story. The original does feature a talking cricket, but he isn't named Jiminy Cricket. After receiving some advice he doesn't like, Pinocchio gets mad and kills the cricket. The talking cricket returns later as a ghost to give Pinocchio additional advice.

1628) On average, a person will die from a complete lack of sleep faster than from starvation. You can live about 11 days without sleep, but you can live weeks without food.

1629) A normal house cat has 18 claws; there are five on each front paw and four on each back paw.

1630) Sweden's official Twitter account is managed by a random citizen chosen each week.

1631) George Reeves, television's original Superman, was one of Scarlett's beaus, Brent Tarleton, in the movie *Gone with the Wind*.

1632) Because they felt it most resembled the surface of the moon, Apollo astronauts trained in Iceland.

1633) The king rat can go longer without drinking than any other land animal; they can go their entire life, three to five years, without drinking.

1634) Gerald Ford is the only U.S. president that wasn't elected president or vice president.

1635) There are 13 witches in a coven.

1636) Q-tips were originally called Baby Gays. They were originally for babies' eyes, ears, nostrils, and gums; the Q stands for quality.

1637) Mexican War hero Zachary Taylor was the first U.S president with no prior political experience.

1638) Lethologica is the word for when you can't remember a word.

1639) In Colombia and other South American countries, movie theaters sell spicy roasted ants that are munched the way American's enjoy popcorn.

1640) George Clinton was the first U.S. vice president to serve under two different presidents; he served as vice president to both Thomas Jefferson and James Madison.

1641) The word scientist was first used in 1833.

1642) Less than 2% of the world's population has red hair, the rarest human hair color.

1643) Due to spinal decompression, you are about one centimeter taller when you wake up in the morning.

1644) Tim Berners-Lee, the inventor of the World Wide Web, regrets putting the double slashes in URLs. It was a programming convention at the time, but it wasn't necessary and has caused a lot of wasted time typing and wasted paper printing.

1645) The name Arctic is from the Greek word "Arktos," meaning bear; in this case, bear is a celestial reference to the Little and Great Bear constellations of the Northern Hemisphere. Antarctica comes from the Greek "Antarktikos," which means the opposite, and therefore, the opposite end of the earth.

1646) Lesotho is the only country that lies completely above 1,000 meters elevation; it has an area of 11,720 square miles.

1647) Insects don't flap their wings. An insect's wings are attached to its exoskeleton; they contract their muscles and force their whole body to vibrate, causing their wings to vibrate.

1648) The slime mold physarum polycephalum is neither a plant, an animal, or a fungus, and it doesn't have two sexes; it has 720. It can also split into different organisms and fuse back together. It is bright yellow and can creep along at a speed of up to 1.6 inches per hour. It can also solve problems, even though it doesn't have a brain. The unicellular being is believed to be about a billion years old, but it first came to the public's attention in May 1973 after a Texas woman discovered a rapidly expanding yellow blob growing in her backyard. Researchers have found that physarum polycephalum can learn to ignore noxious substances and remember that behavior up to a year later. The slime mold is also believed to be capable of solving problems, such as finding the shortest way through a maze and anticipating changes in its environment. It lives on forest floors and thrives in temperatures between 66 and 77 degrees Fahrenheit and humidity levels between 80% and 100%. It is almost immortal; it can be killed by light and drought, but it can hibernate several years when threatened.

1649) The earliest pillows date back 9,000 years to Mesopotamia; they were made from stone, with a curved top, and were designed to keep the head off the ground and prevent insects from crawling into the mouth, nose, and ears.

1650) Ravens, crows, jays, and some songbirds lie in anthills and roll around letting the ants swarm on them, or they chew up the ants and rub them on their feathers. It is called anting, and it isn't understood why they do it.

1651) In 1799, the first U.S. commercial vineyard and winery was established in Lexington, Kentucky.

1652) St. Peter Stiftskulinarium restaurant in Salzburg, Austria, is the world's oldest restaurant and has been in operation since 803 AD.

1653) Writing punctuation as we largely know it today did not exist until the 15th century.

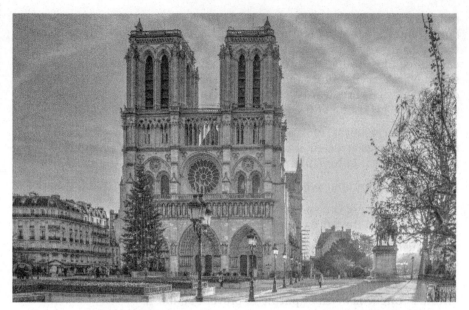

1654) In the 19th century, Notre Dame Cathedral was almost demolished, but it was saved by Victor Hugo's *The Hunchback of Notre Dame*. Hugo wrote the novel partially to save the cathedral from demolition.

1655) A strawberry isn't a berry, but a banana is. Botanically, a berry must have three layers: a protective outer layer, a fleshy middle, and an inner part that holds the seeds. It must also have two or more seeds and come from a flower with only one ovary. Strawberries come from a single flower with more than one ovary, making them an aggregate fruit.

1656) Some people who get bitten by the lone star tick can develop a sudden allergy to red meat. The allergy affects the sensitivity to a carbohydrate called galactose-alpha-1,3-galactose, which is in most mammal cell membranes, so the allergy doesn't extend to poultry or seafood. The lone star tick has been recorded as far north as Maine and as far west as central Texas and Oklahoma.

1657) In 1663, the first magazine ever was launched in Germany; it was a philosophy and literature periodical.

1658) You can fire a gun in the oxygen-free environment of space. Fires can't burn without oxygen, but modern ammunition contains its own oxidizer to trigger the explosion of gunpowder and fire the bullet; no atmospheric oxygen is required.

1659) After going deaf, Beethoven discovered that he could bite on a metal pole connected to the piano he was playing and hear almost perfectly. This process is known as bone conduction; vibrations are transferred into the bones, and the ears pick up the signal with no sound distortion, bypassing the eardrums. We all hear sounds through both our bones and our eardrums; most sounds are air conducted, where the eardrum converts sound waves to vibrations and transmits them to the inner ear. In some cases, vibrations are heard directly by the inner ear, bypassing your eardrums. This is one of the ways you hear your own voice.

1660) On December 9, 1967, Jim Morrison was the first rock star arrested on stage. He was arrested at the New Haven Arena in Connecticut; it was for an incident that took place with a police officer before the show.

1661) Of all paragraphs written in English, 80% contain the word "the."

1662) The Japanese Onagadori chicken has the world's longest feathers; its tail feathers can measure over 10 meters.

1663) Australia has the world's longest fence; the dingo fence was completed in 1885 and is 3,488 miles long.

1664) Since it is exposed to the sun a lot of the time while they eat, a giraffe's tongue is black or purple to prevent sunburn.

1665) The word plagiarism comes from the Latin word "plagiarius," meaning kidnapper.

1666) From a standing position, pigs are physically incapable of looking up toward the sky.

1667) As part of his divorce settlement, Einstein had to give his Nobel Prize money to his ex-wife.

1668) South Africa is the first nation that created nuclear weapons and then voluntarily got rid of them.

1669) Baltimore, Maryland, is the largest independent city in the United States; it is not part of any county.

1670) As much as 95% of all dreams are forgotten shortly after waking. Research suggests that the changes in the brain during sleep do not support the information processing and storage for forming long-lasting memories.

1671) The nursery rhyme *Mary Had a Little Lamb* is based on the true story of Mary Sawyer of Sterling, Massachusetts, who as an 11-year-old was followed to school by her pet lamb. John Roulstone, a student a year or two older, handed Mary a piece of paper the next day with a poem he had written about it. In 1830, Sarah Josepha Hale, a well-known writer and editor, published *Poems for Our Children* that included a version of the poem.

1672) The shortest country names have four letters: Chad, Togo, Mali, Iraq, Iran, Oman, Laos, Niue, Fiji, Cuba, and Peru.

1673) If the earth's history was condensed to 24 hours, humans would appear at 11:58:43 p.m.

1674) Hippos are only territorial in water, not on land.

1675) After the fall of the Roman Empire, the technology to make concrete was lost for 1,000 years. Roman concrete is still more durable than the concrete we make today, and it gets stronger over time. Their concrete was created with volcanic ash, lime, and seawater mixed with volcanic rock; it created a rock-like concrete we haven't been able to duplicate.

1676) Mongolia is the least densely populated country; areas like Greenland have even lower density but aren't independent countries.

1677) Elton John has performed more concerts in Madison Square Garden than any other artist.

1678) Matt Dillon, played by James Arness on *Gunsmoke* from 1955 to 1975, and Detective John Munch, played by Richard Belzer on *Homicide: Life on the Street* from 1993 to 1999 and on *Law & Order: Special Victims Unit* from 1999 to 2013, appeared for more consecutive years than any other male, live-action, primetime characters on U.S. television.

1679) The 3 Musketeers candy bar got its name because it originally came in a package that had three pieces with different nougat flavors: vanilla, chocolate, and strawberry.

1680) There are more insects in one square mile of empty field than there are people in the world.

1681) With less than 400 residents, Ngerulmud, Palau, is the world's smallest population national capital. Palau is an island nation in the Pacific Ocean.

1682) In South Korea, there is an emergency phone number to report spies; it is 113.

1683) Natiform describes something that resembles a butt.

1684) In 1963, the United States launched 500 million whisker-thin copper wires into orbit to create a ring around the earth. It was envisioned as the largest radio antenna ever and a way to protect long-range communications if the Soviet Union attacked; it was called Project West Ford.

1685) Humans have a gaze detection system that is especially sensitive to whether someone is looking directly at you or whether their gaze is averted just a few degrees. Studies have recorded brain activity and found that specific brain cells fire when the gaze is direct; others fire if the gaze is just a few degrees off. Our brain specialization is an indication of how important eye contact is when communicating with others

1686) At 59.9 degrees north latitude, St. Petersburg, Russia, is the world's northernmost city with a population of over 5 million.

1687) Camel milk won't curdle. The structure of the protein in camel milk differs from cows, goats, sheep, and other animals; due to its composition, camel milk does not curdle naturally.

1688) In ancient Egypt, the penalty for killing a cat, even accidentally, was death.

1689) Plato first wrote about the lost civilization of Atlantis in 360 BC.

1690) At normal atmospheric pressure, helium is the only element in the universe that can't freeze; it can't get cold enough.

1691) Almost 3% of the ice in the Antarctic glaciers is from penguin urine.

1692) The Afghan War is the longest war in U.S. history.

1693) In England during WWI, people started wearing pajamas instead of nightgowns, so they would be prepared to run outside in public during air raids.

1694) The bloodhound is the first animal whose evidence is legally admissible in some U.S. courts.

1695) The blue whale is the largest animal that has ever lived. They can be up to 100 feet long and weigh 200 tons.

1696) Babe Ruth wore a cabbage leaf under his cap. To keep cool, he put chilled cabbage leaves under his cap.

1697) In 1863, a military draft was started to provide troops for the Union army during the American Civil War. The draft was set up to allow two ways that you could avoid going; you could pay $300 or find someone else to go in your place. What happened is that people paid $300 to have someone else go in their place. Some people made a career out of taking the money to be a substitute, deserting, and repeating the process.

1698) In the 3rd century BC, Aristarchus of Samos first proposed that the planets orbited the sun. Copernicus developed a fully predictive model in the 16th century, but he wasn't the first to propose the concept.

1699) In 1984, Linda Hunt won a Best Supporting Actress Oscar for *The Year of Living Dangerously*; it was the first Oscar ever for playing the opposite sex.

1700) Due to erosion, Niagara Falls has receded about seven miles over the last 12,500 years.

1701) In 1999, a federal arbitration panel decided that the U.S. government had to pay the heirs of Abraham Zapruder $16 million for his original film of John F. Kennedy's assassination. The acquisition was necessitated by a 1992 federal law that required all records of the Kennedy assassination to be transferred to the National Archives for preservation and research. The Zapruder family still controlled the licensing of images from the film; the issue was the value of the original.

1702) The Indonesian word for water is air.

1703) In the Braille system, there are six dots in each letter.

1704) By area, Manitoulin Island, in Lake Huron, is the world's largest freshwater island; it is over 1,000 square miles and is part of Ontario, Canada.

1705) Arachibutyrophobia is the fear of peanut butter sticking to the roof of your mouth.

1706) Marie Curie (1903 Physics and 1911 Chemistry) and Linus Pauling (1954 Chemistry and 1962 Peace) are the only people to win Nobel Prizes in two different categories.

1707) In 1958 as part of a high school history class project, Robert Heft designed the current 50-star U.S. flag.

1708) Peter the Great ordered the Russian nobility to become more European by shaving off their beards.

1709) The onion is the world's most widely used vegetable.

1710) Velociraptors were nothing like they were portrayed in the movie *Jurassic Park*. They were about 3 feet tall and 6 feet long, including tail; they had feathers and weighed about 30 pounds, the size of a large turkey.

1711) There are at least 24 dialects of English spoken in the United States.

1712) Violet Jessop (1887-1971) survived the collision of the *RMS Olympic* on September 20, 1911, the sinking of the *RMS Titanic* on April 14, 1912, and the sinking of the *HMHS Britannic* on November 21, 1916. She was an ocean line stewardess and nurse.

1713) In medieval manuscripts, it is common to see pictures of knights fighting snails; no one knows why.

1714) The skin on a whale shark's back can be up to four inches thick, and they can make it even tougher by clenching the muscles just beneath the skin. Their underbellies are relatively soft and vulnerable, so they will often turn their belly away when approached.

1715) Iceland had the first openly gay or lesbian prime minister; Jóhanna Sigurðardóttir was prime minister from 2009-2013.

1716) As a defense mechanism, bombardier beetles emit a hot noxious chemical spray that is produced from a reaction between hydroquinone and hydrogen peroxide, which are stored in two reservoirs in the beetle's abdomen. When the solutions are mixed with catalysts, the heat from the reaction brings the mixture to near the boiling point of water and produces gas that drives the ejection. The spray can be fatal to attacking insects. There are over 500 species of bombardier beetles, and they live on all continents except Antarctica.

1717) For the television series *M*A*S*H*, Alan Alda was the first person to win acting, writing, and directing Emmys for the same series.

1718) Founded in 1811, Astoria, Oregon, is the oldest U.S. city west of the Rocky Mountains.

1719) The Great Pyramid of Giza was originally covered in highly-polished white limestone; it was removed over time, so it could be used for other building projects.

1720) Ronald Wayne was the third co-founder and a 10% shareholder of Apple Computer; in 1976, he sold his stake for $800.

1721) On a clear night in a dark area, you can see about 2,000 stars in the sky.

1722) Sharks don't get cavities because the outside of their teeth is made of fluoride.

1723) Franklin D. Roosevelt was the first U.S. president to fly on official business; in 1943, he made a secret trip to Casablanca, Morocco.

1724) On average, female anaconda snakes are 4.7 times larger than males, the largest size difference between sexes of any land vertebrate.

1725) Based on cargo-carrying capacity, the largest current cruise ships are about five times the size of the *Titanic*.

1726) Russia's forested land is larger than Australia.

1727) Scatomancy, the practice of telling the future through someone's poop, was popular in ancient Egypt.

1728) Measured by its share of the world's population, the largest empire in history was the Persian Empire; in 480 BC, it accounted for approximately 44% of the world's population. Comparatively, the British Empire accounted for about 23% of the world's population at its peak.

1729) WWI greatly increased the number of women wearing bras. Before the war, corsets were still the norm, but corset frames were mostly made of metal, which was needed for the war effort, so in 1917, the U.S. War Industries Board asked American women to stop buying them, accelerating the move to bras.

1730) Tsundoku is the act of acquiring books and not reading them.

1731) Horseshoe crab blood is worth $14,000 per quart because its unique chemical properties make it very valuable for bacterial testing. It can coagulate around as little as one part in a trillion of bacterial contamination, and the reaction only takes 45 minutes, instead of two days with mammalian blood.

1732) The giant clam is the largest mollusk and can reach 4 feet in length and weigh more than 500 pounds. They live in the warm waters of the South Pacific and Indian Oceans and can live more than 100 years.

1733) The Pacific Ocean is so large that at some points it is antipodal to itself. Two points are antipodal if they are on diametrically opposite sides of the earth. At some points in the Pacific Ocean, you could go straight through the center of the earth and come out on the other side and still be in the Pacific Ocean.

1734) The word goodbye is a contraction of "God be with ye."

1735) The international distress signal one level less serious than Mayday is Pan-Pan; Securite is the third level.

1736) The Huston and Coppola families have three generations of Oscar winners; Walter, John, and Anjelica Huston and Carmine, Francis Ford, and Sofia Coppola have all won Oscars.

1737) By area, New Mexico is 0.2% water, the lowest percentage of any state.

1738) Franklin D. Roosevelt was put on the dime primarily for his work for March of Dimes, which was originally called the National Foundation for Infantile Paralysis.

1739) In the song "Yankee Doodle," the term macaroni means stylish or fashionable. In late 18th century England, the term macaroni came to mean fashionable; in the song, it is used to mock the Americans, who think they can be stylish by simply sticking a feather in their cap.

1740) Malaria is believed to have killed more people than any other disease in history; it still kills about 1 million people annually.

1741) Thirty-five percent of the world's population drives on the left side.

1742) More than 90% of your serotonin, the neurotransmitter that contributes to feelings of well-being and happiness, is produced in the digestive tract.

1743) Female ferrets can die if they don't mate. The female stays in heat until she mates; if she doesn't, very high levels of estrogen remain in her blood for a long time and can cause aplastic anemia and death. She doesn't have to get pregnant, but she must mate.

1744) *Ben-Hur: A Tale of the Christ* was the first fictional novel blessed by the pope.

1745) Based on his medical records, Adolf Hitler had a huge problem with flatulence. He was regularly taking 28 different drugs to control it. Some of the anti-gas pills he used contained a base of strychnine, which caused further stomach and liver issues.

1746) Ambisinistrous means no good with either hand; it is the opposite of ambidextrous.

1747) About 85% of humans only breathe out of one nostril at a time. They switch between nostrils about every four hours, although it varies by person, body position, and other factors.

1748) A blue whale's arteries are so large that an adult human could swim through them.

1749) Yellowstone National Park has most of the world's geysers.

1750) Idaho was the last state explored by Europeans or Americans (not Native Americans); it wasn't explored until Lewis and Clark entered Idaho in 1805.

1751) Opossums don't play dead. If frightened, they go into shock, which induces a comatose state that can last from 40 minutes to 4 hours.

1752) If you have bloodshot eyes after swimming in a pool, it isn't chlorine causing the reaction; it is urine mixing with the pool's chemicals. The nitrogen in urine combines with the chlorine and forms chloramine that causes eye irritation.

1753) Kentucky produces about 95% of the world's bourbon and has an inventory of 7.5 million barrels, almost two barrels for each of its residents.

1754) Dragonflies may have the best vision of any animal. Humans have three light-sensitive proteins in the eye for red, blue, and green (tri-chromatic vision); dragonflies have up to 33. Their bulbous eyes also have 30,000 facets and can see in all directions at once.

1755) For Thomas Edison's death in 1931, all non-essential lights in the United States were turned off for one minute in his honor.

1756) The shape of a Pringles chip is called a hyperbolic paraboloid; it allows easier stacking and reduces broken chips.

1757) Different cells in the human body have very different lifespans. Sperm cells have a lifespan of about 3 days; colon cells die off after about 4 days; white blood cells live for about 13 days; cells in the top layer of your skin live about 30 days. Red blood cells live for about 120 days; liver cells live about 18 months, and brain cells typically last an entire lifetime.

1758) The practice of quarantine began during the 14th century when ships arriving in Venice from plague-infected ports were required to sit at anchor for 40 days before landing. The word quarantine derives from the Italian words "quaranta giorni," meaning 40 days.

1759) Melanistic animals are the opposite of albinos. They are all black and have an excess of melanin that makes their skin, hair, or fur very dark or black.

1760) In 1893, New Zealand was the first country to allow women to vote.

1761) A Danish journalist covering the 1900 Paris Olympics won a gold medal. He was recruited to replace an ill team member on the combined Sweden/Denmark tug of war team, and they went on to win gold.

1762) The British navy plays Britney Spears music to help scare off Somali pirates.

1763) In 1771, future president James Madison was the first graduate student ever at Princeton University.

1764) Queen Elizabeth II is the world's largest landowner; she technically owns 6.6 billion acres, about one-sixth of the world's land, including Canada and Australia.

1765) Nepetalactone, the essential oil in catnip that gives the plant its characteristic odor, is about 10 times more effective at repelling mosquitoes than DEET, the compound found in most commercial insect repellents.

1766) Cats don't have very good close vision. When they are near water, they may not be able to see the water or the water level; that is why they will frequently paw the water to feel the level or move the dish to cause a disturbance in the water, so they can see it.

1767) *Law & Order: Special Victims Unit* is the only U.S. primetime drama ever spun off from two different shows. It spun off from *Law & Order*, and the character of Detective John Munch came from *Homicide: Life on the Street*.

1768) Louis Armstrong was so hard on his lips with his trumpet playing that he developed lip callouses that he treated with a special salve or even cut off himself. Satchmo's Syndrome is named after Armstrong and is a disorder due to the rupture of the orbicularis oris muscle in the mouth, typically in trumpet players.

1769) *All in the Family, The Golden Girls, Will & Grace,* and *Schitt's Creek* are the only four television series that won Emmys for all their main cast members.

1770) The world's largest recorded turtle was a leatherback turtle that washed up on Harlech Beach, Wales, in 1988. It was estimated to be 100 years old and was almost 9 feet long and weighed 2,016 pounds.

1771) Pen caps have a hole in them to minimize the risk of children inhaling them and choking to death. It is an international safety standard.

1772) At age 69, Jill Biden is the oldest U.S. first lady at the time of election.

1773) In legislation passed in 1975, the U.S. Congress allowed 15 years for voluntary conversion to the metric system.

1774) Founded in 1565, St. Augustine, Florida, is the oldest U.S. city.

1775) Peter Sellers, Alan Arkin, Roger Moore, Roberto Benigni, and Steve Martin have all played Inspector Clouseau in Pink Panther movies.

1776) Hawaii is the only state without a straight line in its border; its borders are entirely defined by natural features.

1777) There are 60 seconds in a minute and 360 degrees in a circle because the ancient Babylonians did math in base 60 instead of base 10 and developed the concepts.

1778) Chang is the world's most common surname.

1779) To avoid dating relatives, Iceland has a phone app that lets users bump phones to see if they are related. Iceland has a relatively small population of over 300,000 people and is somewhat insular, so most people are distantly related. The app emits a warning alarm if people are closely related, so they know not to date.

1780) Spoonfeed is the longest English word with letters arranged in reverse alphabetical order.

1781) You can never recall a single memory by itself; memories are always recalled in packages because that is how the hippocampus stores them.

1782) Excluding man, dolphins have the longest tested memory. Bottlenose dolphins have unique whistles, like names; studies have shown that they remember the whistle of other dolphins they have lived with, even after 20 years of separation.

1783) As a republic and a state, Texas has had 12 different capital cities, including Galveston, Houston, and Austin.

1784) In *To Kill a Mockingbird*, the character Dill Harris, the boy who is visiting for the summer, is based on author Truman Capote. He was a childhood friend and neighbor of author Harper Lee, and they remained lifelong friends.

1785) A Japanese men's marathon runner at the 1912 Stockholm Olympics had an official finishing time of 54 years, 8 months, 6 days, 5 hours, 32 minutes, and 20.3 seconds. When he went to the Stockholm games, Shizo Kanakuri was an experienced runner and held the 25-mile world record; he started the race, but temperatures of almost 90 degrees Fahrenheit forced him to drop out after more than 18 miles. He did not notify the officials, and feeling ashamed that he did not finish, he went quietly back to Japan and was listed as missing in the results. In 1967, a Swedish television show started looking for the missing marathon runner, and at the age of 75, Kanakuri was invited to Sweden for the 55th anniversary of the 1912 games. He was allowed to finish the race and receive an official time.

1786) By area, the five smallest landlocked countries are all in Europe: Vatican City, San Marino, Liechtenstein, Andorra, and Luxembourg.

1787) In the movie *The China Syndrome*, the title refers to a hypothetical catastrophic failure where a nuclear reactor melts through the floor of its containment system and penetrates the earth's surface as if traveling through toward China.

1788) Iceland has the highest per capita electricity consumption; it is about four times higher than in the United States.

1789) Humans need 16 to 20 images per second to perceive something as a moving picture, rather than a flickering image; dogs need 70 images per second. Older televisions could only produce 50 images per second, so dogs would only see flickering images; modern televisions are fast enough to appear as moving pictures to dogs.

1790) The first website was launched by CERN in 1989.

1791) In ancient Egypt, men sat to pee and women stood.

1792) Alcatraz used to be the only U.S. federal prison where inmates got hot showers. They didn't want inmates to get acclimatized to cold water, in case they tried to swim to shore.

1793) Winnie the Pooh's real name is Edward Bear.

1794) Mexico City has more American emigrants than any other city.

1795) Forty percent of schizophrenics are left-handed; only 10% of the total population is left-handed.

1796) Wilmer McLean's homes were involved in both the beginning and end of the American Civil War. On July 21, 1861, the First Battle of Bull Run took place on his farm near Manassas, Virginia. To escape the war, he moved to Appomattox, Virginia, but in 1865, General Robert E. Lee surrendered to Ulysses S. Grant in McLean's house in Appomattox.

1797) The original constitution of the United States included an open invitation for Canada to join the United States. Ratified in 1781, the Articles of Confederation were replaced by the U.S. Constitution in 1789. There was a clause stating if Canada agreed to become a member of the United States, it would automatically be accepted without the consent of the other states.

1798) Mexico has the most emigrants (people living in other countries).

1799) Mickey Mouse first appeared in a Disney animated feature in *Fantasia* (1940).

1800) A group of butterflies is called a kaleidoscope.

1801) The arrector pili muscles, located near the root of human hair follicles, are responsible for goosebumps.

1802) About 99.9% of all commercially grown artichokes come from California.

1803) Twenty-two countries don't maintain an army, including Andorra, Costa Rica, Panama, Grenada, Haiti, Iceland, and Liechtenstein.

1804) Suriname has a higher percentage of forested land than any other country.

1805) The V-shaped formation of a flock of geese is called a skein.

1806) Pregnancy tests have existed for about 3,400 years. Ancient Egyptian women urinated on a bag of barley and a bag of wheat; if the grain in either bag sprouted, she was pregnant. If the barley sprouted first, it would be a boy; if the wheat sprouted first, it would be a girl. In 1963, a test found that the method was accurate about 70% of the time in determining pregnancy but wasn't accurate in determining the baby's gender.

1807) Gene Autry is the only person with a star in each of the five categories (movies, television, music, radio, live performance) on the Hollywood Walk of Fame.

1808) The Harlem Globetrotters are the only sports team to play on all seven continents.

1809) On September 27, 1922, *The Power of Love*, the first 3D movie ever, premiered at the Los Angeles Ambassador Hotel Theater. It could be shown with a single projector, but it required special glasses for viewing.

1810) Wallace's giant bee is the world's largest bee species; it is native to Indonesia and was thought to be extinct for over a century until it was rediscovered in 1981. Females have a 2.5-inch wingspan and are about 1.5 inches long.

1811) Fruit flies produce the largest sperm of any animal. Their sperm is coiled up and unspools to about 2.3 inches, approximately 20 times the length of their body and 1,000 times larger than human sperm.

1812) When her husband was elected president, Eleanor Roosevelt was the editor of the magazine *Babies Just Babies*.

1813) In 1799 in North Carolina, a 12-year-old boy found a 17-pound gold nugget in a creek and took it home; not realizing what it was, the family used it as a doorstop for three years. In 1802, the boy's father sold the nugget to a jeweler, still not realizing what it was. Later, he learned the value of the nugget, and the Carolina Gold Rush, the first gold rush in the United States, started.

1814) The Tom Hanks movie *The Terminal* was inspired by a man who lived at the departure lounge of Charles de Gaulle International Airport for 18 years.

1815) The band Jethro Tull was named after the inventor of the seed drill.

1816) In 2013, the remains of England's King Richard III were found buried under a parking lot in Leicester England; in 1485, he was the last English king to die on the battlefield.

1817) In 1942, Glenn Miller received the first-ever music gold disc for "Chattanooga Choo Choo."

1818) Twelve people have walked on the moon, but only three have been to the deepest part of the ocean. Director James Cameron is one of the three.

1819) While at the opening ceremonies of the 1939 New York World's Fair, Franklin D. Roosevelt was the first U.S. president ever televised.

1820) Peter Finch for *Network* (1976) and Heath Ledger for *The Dark Knight* (2008) are the only two people to win posthumous acting Oscars.

1821) Leonardo da Vinci was the first person to explain why the sky is blue.

1822) Alaska receives the least sunshine of any state.

1823) The left leg of a chicken is more tender than the right. Chickens scratch with their right leg, building up more muscle in that leg and making it tougher than the left.

1824) The Catholic church made Galileo recant his theory that the earth revolves around the sun; it took them 359 years to declare Galileo was right in 1992.

1825) Lake Nicaragua is one of the world's very few freshwater lakes with sharks. Bull sharks can survive in both fresh and saltwater, and they make their way back and forth from the Caribbean Sea to Lake Nicaragua via a 120-mile route through the San Juan River. Researchers have tagged sharks and verified that they move back and forth between the lake and the sea.

1826) There is a basketball court one floor above the U.S. Supreme Court. It is named "The Highest Court in the Land" and was once a spare room to house journals. In the 1940s, it was converted into a workout area for courthouse workers, and backboards and baskets were installed later. It is smaller than a regulation basketball court and is used by clerks, off-duty police officers, and other supreme court employees.

1827) Canada is the only country where more than 50% of its adults have college degrees.

1828) People have surfed for 8 miles and over 30 minutes continuously riding a wave upstream on the Amazon River. The Pororoca is a tidal bore wave that is up to 13 feet high, travels up to 500 miles inland upstream, and has become popular with surfers. The wave occurs during new and full moons when the ocean tide is the highest and water flows in from the Atlantic. The phenomenon is most pronounced during the spring equinox in March when the moon and the sun are in direct alignment with the earth, and their gravitational pull is combined. The wave can be quite destructive as it moves upriver, and the water is filled with debris.

1829) The 1666 Great Fire of London burned for five days and destroyed almost 90% of London's homes, but it only killed eight people.

1830) Abraham Lincoln was 6'4", the tallest U.S. president.

1831) Penguins can swim faster because they have a bubble boost. They fluff their feathers and release bubbles that reduce the density of the water around them; the bubbles act as lubrication that decreases water viscosity.

1832) Annually, more than 1.5 million euros are thrown into Rome's Trevi Fountain; the money is used to subsidize a supermarket for the needy.

1833) Memories continually change. They are malleable and are reconstructed with each recall; what we remember changes each time we recall the event. The slightly changed memory becomes the current memory, only to be reconstructed with the next recall.

1834) To cure a toothache in ancient Egypt, people put a dead mouse cut in half in their mouth.

1835) President Bill Clinton lost the nuclear launch codes for months, and nobody found out. The president must keep the launch codes nearby; every 30 days, a Pentagon staffer is required to check the codes to ensure they're correct, and the codes are replaced every four months. During one of these periods, the Pentagon staffer was told each time they came to check the codes that the president was too busy, and the staffer would leave. At the end of the fourth month, it became clear that Clinton had lost the codes. The procedure has since been changed, and the Pentagon official must physically wait for as long as it takes to verify the codes.

1836) George Washington's salary as U.S. president was $25,000. Based on the change in the consumer price index, it would equate to over $700,000 in today's dollars; today's presidential salary is $400,000.

1837) Medieval chastity belts are a myth; there is no credible evidence that they existed.

1838) Completed in 1885, the world's first skyscraper was Chicago's Home Insurance Building. It was 10 stories and 136 feet tall and was demolished in 1931.

1839) Camels have three eyelids to protect them from the sand.

1840) Eight people took refuge on Noah's ark, Noah and his wife and his three sons and their wives.

1841) Instead of the normal five senses, neuroscientists define 22-33 different senses, known as meta-senses. Some of the common meta-senses are equilibrioception (your sense of balance), proprioception (knowing which parts of your body are where without looking), and thermoception (being able to sense temperature).

1842) Iceland has the world's oldest parliament; it has existed since 930 AD.

1843) At up to 150 pounds, the South American capybara is the world's largest rodent.

1844) It takes an income of $32,400 to be in the top 1% of the world.

1845) The hard piece at the end of a shoelace is called an aglet.

1846) Americans visit Mexico more than any other foreign country.

1847) Richard Nixon once carried three pounds of marijuana for Louis Armstrong. In 1958, Vice President Richard Nixon ran into Louis Armstrong at Idlewild Airport in New York. Since he didn't have to go through customs, Nixon offered to carry Armstrong's luggage. Without knowing it, Nixon carried three pounds of marijuana for Armstrong.

1848) The avocado derives its name from the Nahuatl Indian word "āhuacatl," meaning testicle.

1849) Dwight D. Eisenhower was the first president to govern over all 50 states.

1850) America's first bank robbery occurred in August 1798 at the Bank of Pennsylvania in Philadelphia. The robbers got away with $162,821, and it resulted in a false imprisonment trial, a book, and the real robber depositing some of the stolen money back in the bank. Blacksmith Patrick Lyon became the primary suspect because he had recently installed new locks on the vault doors of the bank; he was arrested and eventually convicted. However, the real robbers were Thomas Cunningham and Isaac Davis. Cunningham was a porter at the bank and the inside man; he died of yellow fever soon after the robbery. Davis was caught after depositing stolen money at banks around Philadelphia, including the bank he robbed. However, he was given a pardon for making a full confession and returning the money; he never spent any time in jail. Lyon served three months in prison before being released; he wrote a book about his experience and sued for wrongful imprisonment. It was one of the first trials in the United States dealing with the concept of probable cause, and he won $12,000 in damages.

1851) On average over their lifetime, a person grows 450 miles of hair on their head.

1852) Napoleon wasn't short for his time. He was about 5'7"; the average adult French male of his time was only 5'5", so he was taller than average. Some of the confusion is the units his height was reported in, and his guards, who he was usually seen with, were required to be quite tall.

1853) *Ben-Hur* is the only Hollywood film to make the Vatican's approved list in the religious category.

1854) A group of elk is called a gang.

1855) Thirty-two countries use the dollar (either the U.S. dollar or other dollar) as their official currency: Australia, Bahamas, Barbados, Belize, Brunei, Canada, Dominica, East Timor, Ecuador, El Salvador, Fiji, Grenada, Guyana, Jamaica, Kiribati, Liberia, Marshall Islands, Micronesia, Namibia, Nauru, New Zealand, Palau, Saint Kitts and Nevis, Saint Lucia, Saint Vincent and the Grenadines, Singapore, Solomon Islands, Suriname, Taiwan, Tuvalu, United States, and Zimbabwe.

1856) Outer space smells most like the burning odor of hydrocarbons; astronauts have reported smelling burned or fried steak after a spacewalk.

1857) The Canary Islands are named after dogs. When the first Europeans arrived, they found large dogs on Grand Canary; canaria is the Latin word for dog.

1858) There were eight U.S. national capital cities before Washington, D.C.: Philadelphia, Pennsylvania; Baltimore, Maryland; Lancaster Pennsylvania; York, Pennsylvania; Princeton, New Jersey; Annapolis, Maryland; Trenton, New Jersey; and New York City, New York.

1859) The company Google was originally called Backrub.

1860) Greece invented cheesecake.

1861) Male pandas perform a handstand when they urinate. By doing the handstand, they get their pee higher up the tree, allowing their scent to be carried further and increasing their mating chances.

1862) A giraffe cleans its ears with its tongue.

1863) Lebanon is the only Middle Eastern country without a desert.

1864) U.S. television allows alcohol to be advertised if no alcohol is consumed in the commercial; it isn't a law or FCC regulation, just a broadcasting standard.

1865) The first arrest for marijuana possession and selling in the United States occurred in 1937 in Colorado.

1866) Pirates wore earrings to improve their eyesight; they believed the precious metals in earrings had healing powers.

1867) Most birds lack a sense of smell.

1868) Coca-Cola didn't entirely remove cocaine as an ingredient until 1929. Most of the cocaine had been eliminated in 1903.

1869) In 1971, *All in the Family* had the first toilet heard flushing on U.S. television.

1870) In 1988, presidential nominee George W. Bush considered bringing on actor and director Clint Eastwood as his running mate.

1871) The word karaoke means empty orchestra.

1872) To absorb urine and feces, both male and female astronauts wear a maximum absorbency garment, an adult diaper with extra absorption material, during liftoff, landing, and extra-vehicular activity. These operations can take a long time or have significant delays, and astronauts can't just get up and go to the bathroom at any time.

1873) During the 1980s, Pablo Escobar's drug cartel was spending $2,500 per month on rubber bands to hold all the cash.

1874) Fuggerei, in Augsburg, Germany, is the world's oldest social housing complex still in use, and the rent for a housing unit has remained the same for 500 years at about $1 per year. It was founded by Jakob Fugger the Younger in 1516 as a place for the needy. The conditions to live there are the same as they were 500 years ago; someone must have lived at least two years in Augsburg, be Catholic, and have become indigent without debt. The rent has always been one Rheinischer Gulden per year as well as three daily prayers for the current owners of the Fuggerei. The housing units are 500-700 square feet and have their own street entrance; the gates to the community are locked every night at 10 p.m., as they have been since the start.

1875) The Statue of Liberty originally also served as a lighthouse.

1876) Because he was afraid of flying, Cassius Clay (Muhammad Ali) wore a parachute on his flight to Rome for the 1960 Olympics.

1877) Annapolis, Maryland, and Albany, New York, are the only two state capitals named for royalty. Annapolis is named for Princess Anne of Denmark and Norway, who became Queen of England; Albany is named for the Duke of York and Albany, who became King James II of England.

1878) Sand dunes cover only about 15% of the Sahara Desert; rock plateaus and coarse gravel cover the majority.

1879) Almost half the gold ever mined has come from Witwatersrand, South Africa.

1880) The peregrine falcon was the first animal placed on the endangered species list.

1881) President Thomas Jefferson is commonly credited with inventing the swivel chair.

1882) Kinderschema is a set of physical characteristics that humans are naturally drawn toward; the characteristics include a rounded belly, big head, big eyes, loose limbs, etc. Puppies, kittens, and other animals, including human babies, trigger kinderschema. Humans have an intrinsic motivation to care for babies and children; these tendencies have developed through millions of years of evolution.

1883) With an estimated 500 million copies sold, *Don Quixote* is the best-selling fiction book of all time; *A Tale of Two Cities* is second at about 200 million copies.

1884) Barbra Streisand is the only person to win Oscars for Best Actress and Best Song; she won the Best Actress Oscar for *Funny Girl* (1968) and the Best Original Song Oscar for "Evergreen" from *A Star is Born* (1976).

1885) Bagpipes were invented in the Middle East.

1886) Grey whales always mate in a threesome with two males and one female; one of the males is dominant, and the other assists.

1887) The expression "red-letter day" derives from an old custom of using red ink on calendars to indicate religious holidays.

1888) Less than 1% of bacteria cause disease in humans.

1889) Adjusted for inflation, *Butch Cassidy and the Sundance Kid* (1969) is the highest-grossing western of all time in the United States.

1890) The lens of the eye continues to grow throughout a person's life.

1891) If Walmart was a country, its revenues would rank it as the world's 25th largest economy.

1892) Playboy founder Hugh Hefner is buried next to Marilyn Monroe in a crypt in Los Angeles' Westwood Village Memorial Park cemetery.

1893) At 20,587 square miles, Alaska's Wrangell-St. Elias National Park and Preserve is the largest national park in the United States.

1894) Walt Disney was head of the committee that organized the 1960 Squaw Valley Winter Olympics opening day ceremonies.

1895) The Caspian Sea is the world's largest enclosed inland body of water; it is considered a lake by some, but it has salt water. It has 3.5 times more water than all the Great Lakes combined.

1896) The first time an NHL team pulled their goalie to have an extra attacker was in 1931. The Boston Bruins pulled their goalie in a playoff game against the Montreal Canadiens.

1897) The footprints left behind by astronauts on the moon could last 10 to 100 million years. The moon has no atmosphere, so there is no wind or water to blow or wash anything away.

1898) Thomas Jefferson did not like public speaking and preferred to remain quiet most of the time. He only made two speeches during his entire eight-year presidency; they were both inaugural speeches and were hardly audible.

1899) You are probably pronouncing Dr. Seuss's name incorrectly. Dr. Seuss was born Theodor Seuss Geisel; Seuss was his mother's maiden name, and it is pronounced as "Soice" (rhymes with voice) by the family.

1900) Human embryos develop fingerprints three months after conception.

1901) Sea otters have the densest fur of all animals; they have up to one million hairs per square inch on the densest parts of their body.

1902) Snail slime is mucus that lubricates the surface and helps them move faster with less friction; they often travel in the mucus trails of other snails to move faster.

1903) Mount Logan, in the Saint Elias range in the Yukon province of Canada, has the world's largest base circumference of any non-volcanic mountain; it has 11 peaks over 5,000 meters (16,400 feet).

1904) Uranus was originally called Planet George, in honor of English King George III.

1905) September's name comes from the Latin "septem," meaning seven. It was the seventh month in the old Roman calendar, where the year started with March; its name was carried over to the Julian and current Gregorian calendars, where it is the ninth month.

1906) When poured, hot water has a higher pitch than cold water. Water changes viscosity with temperature, which affects the sound when poured.

1907) Sulfur gives onions their distinctive smell; when cut or crushed, a chemical reaction changes an amino acid into a sulfur compound.

1908) On December 28th, 1973, the first mutiny in space occurred on *Skylab 4*. The three-man crew turned off radio communications with NASA for a full day and spent the day relaxing. They had already spent as much time in space as anyone ever had and were tired of the demanding schedule NASA had set for them. After the day off, they continued their duties and spent about another month in space, setting the record at the time of 84 days.

1909) Aluminum is the major constituent of rubies.

1910) Europe is the only continent without a significant desert.

1911) In 1967, Frank and Nancy Sinatra had the only number-one song recorded by a father and daughter with "Something Stupid."

1912) Snails slide around on a single foot; the one long muscle acts like a human extremity and helps them grip and push themselves along the ground.

1913) The first chocolate treat was hot chocolate during the Aztec civilization.

1914) Humans make up about 0.01% of the earth's biomass; plants account for about 80%; bacteria account for 13%, and fungi are 2%. In total, animals account for about 0.36%, with insects making up about half of that and fish accounting for another third.

1915) Mr. and Mrs. are abbreviations for master and mistress.

1916) In the 1600s, some doctors recommended their patients fart into jars and store them, so they could later inhale them to ward off the bubonic plague. The idea was that the plague was caused by deadly vapors, so it could be warded off by foul vapors.

1917) An ostrich's eye is bigger than its brain.

1918) The Australian continent has an average elevation of 1,083 feet, the lowest of any continent.

1919) Fred Perry is the only person to be world number one in both table tennis and tennis. He won the 1929 world table tennis championship and was the first tennis player to win a career grand slam, including three straight Wimbledon titles from 1934 to 1936.

1920) The highest blood alcohol level ever recorded that didn't result in death was 0.91%, more than twice the normal lethal level. The typical level for legally drunk is 0.08%.

1921) Before Arnold Schwarzenegger got the part, O.J. Simpson was an early choice to play the title role in The Terminator. Director James Cameron thought he was too likable, among other things.

1922) Bhutan's Gangkhar Puensum is the world's highest unclimbed mountain. It is 24,840 feet high and has been off-limits to climbers since 1994 when Bhutan prohibited all mountaineering above 6,000 meters due to spiritual and religious beliefs.

1923) In pure, powder form, caffeine is white.

1924) At 82.5 degrees north latitude, Canada's Alert Airport is the world's northernmost permanent airport with flights (none scheduled). It is about 520 miles south of the North Pole.

1925) The gender of most turtles, alligators, and crocodiles is determined after fertilization. The temperature of the eggs decides whether the offspring will be male or female; this is called temperature-dependent sex determination.

1926) Without an air circulation system, a flame in zero gravity, even in a pure oxygen environment, will extinguish itself. A typical flame produces light, heat, carbon dioxide, and water vapor; the heat causes the combustion products to expand, lowering their density, and they rise, allowing fresh, oxygen-containing air to get to the flame. In zero gravity, neither buoyancy nor convection occurs; therefore, the combustion products accumulate around the flame, preventing oxygen from reaching it, and the flame goes out.

1927) Yosemite National Park put in a bid to host the 1932 Winter Olympics. The bid went to Lake Placid, New York.

1928) A galactic or cosmic year is the amount of time it takes the sun to orbit once around the center of the Milky Way Galaxy, about 230 million years.

1929) Cartoon character Elmer Fudd was originally called Egghead.

1930) Beetles are the most common type of insect eaten by humans.

1931) The Bible doesn't say Adam and Eve ate an apple. It says they ate the forbidden fruit from the tree of knowledge; nowhere does it say it was an apple.

1932) Inspired by burrs, George de Mestral invented Velcro in the 1940s.

1933) Pablo Picasso's work is stolen more than any other painter.

1934) With an area of 43 square miles, Disney World is about the same size as the city of San Francisco.

1935) If you started with $0.01 and had a 100% daily return on your money, you would be a millionaire in 27 days.

1936) A female octopus can lay tens of thousands of eggs at one time, and when they hatch, she dies. She reproduces only once, and after she lays her eggs, she doesn't eat and puts all her energy into caring for them.

1937) In WWII, Tootsie Rolls were part of soldier rations; they were durable in all weather conditions and were good for quick energy.

1938) If the moon didn't exist, a day on Earth would be 6-8 hours long.

1939) The average pencil has enough graphite to draw a line 35 miles long or write about 45,000 words.

1940) *The Lord of the Rings: The Return of the King* (2003) was the first fantasy film to win the Best Picture Oscar.

1941) Against explicit orders, Portuguese diplomat Aristides de Sousa Mendes issued an estimated 30,000 Portuguese travel visas for Jewish families fleeing Nazi persecution. He was stripped of his diplomatic position and forbidden from earning a living, and his 15 children were also blacklisted and prevented from attending university or finding meaningful work. He died in 1954, and the first recognition of his heroism didn't come until 1966 when Israel declared him to be a "Righteous Among the Nations." In 1986, the U.S. Congress also issued a proclamation honoring his heroic act.

1942) The greatest distance on the earth between the nearest points of land is 994 miles from Bouvet Island in the South Atlantic to Antarctica.

1943) During the American Civil War, women were prohibited from enlisting in both the Union and Confederate armies, but dressed as men, more than 600 women joined the war anyway.

1944) William Shakespeare's *Henry IV, Part 1* is responsible for starlings being introduced in North America. Eugene Schieffelin, chairman of the American Acclimatization Society, wanted to import every bird mentioned in Shakespeare's works, and the starling is only mentioned in *Henry IV, Part 1*. In 1890, he released starlings in New York's Central Park.

1945) German chocolate cake originated in the United States; it was named after American baker Samuel German.

1946) Walmart is the world's largest private employer.

1947) Under daylight conditions, the human eye is most sensitive to the color green; light at that wavelength produces the impression of the greatest brightness.

1948) Currently, an Olympic gold medal is 92.5% silver.

1949) The first recorded worker's strike took place in ancient Egypt in 1152 BC when the artisans of the Royal Necropolis at Deir el-Medina organized an uprising. It took place under the rule of Pharaoh Ramses III and was recorded on papyrus.

1950) Jack Swigert originally said, "Houston, we've had a problem here." The quote is sometimes incorrectly attributed to James Lovell, who repeated, "Houston, we've had a problem," and it is not "Houston, we have a problem," as depicted in the movie.

1951) The elephant probably spends more time standing than any other mammal. In the wild, they live up to 70 years, and they only sleep about two hours a day. They also often sleep standing up, only lying down every few nights.

1952) Vatican City drinks more wine per capita than any other country. They consume about 74 liters per person annually, more than seven times more than the United States.

1953) Instead of the five tastes (sweet, savory, sour, bitter, and salty) that humans can detect, whales and dolphins can only taste salty.

1954) Alaska has all five of the largest land area cities in the United States: Yakutat, Sitka, Juneau, Wrangell, and Anchorage.

1955) France has more visitors annually than any other country.

1956) President John Quincy Adams received a pet alligator as a gift and kept it in the White House East Room bathroom for two months before returning it.

1957) Damascus, Syria, is widely regarded as the world's oldest continuously inhabited city; it has been inhabited for at least 11,000 years.

1958) Humans swallow on average twice a minute, even while sleeping.

1959) In Guinea, wild chimpanzees drink fermented palm sap that contains up to 6.9% alcohol. Some of the chimpanzees consume significant quantities and exhibit signs of inebriation.

1960) In humans, the right lung is always larger than the left. The left lung is smaller to leave room for the heart.

1961) Louis Bonaparte, Napoleon's brother, was called the "King of Rabbits" because he mispronounced the Dutch phrase "I am your King" and instead said, "I am your rabbit," when he took over rule of the Netherlands in 1806.

1962) When they poop, dogs stare at you because they know they are vulnerable at that time, and they are looking to you, a member of their pack, for protection.

1963) Clouds appear to be darker because they are thicker, which prevents more light from passing through; thinner clouds allow more light through and appear white. Seen from an airplane, the top of the cloud will still appear white since the top receives more light. As water droplets and ice crystals in a cloud thicken when it is about to rain, they scatter much less light, and the cloud appears almost black.

1964) "Expletive deleted" came into fashion because of the publication of the Watergate tapes transcript.

1965) The first organ transplants occurred in 800 BC when Indian doctors performed skin grafts.

1966) The cutaneous marginal pouch, informally known as Henry's pocket, is the fold of skin forming an open pouch at the outer base of a cat's ear. Some dogs also have it.

1967) Rome, Italy, is located at about the same latitude as the southernmost point of Canada.

1968) Sandwiches didn't appear in American cookbooks until 1815.

1969) Louis Braille developed the Braille system for the blind at the age of 15 and published the first book about it at age 20.

1970) With nine wins, the movie *Butch Cassidy and the Sundance Kid* holds the British Academy Awards (BAFTAs) record.

1971) Early humans in South America hunted giant armadillos, which were about the size and weight of a Volkswagen Beetle; they used their shells for homes.

1972) At the ancient Olympic games, they used tethered doves as archery targets.

1973) The Greek national anthem "Hymn to Liberty" has 158 verses and is the longest national anthem in the world. It is an 1823 poem by Dionysios Solomos set to music by Nikolaos Mantzaros.

1974) Prairie dogs greet each other by kissing. The kiss involves touching their teeth together to determine whether the prairie dog they are greeting is a member of their social group.

1975) The name IKEA is formed from the founder Ingvar Kamprad's initials (IK), plus the first letters of Elmtaryd (E) and Agunnaryd (A), from the farm and village where he grew up.

1976) Your eardrums move when your eyes move; the reason is unclear.

1977) Researchers have found that most mammals weighing at least 6 pounds take about 21 seconds to urinate. The number seems to be quite consistent, with the urethra scaled to deliver about the same time regardless of the animal size.

1978) The earliest surviving written music dates to 1400 BC, it was a hymn found in Syria.

1979) In a show of dominance, male Indian rhinos can spray urine over 16 feet; this is typically done in the presence of other males or breeding-age females.

1980) Cats and humans have almost identical brain structures, including the region that controls emotion. Cats have temporal, occipital, frontal, and parietal lobes in their brains, just like humans, and the connections within their brains seem to mirror those of humans. Their brains also release neurotransmitters, and they have short and long-term memory.

1981) At 19,714 feet deep, Tibet's Yarlung Tsangpo Canyon is the world's deepest canyon.

1982) The Memphis, Tennessee, Bass Pro Shops Megastore is one of the world's largest pyramids and features a hotel, indoor swamp, aquarium, bowling alley, and the world's tallest freestanding elevator. The pyramid is 321 feet tall and has a 535,000 square foot interior.

1983) The liver is the only human internal organ that can regenerate itself. You can lose up to 75% of your liver, and the remaining portion can regenerate into a whole liver. Therefore, living donor liver transplants can be done where a portion of the liver is taken, and both the donor and recipient's portion regrows into a full liver within about four months. A liver from a deceased donor may also be split and transplanted into two recipients.

1984) In 1958, Nils Bohlin, an engineer at Volvo, invented the revolutionary three-point seat belt used today; to save lives, Volvo gave away the patent for free.

1985) Only once in history has a submerged submarine deliberately sunk a submerged submarine. In 1945, a British submarine sunk a German submarine.

1986) Before 1938, toothbrushes were made using boar hairs.

1987) The green sea slug, which lives off the east coast of the United States, is the first animal ever discovered that is also part plant. The slugs take chloroplasts into their skin, which turns them emerald green and makes them capable of photosynthesis. They can go without eating for nine months or more, photosynthesizing as they bask in the sun.

1988) Adult dogs have 42 teeth; puppies have 28 baby teeth.

1989) A Swedish mathematician calculated that there are 177,147 different ways to tie a necktie knot. The number accounts for variations in exposed knots, wrappings, and windings.

1990) On December 21, 1913, the first published crossword puzzle appeared in the *New York World* newspaper.

1991) The highest and lowest points in the contiguous United States are in the same county. Mount Whitney, at 14,494 feet, and Death Valley's Badwater Basin, at 282 feet below sea level, are separated by 85 miles in Inyo County, California.

1992) The tufts of hair in a cat's ear are called ear furnishings; they help keep out dirt, direct sounds, and insulate the ears.

1993) In the last century, the east coast of the United States has moved about eight feet further away from Europe.

1994) Four is the only number spelled out in English that has the same number of letters as its value.

1995) When written out in English, no number before one thousand contains the letter a.

1996) Owyhee is the original English spelling of Hawaii.

1997) Over 2,300 years ago, Hippocrates described walking as "man's best medicine."

1998) Lyme disease gets its name from Lyme, Connecticut, a small coastal town, where several cases were identified in 1975.

1999) Of the 20 most-watched regular television broadcasts in U.S. history, 19 have been Super Bowl broadcasts; the only other show in the top 20 is the *M*A*S*H* series finale.

2000) Kellogg Corn Flakes were invented in a sanitarium in 1894.

Facts 2001-2500

2001) In 1925, Henry Ford was likely America's first billionaire. John D. Rockefeller is often cited as the first American billionaire in 1916, but his wealth was probably less than a billion at the time.

2002) Sideburns are named after American Civil War general Ambrose Burnside; he was known for having an unusual facial hairstyle with a mustache connected to thick sideburns and a clean-shaven chin.

2003) Disc jockey Alan Freed is generally given credit for coining the term "rock and roll."

2004) In math, a lemniscate shape means infinity; lemniscate is the word for a shape with two loops meeting at a central point.

2005) It takes about 90 minutes to hard boil an ostrich egg.

2006) There are an estimated one million spiders per acre of land; in the tropics, there are closer to three million per acre.

2007) The Congo is the only river that crosses the equator in both a northerly and southerly direction.

2008) The Vatican Bank has the world's only ATM that allows users to perform transactions in Latin.

2009) In the 1700s, about 20% of all women in London were prostitutes. Prostitution was a huge business, generating about $2 billion annually in today's dollars.

2010) Based on its global following, soccer is the world's most popular sport; cricket is second; field hockey is third.

2011) If you ate a polar bear's liver, you would get vitamin A poisoning and could die. Polar bears have 50-60 times the normal human levels of vitamin A in their liver, about three times the tolerable level that a human can intake.

2012) In 1960, *The Flintstones* was the first animated primetime series on U.S. television.

2013) In total darkness, most people naturally adjust to a 48-hour cycle, instead of 24 hours. They have 36 hours of activity followed by 12 hours of sleep; the reasons are unclear.

2014) Dogs normally start sniffing with their right nostril and keep using the right nostril if the smell is something unpleasant or potentially dangerous. If the smell is something pleasant, they will switch to use their left nostril.

2015) Scientists have tracked Alpine swifts, a swallow-like bird found in Europe, Africa, and Asia, that can fly for 200 days straight. They eat and sleep while flying and never leave the air.

2016) An aphthong is a letter or combination of letters in a word that is not pronounced. The "gh" combination in the word night is an aphthong.

2017) Canada has more area devoted to national parks than any other country. There are over 145,000 square miles of national parks, an area larger than Norway.

2018) ESPN's *SportsCenter* has aired the most episodes ever for any U.S. television show. Since 1979, it has broadcast over 50,000 unique episodes.

2019) At 10 years old, Tatum O'Neal is the youngest competitive Oscar winner ever for *Paper Moon* (1973).

2020) Three U.S. presidents got married while in office. John Tyler and Woodrow Wilson remarried after losing their wives; Grover Cleveland got married for the first time in the White House.

2021) More than 1 trillion photographs are taken annually. More photographs are taken every two minutes than were taken in total up through the 1800s.

2022) Excluding eye injuries, pirates likely wore eye patches to see in the dark. They were constantly going above and below deck, and it takes the human eye up to 25 minutes to adapt to seeing in the dark. By wearing a patch, they kept one eye dark adjusted, so they could see in the dark immediately by moving the eye patch.

2023) The Egyptian civilization was the first to divide the day into 24 hours. Ancient Egyptians used a base 12 system, instead of our base 10 system; they counted the knuckles of each finger, using their thumbs as pointers. They had 12 hours of light and 12 hours of darkness, so the length of the hours varied by time of the year. Fixed length hours were proposed by the Greeks in the 2nd century BC, but they did not become common until mechanical clocks first appeared in Europe during the 14th century.

2024) New Zealand has a higher percentage of households with pets than any other country; about 68% of households have a pet.

2025) Turritopsis dohrnii, also known as the immortal jellyfish, is essentially biologically immortal. Once an adult jellyfish has reproduced, it transforms itself back into its juvenile state. Its tentacles retract; its body shrinks, and it sinks to the ocean floor and starts its life cycle all over. They can do it repeatedly, making them essentially immortal unless they are consumed by another animal or struck by disease.

2026) More people die of drowning in the desert than die of dehydration. Flash floods in desert areas kill more people than dehydration.

2027) In 1678, Italian Elena Cornaro Piscopia was the world's first woman to receive a PhD degree.

2028) From 1647-1660, England effectively banned Christmas; Puritans believed that people needed strict rules to be religious and any kind of merrymaking was sinful.

2029) Minnesota has more of the 100 largest U.S. lakes than any other state. It has eight lakes in the top 100: Lake Superior, Lake of the Woods, Red Lake, Rainy Lake, Mille Lacs Lake, Leech Lake, Lake Winnibigoshish, and Lake Vermilion.

2030) The longest period any sports trophy has been successfully defended is 132 years. America's Cup for sailing was held by the United States from its start in 1851 until Australia won in 1983.

2031) The reminiscence bump is the tendency to have increased recollection of events that occurred during adolescence and early adulthood. The bump occurs from about 16 to 25 years of age because memory storage is not consistent through time; it increases during times of change in self and life goals that typically happen during the reminiscence bump years.

2032) Alien hand syndrome, sometimes called Dr. Strangelove syndrome, is a condition where a person's limb acts seemingly on its own without control. It can be caused by the separation of the brain hemispheres and most frequently affects the left hand.

2033) Submarines made their first wartime appearance during the American Revolutionary War. On September 6, 1776, *Turtle*, a submersible built by American David Bushnell, was used in an attempted attack on the British ship *Eagle*. It was a one-man wooden craft that relied on a human-powered hand crank and foot treadle for propulsion. A pedal-operated water tank allowed it to submerge and surface, and lead ballast kept it upright in the water.

2034) At its triple point, a liquid can exist simultaneously as a liquid, solid, and gas. The triple point is the temperature and pressure that puts the three states of matter into a thermodynamic equilibrium, where no state is trying to change into any other state. The boiling liquid causes high energy molecules to rise as a gas; this lowers the temperature of the boiling liquid and makes it freeze. The cycle continues if the triple point temperature and pressure are maintained. For water, the triple point is at 32.02 degrees Fahrenheit and 0.006 atmospheres (normal pressure is 1 atmosphere).

2035) At its peak, the British Empire was the largest empire by area in history; in 1922, it ruled over about 24% of the world's land.

2036) James Bond creator Ian Fleming wrote the book *Chitty-Chitty-Bang-Bang: The Magical Car*, the basis for the movie.

2037) The New Testament was originally written in Greek.

2038) With one ship and seven men, Mongolia has the world's smallest national navy; it is the world's second-largest landlocked country.

2039) Sloths only poop once a week; they also must do it on the ground, making them an easy target for predators. A sloth can lose one-third of its body weight pooping, and it all comes out in one push. They dig a small hole to go in and cover it up when they are done and head back into the trees.

2040) Taumatawhakatangihangakoauauotamateaturipukakapikimaun-gahoronukupokaiwhenuakitanatahu is the world's longest place name; it is a hill in New Zealand.

2041) Of all the text information stored on the world's computers, 80% is in English.

2042) Located in Fez, Morocco, the al-Qarawiyyin library is the world's oldest working library, operating since 859 AD.

2043) Crapulous is the feeling you get from eating or drinking too much.

2044) Everyone who has walked on the moon was born before 1936. Charles Duke, the tenth person to walk on the moon, was born the latest, October 3, 1935.

2045) The top 1% of bands and solo artists earn 77% of all recorded music revenue.

2046) San Marino has the world's oldest surviving constitution; it dates to 1600. The U.S. constitution is the second oldest.

2047) Leeches have 32 brains; each controls a different segment of their body.

2048) During the 50 km cross-country ski race at the 1988 Calgary Olympics, officials were so concerned about Mexican skier Roberto Alvarez that they sent out a search party. He had never skied more than 20 km, and officials thought he was lost or injured; he finished more than an hour behind the next slowest finisher.

2049) Like many royal houses, the Ptolemaic dynasty of Cleopatra often married within the family to preserve bloodline purity. More than a dozen of Cleopatra's ancestors wed cousins or siblings, and her parents were likely brother and sister.

2050) The Mexican free-tailed bat is the world's fastest mammal. It can reach speeds of 100 mph in normal flight.

2051) A poker hand with two black aces and two black eights is known as the "dead man's hand" because it is the hand Wild Bill Hickok was holding when he was killed.

2052) Cal Hubbard was the first person inducted into both the NFL and MLB Hall of Fame. In the 1920s and 1930s, he was an offensive lineman for New York and Green Bay and was on four championship teams; he was also a MLB umpire.

2053) Three dogs survived the *Titanic* sinking, a Pekinese and two Pomeranians.

2054) *The Godfather Part II* and *The Lord of the Rings: The Return of the King* are the only two sequels to win Best Picture Oscars.

2055) Mount Chimborazo, Ecuador, is closer to the moon than any other place on the earth. It is 20,548 feet elevation, but it is very close to the equator, so the bulge in the earth makes it 1.5 miles closer to the moon than Mount Everest.

2056) Bananas, along with other potassium-rich foods like spinach, apricots, salmon, avocados, and mushrooms, are radioactive. K-40 radioactive atoms make up a very small fraction of potassium atoms; they spontaneously decay, releasing beta radiation and gamma rays that are both capable of tissue damage. However, with a half-life of 1.3 billion years, K-40 is not very radioactive, so you would have to eat about 10 million bananas to die of radiation poisoning.

2057) With 24 vertebrae, swans have more neck vertebrae than any other warm-blooded animal.

2058) Bing Crosby was first offered the role of television's Lt. Colombo.

2059) In average lawn or garden soil, a mole can dig 12-15 feet per hour.

2060) Humans produce about 1.5 quarts of mucus per day and swallow most of it.

2061) With speeds up to 242 mph including hunting dives, the peregrine falcon is the world's fastest bird.

2062) To avoid capture, Nedeljko Čabrinović, one of the men involved in the 1914 assassination of Archduke Franz Ferdinand, swallowed a cyanide capsule and jumped into the River Miljacka. Unfortunately, the cyanide pill had expired and failed to kill him, and the River Miljacka was only about four inches deep. He was captured by police, and since he was still a minor, he was sentenced to 20 years in prison, instead of execution; he died in prison of tuberculosis.

2063) Richard Nixon was the first president to visit all 50 states.

2064) Spencer Tracy and Tom Hanks are the only two actors that have won consecutive Best Actor Oscars. Tracy won for *Captains Courageous* (1937) and *Boys Town* (1938), and Hanks won for *Philadelphia* (1993) and *Forrest Gump* (1994).

2065) Ninety percent of all English written material is made up of just 1,000 words.

2066) The odds against any person becoming a saint are 20 million to 1.

2067) Israel has the highest per capita consumption of turkey.

2068) Based on concerns that there were obscene lyrics inserted into the song, the FBI investigated the Kingsmen's 1963 version of "Louie Louie." After three months, they abandoned the investigation; they were unable to discern what the lyrics were.

2069) *My Big Fat Greek Wedding* (2002) is the highest-grossing romantic comedy of all time in the United States.

2070) The Volkswagen Beetle was the first car model to sell 20 million units.

2071) The columella nasi is the fleshy end of your nose that splits your nostrils.

2072) The most common symbol on world flags is a star.

2073) The seahorse and pipefish are the only two species of fish where the male gives birth.

2074) Research shows that all blue-eyed people may be related; they believe the trait comes from a single individual whose genes mutated between 6,000 and 10,000 years ago. Before that, everyone had varying shades of brown eyes.

2075) Great Britain is the only country that is exempt from the international rule that a country's name must appear on its postage stamps. They were the first country with postage stamps and had no name on them and were exempted when the rule was made.

2076) *Midnight Cowboy* is the only X-rated movie to win the Best Picture Oscar. It was X-rated at the time of the award; in 1971, its rating was changed to R.

2077) The term "pixel" is short for picture element.

2078) The logo of New Zealand's Royal Air Force is the kiwi, a flightless bird.

2079) The common cold likely came from camels. Researchers have found that along with being the source of the Middle East Respiratory Syndrome (MERS) virus, camels are the likely source of the common cold that spread to humans thousands of years ago.

2080) Indonesia has the most earthquakes of any country; Japan has the second most.

2081) A giraffe has the highest blood pressure of any animal; it is about 300 over 200.

2082) Male giraffes determine whether a female is fertile and ready to mate by tasting her urine. The male bumps the female until she urinates and then tastes the urine for hormones, indicating she is in heat.

2083) MLB player Joel Youngblood got two hits for two different teams in two different cities on the same day. He was traded from the Mets to the Expos on August 4, 1982; after the Mets day game, he flew to Philadelphia, which was hosting the Expos for a night game.

2084) The word poecilonym is a synonym for synonym.

2085) On April 10, 1996, Tropical Cyclone Olivia produced a 253-mph wind on Barrow Island, Australia, the world's highest surface wind speed ever recorded.

2086) *Lawrence of Arabia* is the only Best Picture Oscar winner without any female speaking roles.

2087) Malta is the only European country that has never had a recorded temperature below freezing.

2088) Despite deaths and injuries, staged train collisions were a spectator attraction from 1896 up until the Great Depression. In 1896, Crush, Texas, was a temporary site established for a one-day publicity stunt of a staged train wreck. It was organized by William George Crush, general passenger agent of the Missouri-Kansas-Texas Railroad. No admission was charged, but the railway charged $2 for every round-trip to get to the site, and there was a restaurant, midway, and medicine show. An estimated 40,000 people attended. For the main event, two unmanned six-car trains crashed into each other at 50 mph. Despite what mechanics had assured, the steam boilers on both trains exploded, creating flying debris that killed two people and injured many others. The spectators had been required to observe the collision from a hill 200 yards away, but they still weren't safe from the flying wood and metal. The staged collisions became popular, and Scott Joplin even wrote the "Great Crush Collision March."

2089) Between 1530 and 1780, over 1 million Europeans were captured and sold as slaves to North Africa.

2090) Orville Wright was the pilot in the first fatal airplane crash.

2091) Minnie Mouse's full first name is Minerva.

2092) Alaska is both the westernmost and easternmost state; parts of Alaska stretch into the Eastern Hemisphere.

2093) A college football game registered as an earthquake. The Earthquake Game was played between LSU and Auburn on October 8, 1988 at LSU's Tiger Stadium with a crowd of 79,431 spectators. Auburn led 6-0 with less than two minutes left when LSU drove down the field and eventually threw an 11-yard touchdown pass on fourth down. The crowd's reaction to the touchdown pass registered as an earthquake on a seismograph located about 1,000 feet from the stadium at LSU's Howe-Russell Geoscience Complex. A seismologist noticed the reading the next day.

2094) Bird's nest soup is made from the nests of swifts; the nest is saliva that has dried and hardened.

2095) Arkansas has the only active diamond mine in the United States.

2096) At 54.8 degrees south latitude, Malvinas Argentinas International Airport, Ushuaia, Argentina, is the world's southernmost international airport.

2097) Crocodiles and alligators can climb trees. Researchers have found adults as high as 6 feet off the ground, and juveniles have been spotted as high as 30 feet.

2098) Born in 1773, Potooooooooo, later shortened to Pot8O's, was one of the greatest racehorses ever and one of the three foundation sires of thoroughbreds today. His name was intended to be Potato or Potatoes, but the stable hand who wrote down his name didn't know how to spell potato and thought it was "pot" plus eight Os.

2099) The term jaywalker originated because jay was a term for an idiot or simpleton and was often applied to rural people; therefore, jaywalking was being stupid, ignoring signs, and crossing the street in an unsafe place.

2100) A group of porcupines is called a prickle.

2101) Longtime NFL placekicker Fred Cox, who played for the Minnesota Vikings from 1963-1977, invented the Nerf football.

2102) The Grand Canyon is the largest canyon in the United States; it is 277 miles long, up to 18 miles wide, and has a maximum depth of 6,093 feet.

2103) The shortest complete English sentence is "Go."

2104) The Easter Island statues have full bodies, not just heads. The remainder of the body is buried; the tallest statue excavated is 33 feet high.

2105) Jane Austen referenced baseball over 40 years before it was invented. In 1797 in her novel *Northanger Abbey*, Austen wrote, "It was not very wonderful that Catherine, who had nothing heroic about her, should prefer cricket, base-ball, riding on horseback, and running about the country at the age of fourteen, to books." Baseball was supposedly invented by Abner Doubleday in Cooperstown, New York, in 1839; however, there are other earlier references to baseball in America. To avoid broken windows, a 1791 bylaw in Pittsfield, Massachusetts, banned the playing of "wicket, cricket, baseball, batball, football, cat, fives or any other game or games with balls" within 80 yards of the town meeting house. The name was certainly in use many decades before the current game was invented; the question is how much different the game was.

2106) Due to a metal shortage during WWII, Oscars were made of painted plaster for three years. Following the war, the Academy invited recipients to trade in their plaster awards for gold-plated metal statuettes.

2107) Marie Curie (1903 Physics and 1911 Chemistry) and her daughter Irene Juliot-Curie (1935 Chemistry) are the only mother and daughter to both win Nobel Prizes.

2108) In 5 BC, Rome was the first city to reach a population of 1 million people.

2109) Before 1859, baseball umpires used to sit in chairs behind home plate; they used rocking chairs that were 20 feet behind the batter.

2110) Horses have weak ciliary muscles that do a poor job of focusing their eyes, so they need to move their heads to adjust the focal length or angle of view until the image falls into view on a portion of their retina.

2111) The whale shark has the world's largest egg, up to 12 inches long; the ostrich has the largest laid egg.

2112) By area, 11 U.S. states are larger than the United Kingdom.

2113) Picasso used house paint in his paintings.

2114) American microbiologist Maurice Ralph Hilleman (1919-2005) is credited with saving more lives than any other medical scientist of the 20th century. He specialized in developing vaccines and developed over 40 in his career, including 8 of the 14 vaccines routinely recommended: measles, mumps, hepatitis A, hepatitis B, chickenpox, meningitis, pneumonia, and Haemophilus influenzae.

2115) Due to a shortage of space in London to bury people, the London Necropolis Railway line was opened in 1854 to carry corpses and mourners between London and the Brookwood Cemetery, 23 miles southwest of London. At the time, it was the world's largest cemetery and was designed to accommodate all London deaths for centuries. The station waiting rooms and the train compartments for both living and dead passengers were partitioned by religion and class to prevent mixing mourners and cadavers from different social backgrounds. By 1941, slightly over 200,000 burials had been conducted in the cemetery, which was far fewer than planned, and the railway line wasn't used again after being damaged during WWII.

2116) If you search for the word askew in Google, the content comes back tilted to the right.

2117) Truth or Consequences, New Mexico, was named for the radio game show. The show offered to broadcast from the first town that renamed itself after the program. In 1950, Hot Springs, New Mexico, won the honor and renamed itself.

2118) Moray eels have two pairs of jaws. They have strong flesh-tearing primary jaws that can cut through bone, and they have a pharyngeal jaw, a second pair of jaws located in their throat. When the eel captures prey with its primary jaws, it can use its secondary pharyngeal jaws to grab the prey and drag it down into its gullet.

2119) The orangutan is the largest tree-dwelling animal; they are up to 4.5 feet tall, weigh up to 200 pounds, and spend nearly all their time in the forest canopy.

2120) For every grain of sand on the earth, there are about 10,000 stars in the known universe.

2121) In 1947, *Mary Kay and Johnny* was the first U.S. television series to ever show a couple sharing a bed; it was the first U.S. sitcom. Couples weren't shown sharing the same bed again until the 1960s.

2122) Your hearing is less sharp after you eat too much.

2123) Bread and beer were the two staples of the ancient Egyptian diet; almost everyone consumed both every day. Laborers would have a morning meal of bread, beer, and often onions, and a heartier dinner of boiled vegetables, meat, and more bread and beer.

2124) The average human heart beats more than 2.5 billion times in a lifetime.

2125) In humans, our two nostrils smell differently. Odors coming in through the right nostril are judged to be more pleasant, and you can describe odors coming in through your left nostril better. The difference is believed to be due to the right nostril being connected to the right brain that deals more with emotions, and the left nostril is connected to the left brain that deals more with language.

2126) Up through the Victorian era, it was common for both boys and girls to wear dresses until the age of seven. Boys wore dresses primarily for practical reasons; dressing and potty training were easier, and dresses weren't as easily outgrown.

2127) The tallest tsunami wave ever recorded was in Lituya Bay, Alaska, in 1958; it was 1,720 feet tall. An 8.0 earthquake dropped 40 to 50 million cubic yards of rock and ice 3,000 feet down into the bay, creating the wave.

2128) At 238 minutes, *Gone with the Wind* is the longest movie to ever win the Best Picture Oscar.

2129) On April 23, 2005, the first video ever uploaded to YouTube was *Meet Me at the Zoo*. It was 19 seconds of a boy explaining that elephants have long tusks.

2130) The furthest distance between any two points in two states is between Hawaii and Florida; it is 5,859 miles from Log Point, Elliot Key, Florida, to Kure Island, Hawaii.

2131) Phytophotodermatitis, also known as margarita photodermatitis, is a condition you can get from spending too much time in the sun after handling limes, lemons, or other plants containing the chemical compound furanocoumarin. In contact with exposed skin and sunlight, the compound creates a phototoxic reaction that looks and feels like a second-degree burn.

2132) Before the early 1500s, the color we know as orange was called geoluhread, meaning yellow-red. Orange wasn't used as a color in English until after the fruit was introduced in Britain.

2133) Before he assumed office, Pope Pius II wrote one of the most popular books of the 15th century; it was an erotic novel, the tale of two lovers.

2134) The first issue of *National Geographic* was published in 1888.

2135) Andrew Jackson was the first Democratic president.

2136) Pencils are typically yellow because it is the traditional color of Chinese royalty. In the 1890s when pencils started to be mass-produced, the best graphite came from China, and manufacturers wanted people to know they used the best quality graphite, so they painted them yellow, the color of Chinese royalty.

2137) China has more bordering countries and territories than any other country; it is bordered by 14 counties and 2 territories.

2138) The Appalachian Mountains used to be as tall as the Rockies and are still shrinking; meanwhile, the Himalayas used to be the size of the Rockies and are still growing.

2139) Hepatitis B is the world's most common infectious disease; more than one-quarter of the world's population is infected.

2140) In 1910, William Howard Taft was the first president to throw out the first pitch at a MLB game.

2141) The Northern Hemisphere is warmer than the Southern Hemisphere by 1.5 degrees Celsius; it is due to ocean circulation.

2142) Michael Crichton is the only author to have his works simultaneously number one in television, film, and books. In 1994, *ER* (television), *Jurassic Park* (film), and *Disclosure* (book) were all simultaneously number one.

2143) Since the earth, our solar system, and our galaxy are all moving through space, you never have been and never will be in the same physical location twice.

2144) Theodore Roosevelt had a pet hyena named Bill, a present from the Emperor of Ethiopia.

2145) In 1869, Arabella Mansfield became the first female lawyer in America.

2146) The force required to topple a domino is less than the force it generates when it falls; this force amplification can be used to topple ever-larger dominos. Each domino can be about 1.5 times larger than the preceding one. Starting with a regular size domino at about 1.875 inches tall and pushing it over, the 25th domino toppled would be about 2,630 feet tall, about the height of the world's tallest building.

2147) Japanese golfers have hole-in-one insurance to pay for the cost of drinks, food, and gifts they are expected to buy if they make a hole-in-one.

2148) Lemons float in water; limes sink. They both have densities close to that of water, but limes are slightly denser, so they sink.

2149) The banana is the world's largest herb plant, with species growing up to 100 feet tall; it doesn't have a true woody trunk like a tree and behaves like a perennial.

2150) There are 293 possible ways to make change for a dollar.

2151) In seven years as a lifeguard at Lowell Park in Dixon, Illinois, future president Ronald Reagan was credited with saving 77 people from drowning in the waters of the Rock River. He started his lifeguard position at the age of 15.

2152) In modern times, the first anti-smoking campaign was launched by the Nazis. Hitler had been a heavy smoker in his twenties, but he later condemned it as "the wrath of the Red Man against the White Man, vengeance for having been given hard liquor." It also played into the Third Reich's propaganda, which labeled tobacco as a genetic poison that would corrupt the German purity.

2153) In the Grimm's fairy tale, the Pied Piper of Hamelin is described as pied because he wears a two-colored coat; pied is thought to come from magpie birds, which are black and white.

2154) During WWI, a Canadian soldier made a black bear his pet and named her Winnipeg. When she became a resident of the London Zoological Gardens, she was known as Winnie, and Christopher Robin, son of Winnie the Pooh author A.A. Milne, adored her and named his teddy bear after her.

2155) The national animal of Canada is the beaver.

2156) Graca Machel is the only person to be the first lady of two countries. She is the widow of both South Africa President Nelson Mandela and Mozambique President Samora Machel.

2157) Eusocial is the highest level of sociality where animals like ants and termites have a single female or caste that produces the offspring, and nonreproductive individuals cooperate in caring for the young.

2158) The size of the average American new home has almost tripled, from 983 square feet in 1950 to 2,600 square feet.

2159) Sphenopalatine ganglioneuralgia is the medical term for brain freeze or ice cream headache.

2160) In languages all over the world, there are more names for warm colors (red, orange, yellow) than there are for cool colors (green, blue, purple).

2161) In 1898, Canada issued the first Christmas stamp.

2162) The kakapo of New Zealand is the only flightless parrot and the heaviest parrot, weighing up to nine pounds.

2163) Not including the United States, seven countries use the U.S. dollar as their official currency: Ecuador, El Salvador, Zimbabwe, Timor-Leste, Micronesia, Palau, and the Marshall Islands -.

2164) Jimmy Carter is the only U.S. president that lived in subsidized housing for the poor. His father was relatively wealthy, but he canceled debts and spread his remaining wealth around widely after his death, leaving Carter with little.

2165) The most sweat glands on the human body are on the bottom of the feet.

2166) After watching workers move timber, Frank Lloyd Wright's son John invented Lincoln Logs.

2167) The human brain uses about 20% of the body's oxygen and blood.

2168) More English words start with the letter s than any other letter.

2169) Atoms are 99.9999999% empty space. If all the empty space was eliminated, the entire human species would fit into the volume of a sugar cube.

2170) Canadian law requires that a skill-testing element must be included for a sweepstakes to be legal. A sweepstakes winner cannot be determined by pure luck; there must be some skill involved. The skill test is often mathematical, involving some combination of addition, subtraction, multiplication, and division that must be performed without a calculator or other aid.

2171) *The Comedy of Errors* is the only Shakespeare play that mentions America.

2172) Monaco is the capital of Monaco; it is both a city and a country.

2173) Without saliva, you wouldn't be able to taste your food. Enzymes in your saliva break down the food and release molecules that are picked up by your taste buds.

2174) When Colgate started mass producing its toothpaste in 1873, it was in a jar; they didn't put it in tubes until the 1890s.

2175) Teeth are the only part of the human body that cannot repair itself.

2176) Liechtenstein is the only country that has won medals in the Winter Olympics but has never won medals in the Summer Olympics.

2177) When touching and microwaved, two whole grapes or a pair of beads made mostly of water concentrate the energy from the microwaves at the point where they make contact and generate a very small hot spot intense enough to spark and generate plasma. The effect seems to be dependent on the size, composition, and shape of the objects.

2178) Ninety percent of all meteorites ever found come from Antarctica.

2179) Four people have won two Nobel prizes: Marie Curie, Linus Pauling, John Bardeen, and Frederick Sanger.

2180) New Jersey has more horses per square mile than any other state.

2181) Thirteen states are entirely north of the southernmost point of Canada: Alaska, Washington, Oregon, Idaho, Montana, North Dakota, South

Dakota, Minnesota, Wisconsin, Michigan, Vermont, New Hampshire, and Maine.

2182) Kim is the most common surname for an Olympic athlete.

2183) Frogs can't swallow with their eyes open. Since they don't have muscles to chew their food, they use their eyes to force their food down their throats. Their eyes sink inside their skull, pushing the food down.

2184) In the 1961-62 NBA season, Wilt Chamberlain averaged more minutes per game than there are minutes in a game. He played every minute of the 80-game season, and with overtime games, he averaged 48.5 minutes played per game.

2185) The combination of a question mark and an exclamation mark is called an interrobang. It was invented in the 1960s by adman Martin Speckter, who wanted to provide punctuation for messages that were both questions and exclamations (e.g. "Got milk?!").

2186) Sex is sometimes dangerous for flies. When some flies mate, they emit a buzzing sound that attracts the attention of predatory bats, so they only copulate briefly.

2187) Even rarer than a double rainbow, a twinned rainbow has two separate and concentric rainbow arcs splitting from a single base. Unlike a double rainbow, both rainbows have their colors in the same order. Twinned rainbows occur with a combination of different size raindrops; due to air resistance, raindrops flatten as they fall, with larger drops flattening more. If there are two rain showers with different size drops, they can combine to form a twinned rainbow.

2188) In the human body, there are about 200 different kinds of cells, and within those cells, there are about 20 different kinds of structures.

2189) In 1835, President Andrew Jackson was shot at twice at point-blank range, but he survived because both guns misfired. It was the first assassination attempt against a U.S. president.

2190) The croissant originated in Austria and not France. It started in Vienna, Austria as early as the 13th century as a denser crescent-shaped pastry called a kipferl and didn't show up in France in its current form until the early 1800s.

2191) While sleeping, people burn an average of 0.42 calories an hour per pound of body weight, so a 150-pound person burns about 63 calories per hour sleeping.

2192) To make it easier to give birth, hammerhead sharks are born with soft hammers bent back toward the tail.

2193) At an elevation of 11,942 feet, La Paz, Bolivia, is the world's highest elevation national capital city.

2194) If you include lake shoreline, Minnesota has more shoreline than Hawaii, California, and Florida combined.

2195) Before the 20th century, lobster was considered a mark of poverty and used for fertilizer and fed to slaves. Its reputation changed when modern transportation allowed shipping live lobsters to urban centers.

2196) The first phone book, consisting of a single piece of cardboard, was published on February 21, 1878, in New Haven, Connecticut; it had 50 listings.

2197) There are 2.3 billion square feet of rental self-storage in the United States, and almost 10% of households rent storage.

2198) Giraffes have seven neck vertebrae, the same as humans.

2199) The sound of pain around the world differs. English speakers typically say "ouch!" or "aww!"; Spanish speakers usually say "uy!" or "ay!"; French speakers say "aïe!"; Germans say "aua!" or "autsch!"; Russians say "oi!"

2200) There are no landlocked countries in North America.

2201) If you are locked in a completely sealed room, you will die from carbon dioxide poisoning before you die from lack of oxygen.

2202) The first Cannes Film Festival was called off after screening only one film because WWII broke out.

2203) A domestic cat can't focus clearly on anything closer than about a foot away.

2204) A group of ravens is called an unkindness or conspiracy.

2205) President Chester A. Arthur is regarded as the most fashionable U.S. president and owned 80 pairs of pants, which he liked to change several times a day.

2206) At 3,964 miles, the Yangtze River is the world's longest river that flows entirely within one country, China.

2207) By the number of members, China has the world's largest legislature; the National People's Congress is a single house with 2,980 members.

2208) In Spanish, the word "esposas" means both wives and handcuffs.

2209) Nikita Khrushchev gave Caroline Kennedy her dog, Pushinka.

2210) Napoleon was attacked by rabbits and had to retreat. In 1807, Napoleon had just signed the Treaty of Tilsit, ending his war with Russia; to celebrate, he went on a rabbit hunt. Hundreds of rabbits had been gathered for the hunt in cages, but when they were released, they swarmed toward Napoleon and his men and started climbing up Napoleon's legs. He was forced to retreat to his coach and depart. Instead of wild rabbits, they had bought tame rabbits from farmers, so they weren't afraid of people and probably thought it was feeding time.

2211) Moon is the scientific name for the moon; unlike other moons in our solar system, it doesn't have any other official name.

2212) Based on revenue, Walmart is the world's largest company.

2213) A shark can have over 30,000 teeth in its lifetime. A shark's teeth are arranged in rows, with each successive row smaller than the last. On average, they have 15 rows of teeth, with some species having up to 50 rows. The row nearest the front is the largest and most used. If a shark loses a tooth, the tooth in the row behind it moves up to take its place. A shark's teeth are not embedded in its jaw; they are attached to the skin covering the jaw. New teeth are continually being grown in a groove in the shark's mouth, and the skin moves the teeth forward into new positions. If they couldn't quickly replace their teeth, they wouldn't have been able to develop such a strong bite that causes them to lose so many teeth.

2214) Mozart wrote numerous letters and an entire song focused on poop; no one is quite sure if it was just his odd humor or a mental issue.

2215) Barbara Bush and Abigail Adams's husbands and sons both served as U.S. president.

2216) The U.S. President lives rent-free at the White House, but they pay for personal and family meals, dry cleaning, hair, and makeup; the federal government pays for state dinners and other official functions.

2217) Of the 48 contiguous states, Olympia, Washington, is the northernmost state capital.

2218) French filmmaker Albert Lamorisse (1922-1970) is best known for creating award-winning short films, such as *The Red Balloon* (1956) that won the grand prize at Cannes and an Oscar, but he also invented the strategic board game Risk in 1957.

2219) In 2019, the first artificial intelligence generated research book was published. The algorithm was designed by researchers from Goethe University in Frankfurt, Germany, and the book is about the state of current research on lithium-ion batteries.

2220) The 1815 eruption of Indonesia's Mount Tambora volcano is the most powerful explosion ever witnessed on the earth. It was equivalent to 800 megatons of TNT, 14 times larger than the largest man-made explosion.

2221) In the 19th century, doctors treated hysteria in women by inducing orgasms; the vibrator resulted from this practice.

2222) William Howard Taft was the first president to use the Oval Office; he made the West Wing a permanent building and had the Oval Office built.

2223) Philip Noel-Baker is the only Olympic medalist to also win a Nobel Prize. He won a silver medal in the 1500-meter run in 1920 and the Nobel Peace Prize in 1959.

2224) A rhinoceros has three toes on each foot.

2225) On taking power in 1959, Fidel Castro banned the board game Monopoly and ordered all sets destroyed; he viewed it as the embodiment of capitalism.

2226) The Statue of Liberty's shoe size would be 879.

2227) As a group, musicians have the life expectancy of Zimbabwe, the lowest of any country.

2228) In 1999 in North Carolina, a female skydiver's life was saved when her chutes didn't open and she landed on a mound of fire ants. She was jumping from 14,500 feet when her main parachute didn't open; her backup chute opened at 700 feet and quickly deflated. She hit the ground at about 80 mph, landing on a mound of fire ants that bit her over 200 times. Fire ants have a toxin-filled painful bite that can cause death in some cases. In this case, doctors determined that the repeated fire ant stings shocked her heart and stimulated her nerves, keeping her heart beating and her organs functioning long enough to reach a hospital. She suffered shattered bones and was in a coma for two weeks, but she recovered fully.

2229) Mozart and Beethoven composed music for the glass armonica instrument, which was invented by Benjamin Franklin. It replicated the sound a wet finger makes when rubbed along the rim of a glass and became very popular. Several composers wrote pieces for it.

2230) *Dumbo* (1941) was the first Disney animated feature set in present day at the time of its release.

2231) Only Michael Jackson, Madonna, U2, and Weird Al Yankovic have had top 40 hits in each of the last four decades (1980s, 1990s, 2000s, and 2010s).

2232) When the first tea bags were developed, the idea was that customers would remove the tea from the bags, but they preferred to brew the tea in the bag.

2233) Jimmy Carter is the longest-lived U.S. president.

2234) Despite scoring 28,596 points in his NBA career, Shaquille O'Neal only made one three-point shot out of 22 attempts in his entire NBA career. His only three-point basket came on February 16, 1996, when the Orlando Magic played the Milwaukee Bucks.

2235) Lasting about 38 minutes, the Anglo-Zanzibar War, between the United Kingdom and the Zanzibar Sultanate, was the shortest war in history; it was fought on August 27, 1896.

2236) St. Lucia is the only country named after a woman; it is in the Caribbean and is named after St. Lucy of Syracuse, who lived in the 3rd century.

2237) King James IV of Scotland paid people to practice dentistry on them. He was an amateur dentist and very interested in medicine; he established the Royal College of Surgeons in Scotland, two centuries before it was established in England.

2238) If they can't find food, ribbon worms will eat themselves. They can eat a substantial portion of their body and still survive.

2239) The oldest surviving paper currency is the Chinese Great Ming Circulating Treasure Note that was initially printed between 1368 and 1398. The value of the currency crashed, and some of the notes were stored away and forgotten.

2240) Since 1980, the birthrate for human twins has increased by about 75%. Part of the reason is that older mothers are more likely to have twins.

2241) Walnuts, almonds, pecans, and cashews aren't technically nuts; they are drupes, which also include peaches, plums, and cherries. Drupes are a type of fruit where an outer fleshy part surrounds a shell or pit with a seed inside. For some drupes, you eat the fleshy part, and for some, you eat the seed inside.

2242) In 1951, Bernie Geoffrion was the first NHL player to use a slapshot.

2243) Honolulu has the only royal palace in the United States.

2244) Kobe Bryant is the only person to win an Olympic gold medal and an Oscar; he won Olympic basketball gold medals in 2008 and 2012 and Best Animated Short Film for *Dear Basketball* (2018).

2245) The time between the Stegosaurus and Tyrannosaurus Rex is larger than the time between the Tyrannosaurus and you. Stegosaurus existed about 150 million years ago; Tyrannosaurus Rex didn't evolve until about 67 million years ago, so the two were separated by about 83 million years.

2246) Sleeping on the job is acceptable in Japan because it is viewed as exhaustion from working hard.

2247) In the *Peanuts* comic strip, Peppermint Patty's real name is Patricia Reichardt.

2248) Three presidents have won Grammys for best spoken word album: Clinton, Carter, and Obama.

2249) Millard Fillmore was the last president who wasn't either a Democrat or Republican; he was a member of the Whig party.

2250) By volume, Tamu Massif is the world's largest volcano, either active or extinct; it is 1,000 miles east of Japan under the Pacific Ocean and is extinct.

2251) Santa Fe, New Mexico, is the only two-word state capital in a two-word state.

2252) India has more post offices than any other country.

2253) The famous Hollywood sign in Los Angeles originally said Hollywoodland. The sign was erected in 1923 as an advertisement for an upscale real estate development called Hollywoodland; in 1949, it was changed to its current form.

2254) There is a southern version of the aurora borealis (northern lights) called the aurora australis; it can be seen from Antarctica, New Zealand, Argentina, and Australia.

2255) Ulage is the unfilled space between a bottle top and the liquid inside.

2256) Uranus' moons are named after characters created by William Shakespeare and Alexander Pope. There are 27 moons: Cordelia, Ophelia, Bianca, Cressida, Desdemona, Juliet, Portia, Rosalind, Cupid, Belinda, Perdita, Puck, Mab, Miranda, Ariel, Umbriel, Titania, Oberon, Francisco, Caliban, Stephano, Trinculo, Sycorax, Margaret, Prospero, Setebos, and Ferdinand.

2257) Oscar Zoroaster Phadrig Isaac Norman Henkle Emmannuel Ambroise Diggs is the real name of The Wizard of Oz.

2258) Flamingos bend their legs at the ankle and not the knee. Their knee is located much higher up, hidden under their feathers. The whole area from the ankle to the toes is a giant foot. The joint that looks like an ankle, near the bottom of their leg, is the beginning of their toes, so about half of what appears to be the flamingo's legs are really its feet.

2259) The bald eagle's name comes from the old English word piebald, meaning white-headed.

2260) Crocodiles don't sweat; they open their mouth, similar to panting, to keep cool.

2261) An ambigram is a word, art form, or other symbolic representation whose elements retain meaning when viewed or interpreted from a different direction, perspective, or orientation. For example, the word "swims" is the same when it is rotated 180 degrees.

2262) Through a process called REM atonia, people don't sneeze while they sleep because the brain shuts down the reflexes that would result in a sneeze.

2263) Its purpose isn't known, but about 39% of the population has a bone in their knee called the fabella. From historical studies, the percentage fell from 17% in 1875 to 11% in 1918, before rising to the current number.

2264) High heels were created in ancient Egypt to keep butcher's feet out of the blood. They became more popular when Persian nobility used them riding horses to help them stay in their stirrups.

2265) Canada eats the most macaroni and cheese per capita of any country.

2266) At the 1908 London Olympics, Italian Dorando Pietri was the first marathon runner to cross the finish line, but he was disqualified because he collapsed from exhaustion while finishing and was helped up and carried across the line by officials.

2267) In 1920, Babe Ruth hit more home runs than any other entire American League team.

2268) Charles Lindbergh was the 19th pilot to fly nonstop across the Atlantic, but he was the first to do it solo. The first nonstop flight across the Atlantic was in 1919, eight years before Lindbergh's flight. British aviators John Alcock and Arthur Brown made the first transatlantic flight from St. John's, Newfoundland, to Clifton, Ireland, in June 1919.

2269) *American Pie* was the name of the airplane Buddy Holly died in; Don McLean used it as the title for his 1972 number-one song.

2270) Many U.S. police departments adopted navy blue uniforms because they were surplus army uniforms from the Civil War.

2271) Johann Sebastian Bach enjoyed coffee so much that he wrote a cantata for it.

2272) Seventeen U.S. presidents didn't have a vice president for all or part of their term: James Madison, Andrew Jackson, John Tyler, Millard Fillmore, Franklin Pierce, Andrew Johnson, Ulysses S. Grant, Chester A. Arthur, Grover Cleveland, William McKinley, Theodore Roosevelt, William H. Taft, Calvin Coolidge, Harry S. Truman, Lyndon B. Johnson, Richard Nixon, and Gerald Ford.

2273) In 1913, Alfred Carlton Gilbert, a 1908 Olympic gold medal pole vaulter, invented the Erector Set toy.

2274) No one is born a citizen of Vatican City. To become a citizen, you must work for the city-state. If you lose your job, your citizenship is revoked, and you automatically become an Italian citizen if you aren't already a citizen of another country.

2275) In about 300 BC, the Roman censor Appius Claudius Caecus removed the letter z from the alphabet because it wasn't used that much and had become archaic. It took about 200 years for it to get added back.

2276) Rio de Janeiro, Brazil, was the only European capital outside of Europe; it was the capital of Portugal from 1808 to 1822. Napoleon was invading Portugal at the time, so the Portuguese royal family moved to Rio, and it became the capital.

2277) The last guillotining in France occurred on September 10, 1977.

2278) In the second half of the 18th century to study the health effects of coffee, King Gustav III of Sweden commuted the death sentence of a pair of twins, on condition that one drank three pots of coffee each day for the rest of their life and one drank three pots of tea each day. He appointed two doctors to supervise the experiment; both doctors and the king died before the experiment was complete. The tea-drinking twin died first, at age 83.

2279) The point in the ocean furthest from the nearest land is 1,670 miles from land; it is called Point Nemo and is in the South Pacific.

2280) The longest recorded time a chicken has flown continuously is 13 seconds; the longest distance chicken flight ever recorded is 301.5 feet.

2281) Only three people have won individual gold medals in the same event in four consecutive Olympics: Michael Phelps (swimming 200-meter individual medley), Carl Lewis (long jump), and Al Oerter (discus).

2282) Grover Cleveland was the only president married at the White House.

2283) Since he was the only U.S. president to never marry, James Buchanan had an adopted niece that took over many of the responsibilities that would normally go to the president's wife.

2284) Mushrooms are more closely related to humans than they are to plants. Animals and fungi branched off from plants about 1.1 billion years ago; later, animals and fungi separated genealogically, making mushrooms closer to humans than to plants.

2285) The pineal gland in the center of the brain is the smallest organ in the human body; it is about the size of a grain of rice and produces and secretes melatonin.

2286) Only two countries formally include "the" at the start of their names: The Gambia and The Bahamas.

2287) The stapes, in the middle ear, is the smallest bone in the human body.

2288) A vast reservoir of water, three times the volume of all the oceans, is located about 400 miles beneath the earth's crust. The water is locked up in a mineral called ringwoodite.

2289) On average, domestic cats sleep 15 hours per day.

2290) In 1898, Morgan Robertson wrote a short novel called *Futility*. It had the *Titan*, a large unsinkable ship with an insufficient number of lifeboats, hitting an iceberg and sinking in the North Atlantic on an April voyage, losing almost everyone on board. Fourteen years later in April 1912, the large unsinkable *Titanic*, with an insufficient number of lifeboats, hit an iceberg and sank in the North Atlantic, losing most of the people on board.

2291) There were 20 years between the first female in space and the first American female in space. Soviet Valentina Tereshkova was the first in 1963; Sally Ride was the first American in 1983.

2292) Russia is the third closest country to the United States.

2293) It is illegal for drug companies to advertise directly to consumers almost everywhere in the world except the United States and New Zealand.

2294) At the time he retired, Wayne Gretzky held 61 NHL records.

2295) In 1956, *The Wizard of Oz* was the first feature film broadcast on U.S. television.

2296) The sign we know as the ampersand (&) was the 27th letter of the English alphabet before being dropped. It wasn't called an ampersand at the time and was referred to as "and."

2297) Queen Elizabeth II has owned more than 30 corgis.

2298) The theme music for television's *Monty Python's Flying Circus* was written by John Philip Sousa; it is "The Liberty Bell March."

2299) The ZIP in ZIP Code stands for Zone Improvement Plan.

2300) Dunce caps originally were a sign of intelligence. John Duns Scotus, a 13th century philosopher, created the idea of the pointy hat as a reverse funnel to spread knowledge into the brain; the hats became popular and were a symbol of high intelligence. In the 1500s, Scotus' ideas fell out of favor, and the pointy hat eventually came to mean the opposite.

2301) The ancient Romans threw walnuts at weddings; they signified hopes for the fertility of the bride.

2302) The Tour de France bicycle race has the world's most in-person spectators of any single sporting event. It attracts 12 to 15 million spectators.

2303) Jacqueline Kennedy Onassis edited Michael Jackson's autobiography *Moonwalk*.

2304) The letter x begins the fewest words in the English language.

2305) During the summer heat, the Eiffel Tower can grow more than six inches from metal expansion. The tower is made up of more than 7,300 tons of iron.

2306) By 70 years of age, the average person will have shed 105 pounds of skin.

2307) The 1900 Paris Olympics had long jump and high jump competitions for horses. The winning long jump was 6.10 meters; the winning high jump was 1.85 meters.

2308) The state of Virginia extends further west than West Virginia.

2309) Coprophagy is the act of eating your own poop; rats and most rodents have simple digestive systems and eat their own poop to recover additional nutrients.

2310) Windsor Castle is 590,000 square feet, making it the world's largest inhabited castle.

2311) Birds don't urinate. They convert excess nitrogen to uric acid, instead of urea; it is less toxic and doesn't need to be diluted as much. It goes out with their other waste and saves water, so they don't have to drink as much.

2312) By area, Libya is 99% desert, the highest percentage of any country.

2313) Your fingers don't contain any muscles. The muscles that bend the finger joints are in the palm and mid-forearm and are connected to the finger bones by tendons that pull on and move the fingers.

2314) Based on the volume of the average human body, the world's population could fit in a cube 2,577 feet on each side, about 0.116 cubic miles.

2315) Ostrakismos, meaning ostracism, was a process in ancient Greece where any citizen could be voted out and expelled for 10 years. In some instances, it was used to express popular anger against an individual, but it was often used preemptively to remove someone who was thought to be a threat to the state.

2316) At 4,300 miles long, the Andes are the world's longest above-water mountain range, but the mid-ocean ridge, at 25,097 miles, is the longest if you include underwater ranges. The mid-ocean ridges of all the world's oceans are connected.

2317) There is a very rare third type of human twin called sesquizygous (semi-identical). Monozygotic (identical) twins result from a single fertilized egg that splits in two and forms two identical boys or girls that share 100% of their DNA. Dizygotic (fraternal) twins form from two eggs that have been fertilized by two of the father's sperm, creating two genetically unique siblings that share 50% of their DNA. Semi-identical twins are so rare that only two cases have ever been identified; they share between 50% and 100% of their DNA and are formed when a single egg is fertilized by two sperm. This shouldn't happen; once a sperm enters the egg, the egg locks down to prevent another sperm from entering. Even if a second sperm entered, an embryo with three, rather than the normal two, sets of chromosomes won't survive. To produce semi-identical twins, the egg splits the three sets of chromosomes into two separate cell sets.

2318) Along with murdering his mother and his first two wives, Roman emperor Nero married a boy slave, Sporus, who was designated a puer delicatus, which were slaves of important Roman citizens chosen because of their beauty. Nero freed Sporus and married him; he also had him castrated, as was customary with puer delicatus, so his boyish looks wouldn't change. Sporus was Nero's formal wife in the eyes of everyone and dressed as an empress.

2319) During the Victorian period on both sides of the Atlantic, fern mania, known as pteridomania, was a huge fad. Almost every house had a potted fern. People would collect rare ferns; there were fern books and fern societies, and florists bulked out floral arrangements with ferns.

2320) Sacagawea has more U.S. statues in her honor than anyone else.

2321) At age 21, Marlee Matlin is the youngest Best Actress Oscar winner for *Children of a Lesser God* (1986).

2322) English has more words than any other language.

2323) At 5'11" tall, Melania Trump, Michelle Obama, and Eleanor Roosevelt are tied as the tallest U.S. first ladies.

2324) Montpelier, Vermont, is the only state capital without a McDonald's.

2325) Genghis Khan fathered countless children; while we will never know exactly how many offspring the Mongol leader had, scientists now believe that about 1 in every 200 men are his direct descendants.

2326) *Rocky*, *Chariots of Fire*, and *Million Dollar Baby* are the only three sports-related movies that have won the Best Picture Oscar.

2327) Due to its unique chemical qualities, honey can remain edible for centuries; 3,000-year-old edible honey has been found in tombs.

2328) On average, it takes about a minute for human blood to circulate through the entire body.

2329) Academy Awards are called Oscars because Margaret Herrick, Academy librarian and future executive director, thought the statue looked like her uncle Oscar.

2330) At the age of 16, the famous poet Maya Angelou was San Francisco's first African American female streetcar conductor.

2331) The first pedestrian ever killed by a car occurred on August 17, 1896. Bridget Driscoll was struck by a demonstration car that was traveling at 4 mph.

2332) On *Sesame Street*, the Cookie Monster's real name is Sid.

2333) The longest gloved boxing match in history was in 1893 and lasted for 110 three-minute rounds, for a total of 7 hours and 19 minutes. It was a lightweight match between Andy Bowen and Jack Burke in New Orleans, Louisiana, and began around 9 p.m. and finished after 4 a.m. There was no winner, as both fighters were too exhausted to continue.

2334) In *Star Wars Episode V: The Empire Strikes Back*, Darth Vader never says, "Luke, I am your father." Instead, he says, "No, I am your father."

2335) Based on the number of participants, soccer is the world's most popular sport; badminton is second, and field hockey is third.

2336) William Howard Taft is the only man to have been both Chief Justice of the U.S. Supreme Court and U.S. president.

2337) Wooly mammoths were still alive about 900 years after the Great Pyramid of Giza was built. The last mammoths died out about 1650 BC on Wrangel Island in the Arctic Ocean; the Great Pyramid was completed in about 2560 BC.

2338) Unconsciously, native English speakers say adjectives preceding nouns in a specific order: opinion, size, age, shape, color, origin, material, and purpose. That is why we say things instinctively like "big, old, black, leather chair" instead of "black, leather, old, big chair," which doesn't sound right.

2339) At some points in history, money was designed to discourage people from having too much. According to Greek historian Plutarch, the Spartans used long, heavy iron rods as their currency to discourage people from pursuing great wealth. The currency was called obeloi and was so cumbersome that carrying multiple pieces required help.

2340) William Shakespeare's only son was named Hamnet.

2341) Written out in English, eight billion is the second number alphabetically, no matter how high you go.

2342) You can get from Norway to North Korea by land going through one country, Russia.

2343) An average alligator can go through 2,000 to 3,000 teeth in a lifetime. An alligator has roughly 80 teeth, and as the teeth wear down, they are replaced.

2344) Piggy banks got their name because they were originally made from pygg, an orange-colored clay. During the Middle Ages, the clay was used to make bowls and jars and other containers that people started to store change in; the containers were not made into pig shapes until much later.

2345) The pizza served in the United States each day would cover an area of about 100 acres.

2346) The Brooklyn Bridge was under construction when Custer was defeated at the Battle of Little Bighorn in 1876.

2347) Chocolate is the only edible substance that melts just below human body temperature. Chocolate melts at 93 degrees, which is why it melts in your mouth.

2348) The Pentagon, headquarters for the U.S. Department of Defense, was originally designed to fit on a piece of land that was bordered on five sides by roads. It was decided that the original site was too close to Arlington Cemetery, so it was moved to its current location. Since the design was already complete, it was slightly modified, but it kept its pentagon shape, even though it wasn't essential any longer.

2349) The standard U.S. railroad width of 4 feet 8.5 inches is directly derived from the width of Roman war chariots. The English expatriates who designed the U.S. railroad system based their measurements on the pre-railroad tramways built in England, which were built using the same tools used to build wagons. To avoid breaking down during long treks across the old English roads created by the Romans, wagons were built to fit the ruts carved out by Roman war chariots, and all Roman chariots were built to a standard width of 4 feet 8.5 inches.

2350) Up until the 1970s, the mental disorder sluggish schizophrenia was diagnosed as a made-up disorder the Soviet Union used to confine dissenters. It was supposedly a very slow developing schizophrenia, so they could use the diagnosis on anyone.

2351) At one point in the year, it is the same local time for people living in Oregon and Florida. A small part of eastern Oregon is in the Mountain Time Zone, and a small part of western Florida is in the Central Time Zone. When the change from daylight saving time to standard time is made, these two areas share the same time for one hour after the Central Time Zone has fallen back to standard time and before the Mountain Time Zone has.

2352) Albert Einstein's 1921 Nobel Prize in Physics was for the photoelectric effect, not for his work on relativity. He suggested for the first time that light is both a wave and a particle and established the existence of photons.

2353) Richard Rogers and Marvin Hamlisch are the only two people ever to win an Oscar, Emmy, Tony, Grammy, and Pulitzer.

2354) Greenland is part of the Kingdom of Denmark; if you include it as part of Denmark's area, Denmark is the 12th largest country.

2355) Ecuador is the only point on the equator with snow on the ground.

2356) Hippo milk is bright pink. Hippos secrete two unique acids, hipposudoric acid and norhipposudoric acid, that function as a natural sunscreen and antimicrobial agent. The acids are red and orange, and when mixed with a hippo mother's milk, they turn it bright pink.

2357) In 1941, the first U.S. television commercial ever broadcast was for Bulova watches.

2358) The Statue of Liberty is made of copper; about 62,000 pounds of copper were used to create it, and it looked like a new penny when it was first created.

2359) A pangram is a sentence or verse that contains all letters in the alphabet at least once, such as "The quick brown fox jumps over a lazy dog."

2360) The use of the word "bucks" for dollars dates to the 1700s when deerskins were commonly used for trading. A trading record from 1748 notes the exchange of a cask of whiskey for 5 bucks. The term stayed around after the dollar became the U.S. standard currency in 1792.

2361) Sharks have been around longer than trees. The first sharks appeared about 450 million years ago; the first trees were about 385 million years ago.

2362) A male dog lifts his leg to pee because he wants to leave his mark as high as possible, as a sign of size and status. He also prefers to pee on vertical objects because the scent lasts longer.

2363) Japan and Russia still haven't officially signed a peace treaty between them ending WWII; they have a dispute over the Kuril Islands.

2364) Researchers have found that cats can recognize their names, but they are also willing to ignore you.

2365) Human babies are born without kneecaps; at three to five years old, the cartilage in their knee ossifies into kneecaps.

2366) Snails move at a steady pace with a maximum speed of about 50 yards per hour, or 0.03 mph.

2367) The whip was the first man-made object to break the sound barrier. The crack a whip makes is due to a small sonic boom.

2368) A blue moon is defined as the second full moon in a calendar month. It happens about every three years, giving the expression "once in a blue moon" for something that doesn't occur very often.

2369) Australia is the only continent without an active volcano.

2370) Despite the fact the William Shakespeare has become the accepted spelling of the writer's name, he never once spelled it that way, and it was spelled in over 80 variations by his contemporaries, including several by Shakespeare himself.

2371) Even though it is known worldwide for its casinos, Monaco doesn't allow its citizens to even step foot in its casinos unless they work there. This law excludes foreign nationals that reside in Monaco and account for about 80% of the population.

2372) A double rainbow happens when light is reflected twice in the raindrop. You see two different reflections coming from different angles, and it also reverses the order of the colors on the secondary rainbow.

2373) In the 15th century, King Louis XI of France ordered Abbot de Beigne to create a musical instrument using the voices of pigs. He built a keyboard that jabbed a spike into the rumps of pigs to produce a squeal.

2374) In 1964, grad student Donal Rusk Currey got his tree corer stuck in a bristlecone pine, and a park ranger helped him remove it by cutting the tree down. When Currey counted the rings, he found out the tree was almost 5,000 years old, the oldest ever recorded at that time.

2375) The Meganeura is the largest known flying insect ever. It lived more than 300 million years ago during the Carboniferous Period and was a dragonfly-like insect with a wingspan of about 2.5 feet. It was a carnivore and fed on other insects and small amphibians.

2376) To ensure global supply in the case of an emergency, Canada has a strategic maple syrup reserve. The reserve contains about 2.4 million gallons of syrup. Quebec province produces about 75% of the global supply of maple syrup.

2377) Bingo is the name of the dog on the Cracker Jack box.

2378) Deaf-mute MLB player William Hoy inspired the non-verbal signs used in baseball and stole over 600 bases in his career; he started his career in 1888.

2379) Until the 19th century, the word hypocrites referred to actors.

2380) Human bodies can continue to move for more than a year after death. Through time-lapse photography, researchers found that bodies can continue to move significantly; the movements are believed to be due to the process of decomposition as the body mummifies and the ligaments dry out.

2381) English is the official language of the most countries.

2382) In traditional vampire folklore, one of their weaknesses is arithmomania, a compulsion to count things. This weakness can be used to defend against them by placing grains of rice or sand out that they will be compelled to count. Therefore, *Sesame Street's* Count von Count's love of counting is part of being a vampire.

2383) The blackest man-made object is made from vertically aligned carbon nanotubes grown on a surface of chlorine-etched aluminum foil. The foil captures at least 99.995% of any incoming light, making it the blackest material ever recorded.

2384) Beetles are the most common group of insects. Flies are the second most common, and bees and ants are third.

2385) The first automobile speeding ticket was issued in 1896 in England. The car was going 8 mph; the speed limit for cars was 2 mph. You could go over 2 mph if you had someone walk in front of the car waving a red flag to alert people.

2386) With over 300,000 people, Murmansk, Russia, is the most populous city north of the Arctic Circle.

2387) In the 14th century, the bubonic plague killed so many people that the world population did not reach the same levels again until the 17th century.

2388) Starfish don't have blood; their circulatory system is primarily made of seawater.

2389) A cluster of 10-20 bananas is called a hand.

2390) Sea otters hold hands while they are sleeping, so they don't drift apart.

2391) The tongue is the fastest healing part of the human body.

2392) Mars is red because it is covered in iron oxide (rust).

2393) Pizza Hut is the oldest pizza chain in the United States; it was founded in 1958.

2394) The tall, pleated chef's hat is called a toque; the 100 folds in it are said to represent 100 ways to cook an egg.

2395) *The Shape of Water* (2017) was the first science fiction film to win the Best Picture Oscar.

2396) The Declaration of Independence wasn't signed on July 4, 1776. It was signed on August 2, 1776; it was adopted by Congress on July 4, 1776.

2397) American Eddie Eagan is the only person to win gold medals in both the Winter and Summer Olympics. He won for boxing in 1920 and bobsled in 1932.

2398) The cat is the only domestic animal not mentioned in the Bible.

2399) Built between 1825 and 1843, the world's first underwater tunnel was under London's Thames River.

2400) If you wrote out every number in English (one, two, three, etc.), you wouldn't use the letter b until you reached one billion.

2401) Sam Snead was the first PGA golfer to shoot their age in a tournament round; he shot a 67 at the 1979 Quad Cities Open.

2402) The average person walks about 75,000 miles in their life.

2403) The Arabian Desert contains the world's largest continuous body of sand. The contiguous sand body, known as the Rub 'al-Khali or the "Empty Quarter," is about 250,000 square miles.

2404) Lhasa Apsos originated in Tibet and were originally kept exclusively by nobility and holy men of Tibet; they lived in the palace of the Dalai Lama and the surrounding monasteries.

2405) Early Americans used corn cobs for toilet paper. Dried corncobs were plentiful, efficient, and are softer and more flexible than you might think.

2406) Nudiustertian means the day before yesterday.

2407) An autological word is a word that describes itself; some examples include word, noun, polysyllabic, unhyphenated, and suffixed.

2408) Drupelets are the individual bumps making up a raspberry or blackberry.

2409) On a per-capita basis, Alaska produces more serial killers than any other state.

2410) In April 1933, Amelia Earhart and Eleanor Roosevelt snuck out of a White House event, commandeered an airplane, and went on a joyride.

2411) Rin Tin Tin was born in a bombed-out French village during WWI and was voted the most popular film performer in the United States in 1926.

2412) The national capital city of La Paz, Bolivia, is one of the world's most fire-safe cities. At an elevation of 11,800 feet, it is difficult for fires to spread due to the low oxygen level.

2413) Scotland has the highest percentage of natural redheads of any country, about 13%.

2414) South Africa has three national capital cities. Pretoria is the administrative capital; Cape Town is the legislative capital, and Bloemfontein is the judicial capital.

2415) Pareidolia is the term for seeing patterns in random data. Some common examples are seeing a likeness in the clouds or an image on the surface of the moon.

2416) The Sargasso Sea is the only sea without a coastline (no land border). It is in the North Atlantic, off the coast of the United States, and is defined by currents.

2417) Jane Addams was the first American woman to win a Nobel Prize; she shared the 1931 Nobel Peace Prize.

2418) TV dinners were first sold in 1954. Swanson had 260 tons of leftover frozen turkeys from Thanksgiving. Inspired by the food trays on airlines, they created a meal of turkey, cornbread dressing, gravy, peas, and sweet potatoes.

2419) More national capital cities start with the letter "B" than any other letter: Baghdad, Baku, Bamako, Bandar Seri Begawan, Bangkok, Bangui, Banjul, Basseterre, Beijing, Beirut, Belgrade, Belmopan, Berlin, Bern, Bishkek, Bissau, Bogotá, Brasília, Bratislava, Brazzaville, Bridgetown, Brussels, Bucharest, Budapest, and Buenos Aires.

2420) President William Howard Taft had a special bathtub, big enough to hold four men, installed in the White House.

2421) Osmium is the densest naturally occurring element; it is about 25 times denser than water.

2422) As part of its reproductive process, the jewel wasp will sting a cockroach twice, first in the thorax to partially immobilize it and then in the head to block its normal escape reflex. The wasp is too small to carry the cockroach, so it leads it back to its burrow by pulling on one of its antennae. Once in the burrow, the wasp lays one egg on the roach's abdomen and exits and fills in the burrow entrance with pebbles. With the effect of the wasp venom, the roach rests in the burrow, and in about three days, the wasp's egg hatches, and the larva begins feeding on the roach for four to five days before chewing its way into the roach's abdomen. It continues to reside inside the roach, and over eight days, it consumes the roach's internal organs in an order that maximizes the time the roach is still alive. The larva enters a pupal stage and forms a cocoon inside the roach, and the fully-grown wasp eventually emerges from the roach's body, completing the reproductive cycle.

2423) Portland cement gets its name from England; it was created in the mid-19th century and is named because of its similarity to Portland stone that was quarried on the Isle of Portland, off the coast of England.

2424) Phoenix, Arizona, has the largest population of any state capital.

2425) Sunsets on Mars are blue.

2426) Jupiter is the fastest spinning planet in our solar system; at the equator, it rotates at 28,273 mph; comparatively, the Earth rotates at 1,038 mph.

2427) In Iceland, you can swim between the European and North American tectonic plates. The Silfra fissure is a crack between the two continental plates and is the only spot in the world where you can swim directly between the North American and European continents. The crack is filled with extremely clear, cold water that remains about 35 to 39 degrees Fahrenheit all year.

2428) With about 200 million copies printed annually, the IKEA catalog is the world's most printed book.

2429) Thomas Jefferson wrote his own translation of the Bible. He didn't agree with some of the supernatural elements of the Bible and wrote his own version, eliminating what he didn't agree with.

2430) Worldwide, the average human weighs about 137 pounds.

2431) Andorra has no standing army, but it requires that the eldest, able-bodied man in each household must have a rifle for national protection if needed.

2432) After aardvark, the aardwolf, a member of the hyena family that looks like a small striped hyena, is the second animal alphabetically. It is native to eastern and southern Africa and feeds on insects, primarily termites.

2433) Istanbul, Turkey, is the only major city located on two continents, Europe and Asia.

2434) During WWI, starving wolves, displaced by the war, amassed in such numbers that the Germans and Russians agreed to a temporary cease-fire to jointly battle the wolves.

2435) Everyone alive when the oldest living person was born is dead.

2436) At 970,000 square miles, the Tibetan Plateau in China and Pakistan is the world's largest plateau.

2437) The sport of cricket originated the term hat trick. The term first appeared in 1858 when H. H. Stephenson took three wickets with three consecutive balls; fans held a collection for him and presented him with a hat, which was bought with the proceeds.

2438) As a gas, oxygen is odorless and colorless; in its liquid and solid forms, it is pale blue.

2439) Paraguay is the only country with a two-sided (different designs on each side) flag.

2440) A desert locust swarm can cover 460 square miles and contain billions of locusts that can eat their weight in plants each day, consuming potentially hundreds of millions of pounds of vegetation per day.

2441) During the Boer War from 1900 to 1902, Great Britain originated the concept of the concentration camp.

2442) Extant is the opposite of extinct.

2443) Uncoiled, a Slinky is 87 feet long.

2444) At about 65 million years old, Kazakhstan's Lake Zaysan is the world's oldest lake.

2445) The surface area of Pluto is only about 3% larger than Russia.

2446) Charles Darwin ate many of the animal species he discovered.

2447) At age 42, Satchel Paige was the oldest Major League Baseball rookie.

2448) The 2016 Rio de Janeiro Olympics was the first Summer Olympics held entirely during the winter. The other two Summer Olympics in the Southern Hemisphere had taken place at least partly in the spring.

2449) The difference between antlers (found on deer, elk, and moose) and horns (found on pronghorn antelope, bighorn sheep, and bison) is that antlers are an extension of the animal's skull, and they are true bone that is shed and regrown each year. Horns are composed of an interior bone that is an extension of the skull; they are covered by an exterior sheath, grown by specialized hair follicles. They aren't shed and continue to grow throughout the animal's life. The exception is the pronghorn antelope, which sheds and regrows its horn sheath each year.

2450) Men wore high heels before women did; it was a sign of status. In the 1600s, women started to wear high heels as a way of appropriating masculine power; it then filtered down to the lower classes. When it was no longer a power symbol, men eventually quit wearing high heels.

2451) Benito Mussolini wrote a historical romance novel, *The Cardinal's Mistress*.

2452) When you wake up with a jolt, it is called a hypnic jerk. It is an involuntary twitch that occurs when you are beginning to fall asleep, causing you to jump and awaken suddenly for a moment.

2453) Boston and Austin are the only two U.S. state capitals with rhyming names.

2454) In the 13th century, Pope Gregory IX believed that black cats were an instrument of Satan; he condemned cats across Europe, and they were hunted down and killed.

2455) There are 45 miles of nerves in the human body.

2456) Charles Addams' *New Yorker* cartoons of a spooky husband and wife were the inspiration for *The Addams Family* and Boris Badenov and Natasha Fatale of *Rocky and Bullwinkle and Friends*.

2457) At 16 letters, unprosperousness is the longest English word where each letter occurs at least twice.

2458) The mouthwash Listerine was created as a surgical disinfectant.

2459) The Brothers Grimm version of *Cinderella* is a much darker story. To fit into the shoe, the stepsisters cut off their toe and a part of their heel, and they try to go to Cinderella's wedding and get their eyes plucked out by birds.

2460) Bug spray doesn't repel mosquitos. Ingredients like DEET mask what you smell like, creating a barrier on your skin that interferes with the mosquito's detection of the lactic acid and carbon dioxide they're attracted to.

2461) One million dollars in $100 bills weighs about 20.4 pounds.

2462) France's *The Artist* (2011) was the first movie from a non-English speaking country to win the Best Picture Oscar.

2463) The can opener was invented 45 years after tin cans were invented.

2464) The Russian army didn't wear socks until 2013. Since the 17th century, the army had worn portyanki, a square of cloth (cotton for summer, flannel for winter), that they wrapped their feet in. Portyanki were far cheaper to make than socks, and they were quicker and easier to wash, dry, and mend, but they had to be worn correctly and wrapped tightly, or they could cause blisters. You also had to be able to put your portyanki on fast; regulations required soldiers to be fully dressed in 45 seconds.

2465) In 1892, Gallaudet University, a school for the deaf, originated the football huddle. They huddled to avoid the other team seeing their sign language.

2466) Ice worms are related to common earthworms, but they spend their entire lives in glaciers and require below freezing temperatures to survive. They are found across the northern United States and Canada and come to the glacier surface to feed on snow algae. At temperatures even five degrees above freezing, their internal membranes start to fall apart, and they essentially liquefy and die.

2467) Macy's was the first U.S. department store; it opened in 1858.

2468) In ancient Rome, it was considered a sign of leadership to be born with a crooked nose.

2469) In Switzerland, it is illegal to own just one guinea pig. They are social animals, and it is considered animal cruelty to deny them companionship.

2470) Crab, in *Two Gentlemen of Verona*, is the only named dog in any Shakespeare play.

2471) The feeding of the 5,000 is the only miracle mentioned in all four Bible gospels.

2472) The oldest known advertising dates from about 3000 BC. In Thebes, Greece, a fabric seller announced a reward for the return of his slave to his store, where the most beautiful fabrics are woven for each person's taste.

2473) The Amazon River has the world's largest discharge volume. At an average of about 55 million gallons per second, its discharge is larger than the world's next seven largest rivers combined and accounts for 20% of the total global river discharge to the oceans.

2474) Time, person, and year are the three most used English nouns.

2475) Marie Curie is the only person to win Nobel Prizes in two different areas of science, physics and chemistry.

2476) Up until a 1747 proclamation by Spain's King Ferdinand VI, many Europeans believed California was an island. The misconception started in 1510 when Spanish novelist Garci Rodríguez de Montalvo wrote *Las Sergas de Esplandián*, a novel about a mythical island called California. His work formed the basis for naming California, and the name propagated the idea it was an island.

2477) Antepenultimate means the third to last thing.

2478) The probability that any single glass of water contains at least one molecule of water drunk by Cleopatra is almost 100%. There are about 1,000 times as many molecules of water in a glass as there are glasses of water in the earth's water supply. If water molecules spread through the entire water supply, any given glass of water should contain 1,000 molecules of water from any other glass.

2479) The giant eland is the largest species of antelope and can be almost 6 feet at the shoulder and weigh up to 2,200 pounds.

2480) Moths rest with their wings open flat; butterflies rest with their wings together.

2481) *Gone with the Wind* screenwriter Sidney Howard won the first posthumous Oscar ever awarded.

2482) The lunula is the white crescent near the base of your fingernail.

2483) Some spiders produce a milk-like substance for their young. Researchers have found that the jumping spider secretes a nutritious milk-like substance to feed its offspring. The spider also continues to care for its young as they mature and become independent, so maternal care may be more widespread than has been assumed in the animal world.

2484) The sport of cricket originated the term home run.

2485) A sneeze sounds different in different parts of the world. Americans typically say "achoo!"; for Germans, it is "hatschi!"; for Spanish, it is "achis!"; for Japanese, it is "hakashun!"; for Russians, it is "apchkhi!"; for French, it is "atchoum!"

2486) Zambia has a larger percent of its area devoted to national parks than any other country; national parks make up 32% of its area.

2487) Boxing originated the term southpaw. Left-handed fighters were said to use a southpaw stance; no one is quite sure why, but hitting someone with a left came to be known as a southpaw punch.

2488) Google is the world's most visited website.

2489) "Make Your Wet Dreams Come True" was once a U.S. presidential campaign slogan. In 1928, former New York Governor Al Smith ran for president against Herbert Hoover; a major debate was over whether the prohibition alcohol ban should continue. Those against prohibition were known as Wets, and those in favor were known as Drys. Smith campaigned against prohibition, so they produced buttons bearing the slogan.

2490) Norway, Austria, and Liechtenstein are the only countries that have won more medals at the Winter Olympics than at the Summer Olympics.

2491) A rat can tread water for three days and survive being flushed down the toilet.

2492) The largest cell in the human body is the egg; it is about 30 times larger than the smallest cell, the sperm.

2493) The Decalogue is more commonly known as the Ten Commandments.

2494) At the outbreak of the American Civil War, future U.S. president Andrew Johnson was the only southern senator to keep his seat in Congress. He was pro-slavery but disagreed with secession and stayed loyal to the Union.

2495) Other than leap day, the least common U.S. birthday is December 25.

2496) In terms of how long it takes to process input, the fastest human sense is hearing; it takes as little as 0.05 seconds to process.

2497) The king cobra is the only snake that builds a nest. They can lay up to 40 eggs at once; the nest is built from vegetation and helps keep the eggs safe.

2498) On average, the moon is 238,900 miles from the earth.

2499) The disclaimer that appears at the end of virtually every film that states the movie is a work of fiction and any similarity to actual persons living or dead or actual events is purely coincidental is a result of Rasputin's murder. In the 1933 MGM film *Rasputin and the Empress*, Felix Yusupov, the man who assassinated Rasputin, and his wife Irina were portrayed under different names, and they were both still alive. They were unhappy with how they were portrayed, but since Felix had confessed to the killing, it was more difficult to prove a libel case around him, so Irina sued the studio for libel and won. Part of the problem for MGM was that they implied at the beginning of the film that it depicted real people and events. A judge in the case told MGM that the studio would have stood a better chance had they incorporated a disclaimer stating the opposite, so that is why the disclaimer exists on films today.

2500) In 1912, Merck invented the drug ecstasy. They wanted to develop something to stop abnormal bleeding, and they synthesized MDMA to avoid a Bayer patent. There was no real interest in the drug at the time, and it wasn't until 1975 that he psychoactive effects of the drug were seriously considered.

Facts 2501-3100

2501) In about 1840, naturalist Charles Darwin is credited as being the first person to put wheels on an office chair.

2502) The Amazon is the world's widest river; it is almost 25 miles wide during the wet season.

2503) At 18,009 feet, Alaska's Mount Saint Elias is the second-highest mountain in the United States.

2504) The year 1 BC was followed by 1 AD.

2505) In 1991, *L.A. Law* had the first romantic kiss between two women on U.S. primetime television. Female characters Abby, played by Michele Greene, and C.J., played by Amanda Donohoe, kissed.

2506) Your taste buds are replaced every 10-14 days.

2507) The name M&M's stands for Mars & Murrie, the co-creators of the candy. Forest Mars, son of the Mars Company founder, and Bruce Murrie, son of the Hershey Chocolate president, went into business together in 1941 to develop the candy. Until 1949 when the partners had a falling out and

Mars bought back Murrie's share of the business, M&M's contained Hershey's chocolate.

2508) The Greenland shark has the longest known lifespan of all vertebrate (with a backbone) animal species. They can live up to 400 years.

2509) A female cat is called a molly; after she becomes a mother, she is called a queen.

2510) Apple founder Steve Jobs was adopted at birth; later in life, he decided to find his biological family. He found his mother and sister, and his sister found their father, a Syrian immigrant and California restaurant owner. When his sister went to meet their father, Jobs asked her not to mention anything about him. When talking to her father, he mentioned that famous people came to his restaurant and mentioned Steve Jobs as one of them. When his sister told Jobs this, he remembered meeting the restaurant owner multiple times. The two never met in person after knowing who each other was.

2511) A group of rattlesnakes is called a rhumba.

2512) According to recent studies, there may be about one trillion species of microbes, and 99.999% of them have yet to be discovered.

2513) The sun has made about 20 orbits around the center of the Milky Way Galaxy in its life.

2514) In the last battle Liechtenstein ever participated in, they sent out an army of 80 men for the Austro-Prussian War in 1866; they came back with 81 men. They had no casualties and picked up an extra soldier along the way.

2515) Richard Anderson and Martin E. Brooks were the first actors in U.S. television history to play the same characters on two different series on two different networks at the same time. They played Oscar Goldman and Dr. Rudy Wells on *The Six Million Dollar Man* and *The Bionic Woman*; both shows were originally on ABC. In 1978, *The Bionic Woman* moved to NBC, and they continued their roles on both shows.

2516) Polo is played on the largest field of any sport; the field is 300 yards by 160 yards.

2517) Fortune cookies were invented in the United States.

2518) The monkeys Mizaru, Kikazaru, and Iwazaru are better known as see no evil, hear no evil, and speak no evil.

2519) "The Twist" by Chubby Checker is the only single by the same artist to go to number one twice, in 1960 and 1961.

2520) With speeds up to 68 mph, the sailfish is the fastest fish.

2521) Babe Didrikson is the only person named Associated Press athlete of the year in two different sports; she was named for track and field in 1932 and for golf in 1945, 1946, 1947, 1950, and 1954.

2522) Amen is in 1,200 different languages without change.

2523) Even though it is almost 300 miles from the ocean, Reno, Nevada, is about 86 miles further west than Los Angeles.

2524) Mosquitos don't have teeth, but a mosquito's proboscis has 47 sharp edges on its tip that help it cut through skin and even clothing. The pain you feel from a mosquito bite is from the initial stab of sticking its proboscis into you.

2525) In August 1864, Abraham Lincoln was riding a horse to the Soldiers' Home outside of Washington, D.C., where the president and his family stayed to escape the summer heat. There was a gunshot, and his horse bolted; Lincoln lost his hat, which he believed was due to his horse jerking. When they went back to find his hat, they found a bullet hole in it; the assassination attempt was about eight months before John Wilkes Booth assassinated Lincoln.

2526) Mercury was used in the production of felt used in hats; this led to the expression "mad as a hatter," due to mercury poisoning.

2527) Mobster Al Capone offered a $10,000 reward for information leading to the capture of the Lindbergh baby kidnapper; he also offered that he and his men would search for the perpetrators if he was released from prison.

2528) On *Sesame Street*, Big Bird is 8'2" tall.

2529) President John Quincy Adams believed that the earth was hollow and signed off on an expedition to explore the hollow core; the expedition never took place.

2530) Ohio's Kenyon College won the NCAA Division III men's swimming and diving championship 31 consecutive years (1980-2010). It is the most consecutive national championships for any men's or women's team in any NCAA division.

2531) In 1828, Ioannis Kapodistriasthe, the first governor of Greece, spread the potato as a Greek crop by getting people to steal them. He tried to introduce potatoes as a crop to help with the Greek hunger problem, but when he offered potatoes to anyone interested, no one wanted them, so he ordered the shipment of potatoes put on public display under guard. People assumed the potatoes must be important since they were guarded and began to steal them, which the guards allowed. They took all the potatoes and spread the potato as a Greek crop.

2532) From the mid 5th to the early 13th century, Constantinople was one of the largest and wealthiest cities in Europe; it had survived many attacks and sieges and was regarded as one of the most impregnable cities, with an outer ditch and three rings of walls. In 1453, the city was besieged by the Turks, and someone accidentally left one of the small gates open, allowing the Turks to get in. The city may have fallen regardless, but the open gate quickened its demise. The inhabitants were killed or enslaved, and Emperor Constantine XI was killed.

2533) Frenchwoman Micheline Ostermeyer, a professional concert pianist, won the 1948 London Olympics shot put and discus gold medals. She had never picked up a discus until a few weeks before winning the Olympic title; she also won bronze in the 80-meter hurdles.

2534) Stevie Wonder is the youngest solo artist to have a number-one hit on Billboard's Hot 100. In 1963, he was 13 when "Fingertips Part 2" was number one.

2535) We don't know how many insect species exist; new beetles are discovered at a rate of one an hour. There are 350,000 named beetles, plus perhaps 8 million more unnamed.

2536) The placebo effect works even if people know it is a placebo. In studies, if people were told the pill they were taking was a placebo but were also told that placebos can have an effect, they experienced the same outcome as those unknowingly taking a placebo.

2537) In 1861, Abraham Lincoln imposed the first U.S. federal income tax. It was implemented to pay for the Civil War.

2538) The first internet domain name was registered in 1985.

2539) Alaska has about 365,000 miles of rivers, more than any other state and almost twice as much as second-place Texas.

2540) Humans have managed to explore only about 5% of the ocean floor.

2541) It is illegal to take pictures of the Eiffel Tower at night. French copyright law gives the original creator of an object exclusive rights to its sale and distribution; this includes buildings and lasts for 70 years after death. Gustave Eiffel, the tower creator, died in 1923, which means the copyright ran out in 1993. The Las Vegas replica wasn't built until 1999. However, night photos are still protected by copyright because the Eiffel Tower lights were installed in 1985 and are considered a separate artistic work by their creator, Pierre Bideau. They are protected by copyright until 70 years after his death.

2542) Early versions of the computer mouse were referred to as a turtle, presumably because of its hard shell on top.

2543) A rat can fall 50 feet uninjured.

2544) New Hampshire consumes more alcohol per capita than any other state; its consumption is 103% higher than the national average and more than one gallon per capita higher than the second-highest state, Delaware.

2545) The button on the top of a baseball cap is called a squatchee.

2546) Alice in Wonderland Syndrome is a neuropsychological condition where people may perceive objects to be larger or smaller than they are or nearer or farther away than they are. It can also affect the perception of the passage of time and other senses. It is often associated with migraines, brain tumors, and psychoactive drug use.

2547) Ancient Rome's population density was about eight times greater than modern New York City.

2548) *Gone with the Wind* was the first full-color film to win the Best Picture Oscar.

2549) An adult blue whale's stomach can hold 2,200 pounds of krill at a time, and they require almost 9,000 pounds of krill a day.

2550) In search of perpetual motion, Blaise Pascal invented the roulette wheel in the 17th century.

2551) When attacked, the horned toad squirts blood from its eyes.

2552) Poena cullei, meaning "penalty of the sack" in Latin, was an execution punishment in ancient Rome for parricide, killing a parent. It consisted of being sewn up in a sack with a variety of live animals, such as a monkey, dog, snake, and chicken, and then being thrown into a river. Before being put in the bag, the person was beaten with rods, and their head was covered in a bag made of wolf hide.

2553) The Snickers candy bar is named after the creator's horse.

2554) While he was in office, President Franklin Pierce was arrested for running over a woman with his horse; the charges were dropped due to lack of evidence.

2555) With 17 million units sold, the Commodore 64, introduced in 1982 with a 1 MHz processor and 64K of memory, is the largest selling personal computer model of all time.

2556) Almost the entire continent of South America is east of the easternmost point of Florida. Mainland South America and Florida only overlap for a little more than one degree of longitude.

2557) Mount Rushmore cost less than $1 million to build; construction took 14 years, from 1927 to 1941, and employed 400 people.

2558) The philtrum is the groove in your upper lip that runs from the top of the lip to the nose.

2559) The saltwater crocodile is the world's largest reptile. They are up to 20 feet long and weigh up to 3,000 pounds.

2560) Although it had been proposed in some form for over 50 years, the scientific community didn't agree on plate tectonics until 1967, two years before we landed on the moon.

2561) In January 1919, a 50-foot-tall holding tank burst open sending a 15-foot-tall wave of molasses through the streets of Boston, Massachusetts. It crushed houses, killed 21 people, and injured 150.

2562) To get a narcotic hit and ward off insects, lemurs in Madagascar capture large red millipedes. When millipedes are picked up, they secrete a toxic combination of chemicals, including cyanide, as a defense mechanism. Lemurs pick up a millipede and bite it gently and throw it back on the ground; they rub the millipede secretion all over their fur, which functions as a natural pesticide and wards off malaria-carrying mosquitos.

The secretion also acts as a narcotic that causes the lemurs to salivate profusely and enter a state of intoxication.

2563) According to the CDC, 50% of American adults will develop at least one mental illness in their lifetime.

2564) *Dune*, the bestselling science fiction book of all time, was rejected by more than 20 publishers before being published by Chilton Books, a little-known printing house best known for its auto repair manuals.

2565) Eunoia is the shortest English word that contains all five vowels. It means goodwill towards an audience, either perceived or real.

2566) The earliest indications of cannabis smoking are from China, about 2,500 years ago; the plant may have first grown millions of years ago in China.

2567) Four U.S. presidents have won the Nobel Peace Prize: Theodore Roosevelt, Woodrow Wilson, Jimmy Carter, and Barack Obama.

2568) Termites are the only insect that has both a king and a queen. The king helps found the colony with the queen and will mate with the queen during his life. There may be more than one pair of kings and queens in the termite mound.

2569) Ancient gladiators were mainly vegetarian; their diet was grain-based and mostly meat-free.

2570) $1.19 (three quarters, four dimes, and four pennies) is the most money you can have in change and not be able to make change for a dollar.

2571) Arabian horses have a greater bone density than other horses; they also have a shorter back with one fewer lumbar vertebra and one fewer pair of ribs.

2572) At 69.7 degrees north latitude, Tromsø Golfpark at Breivikeidet, near Tromsø, Norway, is the world's northernmost 18-hole golf course.

2573) The world's largest gold depository is the Manhattan Federal Reserve Bank; it houses 7,700 tons of gold.

2574) In 1872, P.B.S. Pinchback became the first African American state governor. He had been a Louisiana state senator and was serving as lieutenant governor when Governor Henry Clay Warmoth had to step down temporarily while he battled impeachment charges for election tampering. Pinchback served as governor for 36 days; there wouldn't be another African American governor until 1990.

2575) Astronomers have discovered the largest reservoir of water ever detected in the universe; it has the equivalent of 140 trillion times the water in the earth's oceans and surrounds a huge black hole, more than 12 billion light-years away.

2576) Maine is the only state that borders just one other state.

2577) We won't always have the same North Star. In 13,000 years, Polaris, the current North Star, will be replaced by Vega, and 26,000 years from now, Polaris will be back as the North Star. This is because the direction the earth's axis points changes due to a motion called precession. If you think of a spinning top given a slight nudge, the top traces out a cone pattern; that is how the earth moves on its axis. The earth bulges out at the equator, and the gravitational attraction of the moon and the sun on the bulge causes the precession that repeats in a 26,000-year cycle.

2578) James Buchanan was the only U.S. president that never married. Historians speculate that he may have been the first gay president. He developed a very close relationship with William Rufus King, an Alabama senator who was Franklin Pierce's vice president. Buchanan and King lived together and were openly close with each other, causing people to refer to King as Buchanan's better half.

2579) George Washington was the only U.S. president to never live in Washington, D.C.

2580) Five surnames have been shared by more than one president: Adams, Harrison, Johnson, Roosevelt, and Bush. Only Andrew and Lyndon Johnson weren't related.

2581) Margaret Abbott was the first American woman to win an Olympic gold medal; she won the 1900 Paris Olympics golf tournament.

2582) By area, 38% of the United States is further north than the southernmost point of Canada. Middle Island, in Lake Erie at 41.7 degrees north latitude, is the southernmost point of Canada and is about the same latitude as Chicago.

2583) The Ruppell's Griffon vulture is the highest-flying bird species ever recorded. They have been spotted at 37,000 feet and have special hemoglobin that makes their oxygen intake more effective.

2584) As a mosquito sucks your blood, they also pee on you. As they suck blood, mosquitoes need to get rid of excess fluid and salts, so they urinate to maintain their fluid and salt balance.

2585) George Washington grew hemp at Mount Vernon for rope and canvas making.

2586) The cast of the television series *Glee* has 207 Billboard Hot 100 entries, more than any other artist or group.

2587) About 100 cats roam free at Disneyland; they keep the rodent population down and have been in the park since it opened in 1955. They have feeding stations, veterinary care, and are taken care of by the workers.

2588) A digamy is a legal second marriage after death or divorce.

2589) Before clocks, there were candle clocks that showed the passage of time by how far a candle burned. They could even be turned into an alarm clock by pushing a nail in at the desired point; the nail would fall and clank when the candle burned down to that point.

2590) Yuma, Arizona, is the world's sunniest city. It averages 4,015 hours of sunshine annually, about 90% of daylight hours.

2591) There is no cellphone or Wi-Fi service in Green Bank, West Virginia, because it could interfere with the operation of the National Radio Astronomy Observatory's radio telescope. The National Radio Quiet Zone was created in 1958 as an area where radio transmissions are heavily restricted by law. Straddling West Virginia's border with Virginia and Maryland, it covers a 13,000 square mile area. Restrictions apply to the entire area, but they are most severe the closer you get to the Green Bank Observatory.

2592) Your fingernails grow 2-3 times faster than your toenails, and the fingernails on your dominant hand tend to grow faster than on your other hand.

2593) Five U.S. presidents haven't had any recognized biological children: Washington, Buchanan, Polk, Jackson, and Harding.

2594) In 1917, the Seattle Metropolitans were the first U.S. hockey team to win the Stanley Cup. The Stanley Cup was first awarded in 1893.

2595) According to the *Guinness Book of World Records*, Scientology founder L. Ron Hubbard has 1,084 published works, the most of any single author.

2596) The ancient Romans called early Christians atheists because they didn't worship pagan gods.

2597) In France, most toilet paper sold for home use is pink.

2598) Bill Clinton, George W. Bush, and Donald Trump were all born in 1946, the only year three future presidents were born.

2599) Andrew Jackson was the first U.S. president physically attacked while in office; a man punched him and ran away.

2600) *Oliver!* (1968) is the only G-rated movie to win the Best Picture Oscar.

2601) Florence Nightingale carried a pet owl in her pocket.

2602) Leonardo da Vinci could write with both his left and right hand simultaneously.

2603) Demodex mites live on your face, and you are more likely to have them the older you get. They are sausage-shaped with eight legs clustered in their front third and are up to one-third of a millimeter long. They spend most of their time buried head down in your hair follicles and are mostly found in your eyelids, nose, cheeks, forehead, and chin. They like areas that have a lot of oils, which is why they prefer the face. They can leave the hair follicles and slowly walk around on the skin, especially at night since they try to avoid light. The mites are transferred from person to person through contact with hair, eyebrows, and the sebaceous glands of the face. They eat, crawl, and reproduce on your face; the entire cycle from reproduction through death is about two weeks.

2604) Only one person in modern recorded history has been struck dead by a meteorite. In 2016, a 40-year-old man was relaxing outside at a small engineering college in India when there was the sound of an explosion; he was found next to a two-foot crater and later succumbed to injuries he sustained.

2605) The Egyptian pyramids were built by paid laborers, not slaves.

2606) There are multiple times more deaths caused by taking selfies each year than there are by shark attacks.

2607) Each minute, an adult male human loses about 96 million cells that are replaced by cells dividing.

2608) Sharks have a very well-developed sense of hearing. Their ears are small holes on the sides of their head that lead directly to the inner ear.

They are particularly good at hearing low-frequency noises, such as an injured fish would make, and at finding out where a noise is coming from.

2609) There are far more fake flamingos than real ones. There are just under 2 million flamingos in the wild; there are many millions of plastic ones.

2610) The wheel was invented in about 3500 BC.

2611) The cockroach is possibly the largest methane producer relative to its body size; they emit up to 43 times their weight in methane annually.

2612) The "DC" in DC Comics stands for Detective Comics.

2613) Joseph A. Walker was the first person to fly into space twice; he did it in 1963 aboard an X-15 winged aircraft. Space is defined as 62 miles above the earth.

2614) Miguel de Cervantes, the author of *Don Quixote*, was captured by Turkish pirates and held as a slave for five years in Algiers.

2615) Miami is the only major U.S. city founded by a woman; Julia Tuttle was a businesswoman and the original owner of the land where Miami was built.

2616) According to suffragette Susan B. Anthony, the bicycle had "done more to emancipate women than anything else in the world."

2617) J.P. Morgan, one of the wealthiest and most powerful men in America during the late 19th and early 20th centuries, offered a $100,000 reward to anyone who could explain or cure his very red face and huge, purple nose. Nobody ever came forward with an answer, and Morgan died in 1913 before the condition would've been diagnosed as rhinophyma, a skin disorder characterized by a large, red, bumpy, or bulbous nose. Its exact cause is unknown, but it's considered a subtype of severe rosacea.

2618) A gallon of gasoline contains about 31,000 calories; if you could drink gasoline as fuel, you could ride a bicycle at 15 mph for about 912 miles on a gallon of gas.

2619) James Earl Jones was the first celebrity to make a guest appearance on *Sesame Street*; he appeared on the show's second episode.

2620) By area, Saudi Arabia is the largest country that doesn't have any natural rivers; it is the 12th largest country.

2621) Five rivers in the world are over 3,000 miles long: the Nile, Amazon, Yangtze, Yellow, and Parana.

2622) Spraint is the dung of an otter.

2623) Ohio has the only non-rectangular state flag; it is a swallowtail shape.

2624) Bowler hats were designed by London hatters Thomas and William Bowler and were invented to keep a horse rider's head safe from branches and other obstacles.

2625) Sex therapist Dr. Ruth trained as a sniper in the Israeli army; they thought her short stature, 4'7", would make her hard to see; she had an affinity for it.

2626) Mapmakers have a long tradition of putting slight inaccuracies in their maps to catch people who try to copy their work. Typically, it is something small, like a nonexistent dead-end, fake river bend, or adjusted mountain elevation. However, in one case, a mapmaker put in the fictional town of Agloe, New York. When a store was built in the corresponding location, the owner read the map and named it Agloe General Store, assuming it was a real area name, so a fictional location became real.

2627) On average, the Netherlands has the world's tallest people, with an average of 5'11 1/2" for men and 5'6 1/2" for women.

2628) Tycho Brahe, a 16th century Danish astronomer, alchemist, and nobleman, had a pet moose that liked to drink beer; it died when it drank too much beer and fell down a flight of stairs.

2629) Most artificial banana flavoring is based on an older variety of banana that is no longer grown in bulk, so it doesn't taste very similar to the bananas you eat. The bananas you eat today are mostly the Cavendish variety, but banana flavoring is based on the Gros Michel, a sweeter variety. The Gros Michel is no longer grown in bulk because it is susceptible to a fungus.

2630) A group of unicorns is called a blessing.

2631) The words bulb, angel, and month have no rhyming words in the English language.

2632) The last public execution in the United States was in 1936 in Kentucky.

2633) There are five debt-free countries: Macau, British Virgin Islands, Brunei, Liechtenstein, and Palau.

2634) Humans and dogs are the only two animal species known to seek visual clues from another animal's eyes, and dogs only do it with humans.

2635) Caffeine is lethal in high enough doses; it would take about 70 cups of coffee to kill a 150-pound person.

2636) The Milky Way Galaxy is likely filled with thousands of tiny black holes.

2637) Emma Thompson was the first person to win Oscars for acting and writing; she won the Best Actress Oscar for *Howards End* (1992) and the Best Adapted Screenplay Oscar for *Sense and Sensibility* (1995).

2638) Forty is the only number spelled out in English that has its letters in alphabetical order.

2639) About 90% of the coal we burn today came about because wood-eating bacteria didn't evolve until about 60 million years after trees existed. For tens of millions of years, all the dead tree material remained intact; trees would fall on top of each other, and the weight of the wood would compress the trees into peat and then into coal. Had wood-eating bacteria been around, they would have broken the carbon bonds and released carbon and oxygen into the air; instead, the carbon remained in the wood. This era from 359 to 299 million years ago is known as the Carboniferous Period because of the large amounts of coal formed.

2640) Danny Ainge is the only person named a first-team high school All-American in football, basketball, and baseball. He went to high school in Eugene, Oregon, and went on to play professional baseball for the Toronto Blue Jays and won two NBA championships with the Boston Celtics.

2641) There is enough water in Lake Superior to cover all the land in North and South America in one foot of water.

2642) Seven basketball players have won NCAA, Olympic, and NBA championships: Clyde Lovellette, Bill Russell, K.C. Jones, Jerry Lucas, Quinn Buckner, Michael Jordan, and Magic Johnson.

2643) A group of hippos is called a bloat.

2644) The first screen kiss between two men occurred in the 1927 movie *Wings*; it didn't cause any stir at the time.

2645) *Saturday Night Live* was the first U.S. network television show to use the "F" word.

2646) The Coriolis effect does not cause toilet water in the Southern Hemisphere to rotate in the opposite direction compared to the Northern Hemisphere. The Coriolis force is a real effect and is why large systems, like hurricanes, rotate in different directions in the two hemispheres, but it is proportional to velocity, and its effect on a toilet flushing is minuscule, compared to the water jets and other irregularities.

2647) Colorado has 53 mountains at least 14,000 feet tall, more than any other state.

2648) The Tower of Pisa took 177 years to build, but it started leaning, due to soil subsidence, just 10 years after its completion in 1372. The lean was 5.5 degrees before a 2010 restoration reduced it to 4 degrees.

2649) Orlando, Florida, is the most visited U.S. city; New York City is second.

2650) Gnurr is the word for pocket lint.

2651) According to the Bible, Goliath was six cubits tall, about nine feet.

2652) The foam on beer is called barm.

2653) The Great Barrier Reef is the world's largest living structure. Situated off the northeastern coast of Australia, it stretches for 1,429 miles and covers approximately 133,000 square miles.

2654) The average major league baseball lasts for six pitches.

2655) The Bluetooth wireless technology is named after King Harald "Bluetooth" Gormsson, the 10th-century ruler of Denmark.

2656) Vitali Klitschko is the first world boxing champion to hold a PhD degree. He was a three-time world heavyweight champion, between 1999 and 2013, and got his PhD in sports science in 2000. He also served as mayor of Kyiv and was in the Ukrainian parliament.

2657) Camels store water in their bloodstream, not in their hump; they can drink up to 20 gallons at a time. The hump is almost all fat and serves as an alternative energy source and helps regulate body temperature. By concentrating fat in the hump, as opposed to being spread over their body, they are better able to handle hot climates.

2658) On his television show, Ed Sullivan made the Rolling Stones sing "Let's Spend the Night Together" as "Let's Spend Some Time Together."

2659) McDonald's uses over 10% of the potatoes harvested in the United States annually.

2660) In 2013, Mississippi was the last state to officially ratify the 13th amendment to the U.S. Constitution abolishing slavery. Mississippi ratified the amendment in 1995, but it didn't notify the U.S. archivist and didn't officially complete the process until 2013.

2661) Almost one-third of the world's languages are only spoken in Africa.

2662) Treason, piracy, and counterfeiting are the only three crimes mentioned in the U.S. Constitution.

2663) After *Apollo 11* landed on the moon and before anyone set foot on the moon, Buzz Aldrin took communion; NASA did not want it broadcast or made public.

2664) The movie *Romancing the Stone* centers around an American kidnapping in Colombia; ironically, an increase in American kidnappings in Colombia caused the filming to be moved to Mexico.

2665) As a defense mechanism when threatened, sea cucumbers can eviscerate themselves and shoot out their internal organs. Sea cucumbers are echinoderms, which also include marine animals like starfish and sea urchins; depending on the species, they can shoot the organs out their head or butt, but they can regrow the organs. Through a process called dedifferentiation, certain cells in their bodies lose their specialized functions and move around the sea cucumber's body and become whatever type of cell is needed to regrow the lost organs.

2666) In 1889, Germany was the first country to introduce old-age pensions.

2667) Author James Patterson has the most entries on the New York Times best-seller list.

2668) India has more paid newspapers than any other country.

2669) In 1930, the first television was installed at the British Prime Minister's residence at 10 Downing Street, London. Prime Minister Ramsay MacDonald and his family watched the first television drama ever on it.

2670) Sweden has the largest permanent scale model of the solar system. The sun is in Stockholm and is represented by the world's largest hemispherical building; the model is on a 1:20 million scale and stretches for 590 miles.

2671) Human boogers are just dried mucus. Most mucus is swept by the nose cilia hair to the back of the throat, but near your nostrils, it can begin to dry out first and become too thick to be swept by the cilia. If it sits long enough, it dries further and becomes a booger.

2672) Golf balls were originally made of wood; in the early 17th century, wood was replaced by boiled feathers compressed inside a stitched leather cover.

2673) Satan is the Hebrew word for adversary.

2674) Every second, the sun produces as much energy as over 90 billion one-megaton nuclear bombs.

2675) Frozen seawater contains only about one-tenth of the salt content found in liquid seawater because most of the salt separates from the water as it freezes. Due to the salt content, seawater freezes at about 28.4 degrees Fahrenheit.

2676) Caterpillars essentially dissolve themselves to become butterflies. In the cocoon, the caterpillar releases enzymes that dissolve all its tissues; it then begins rapid cell division to form an adult butterfly or moth.

2677) Cats are such picky eaters because they seem to be naturally driven to eat foods with about equal energy from protein and fat. They will seek out these ratios, even overriding taste preferences; science has no idea how they know what food provides the correct ratio.

2678) Joseph Biden was the first Roman Catholic U.S. vice president.

2679) Since she was still married to her former husband, President Andrew Jackson's wife was technically a bigamist. In 1790, his wife had separated from her first husband, but she never finalized the divorce before marrying Jackson. Once the divorce was finalized in 1794, she remarried Jackson.

2680) John Quincy Adams served in the U.S. House of Representatives after he served as U.S. president.

2681) About 20% of the world's households don't have a television.

2682) When playing with female puppies, male puppies will often let the female win, even if they have a physical advantage.

2683) Due to continental drift, New York City moves one inch further away from London each year.

2684) Because the moon rotates on its axis at the same rate that it orbits the earth, only one side of the moon is visible from the earth; this is known as synchronous rotation or tidal locking.

2685) Four state capitals are named after presidents: Lincoln, Jefferson City, Jackson, and Madison.

2686) The Walt Disney Company is the world's largest consumer of fireworks and the second-largest purchaser of explosive devices, behind the U.S. Department of Defense.

2687) In 1877, Lucy Webb Hayes was the first U.S. president's wife to be referred to as the first lady.

2688) In 1975, *Jaws* was the first movie to make $100 million at the box office.

2689) John Tyler was the only U.S. president to serve in the Confederate Congress. He represented Virginia from 1861 until just before he died in 1862; his term as president was from 1841-1845.

2690) The word orchid is Greek and means testicle.

2691) When Thomas Jefferson sent Lewis and Clark on their expedition, he asked them to look for wooly mammoths; Jefferson believed there might be wooly mammoths still living in the west.

2692) In 1980, new Iraqi President Saddam Hussein was awarded the key to the city of Detroit for donating $250,000 to a local church.

2693) In the movie *Lifeboat*, Alfred Hitchcock couldn't make his usual in-person cameo appearance because the film was set in a lifeboat, so he appears as a before and after picture in a newspaper weight loss ad.

2694) Thomas Jefferson had the largest personal book collection in the United States and sold it to become part of the Library of Congress after the library was destroyed in the War of 1812.

2695) In 1943, the Slinky was invented accidentally by Richard James, a mechanical engineer. He was devising springs that could keep sensitive ship equipment steady at sea, and after accidentally knocking some samples off a shelf, he saw a spring right itself.

2696) In three 1963 television advertisements, future *Today Show* weatherman Willard Scott was the first person to play Ronald McDonald.

Scott was a local radio personality in Washington, D.C., and had played Bozo the Clown on television from 1959-1962.

2697) Hong Kong has more skyscrapers than any other city; New York City is second; Dubai is third. There is no exact definition of a skyscraper, but they are generally considered to be 150 meters or taller.

2698) Eighty percent of the world's population eats insects as part of their regular diet.

2699) Thomas Andrews, one of the designers of the *Titanic*, was on board when it sank, and his body was never recovered. His suggestions that the ship should have 46 lifeboats instead of 20, a double hull, and a larger number of watertight bulkheads were overruled.

2700) The 10,000-ton meteor that struck Russia in 2013 had an estimated impact energy of 500 kilotons and affected a 77,000 square mile area. The atomic bomb dropped on Hiroshima was about 33 times smaller.

2701) The S in Harry S. Truman's name didn't stand for anything; it was in honor of both his grandfathers but didn't stand for a middle name.

2702) Cassowaries are the world's second-largest bird, standing up to 6 feet tall and weighing up to 130 pounds. They are also known as the world's most dangerous bird; they have a four-inch, dagger-like claw on each foot that can slice open a predator with a single kick, and they have killed humans. They can also run up to 31 mph and jump up to 7 feet in the air. They are native to the tropical forests of Papua New Guinea, Indonesia, and northeastern Australia.

2703) A sapiosexual is sexually attracted to intelligence in others.

2704) Cicadas flex their muscles to buckle a series of ribs one after another to produce their loud sound. Every time a rib buckles, it produces a click; many clicks produce the buzzing sound. The series of ribs are called a tymbal.

2705) It would take 1.2 million mosquitoes, each sucking once, to drain the average human of all their blood.

2706) In the early 19th century, some of the most stylish men in London and Paris polished their shoes with champagne. Beau Brummell, the preeminent example of an English dandy at that time, swore by the method to make his shoes the blackest black.

2707) Olivia de Haviland and Joan Fontaine are the only sisters to win acting Oscars.

2708) All seven dwarfs except Dopey have a beard.

2709) NASA accidentally erased and reused the original 1969 *Apollo 11* moon landing tapes. The tapes were reused as part of a money-saving effort.

2710) Luise Rainer and Katharine Hepburn are the only two actresses that have won consecutive Best Actress Oscars. Rainer won for *The Great Ziegfeld* (1936) and *The Good Earth* (1937); Hepburn won for *Guess Who's Coming to Dinner* (1967) and *The Lion in Winter* (1968).

2711) In 1912, a Paris foundling hospital held a raffle of live babies; it was designed as a fundraiser and a way to find homes for orphaned children. The management of the hospital held the raffle with the consent of authorities; the raffle proceeds were divided among several charities.

2712) According to the Old Testament, Noah planted the first vineyard.

2713) Adjusted for inflation, *Gone with the Wind* is the all-time highest-grossing movie in the United States; it is followed by *Star Wars*, *The Sound of Music*, *E.T. the Extra-Terrestrial*, and *Titanic*.

2714) With an area of 8.1 square miles, Nauru is the smallest island nation.

2715) Montana's Roe River is recognized as the world's shortest river; it flows for 200 feet between Giant Springs and the Missouri River, near Great Falls, Montana.

2716) Almost 100% of Iceland's domestic electricity production is from renewable sources, and about 85% of its overall energy consumption is from renewable sources, the highest of any country.

2717) *The Howdy Doody Show* (1947-1960) was the first U.S. nationally televised children's show.

2718) Scientists believe the world's most abundant vertebrate (animal with a backbone) species is the bristlemouth fish. They are small, deep-sea fish that are only about 3 inches long and live at depths from 3,000 feet to 3 miles. They likely number in the quadrillions.

2719) Adjusted for inflation, *Snow White and the Seven Dwarfs* (1937) is the earliest movie made that has grossed $1 billion in the United States.

2720) Bullwinkle Moose is originally from Moosylvania; it is a small island in Lake of the Woods that neither the United States nor Canada wants to claim.

2721) The little paper tail sticking out of a Hershey's Kiss is called a niggly wiggly.

2722) Dr. Seuss was the first to use the word "nerd" in print; it is the name of a creature in *If I Ran the Zoo*, published in 1950.

2723) Before devoting his life to philosophy, Socrates was a mason or stonecutter.

2724) Eighteen countries don't have any natural rivers: Bahamas, Bahrain, Comoros, Kiribati, Kuwait, Maldives, Malta, Marshall Islands, Monaco, Nauru, Oman, Qatar, Saudi Arabia, Tonga, Tuvalu, United Arab Emirates, Vatican City, and Yemen.

2725) Of cities of 1 million or more population, Auckland, New Zealand, is furthest away from another city of 1 million or more population; it is 1,347 miles away from Sydney, Australia.

2726) *The Passion of the Christ* (2004) is the highest-grossing foreign language or subtitled film ever in the United States.

2727) In 1946, Nutella was invented by an Italian pastry maker looking for a cheaper alternative to chocolate that was in short supply due to WWII, so he mixed hazelnuts with some cocoa.

2728) Zero can't be represented in Roman numerals.

2729) By picking up chemical signals from human sweat, dogs can smell human fear.

2730) With 11 wins each, *Ben-Hur*, *Titanic*, and *The Lord of the Rings: The Return of the King* are tied for the most Oscars.

2731) With an area of 735,400 square miles, Indonesia is the largest island nation.

2732) In space, the mucus that normally empties through your nose and drains down the throat backs up in the sinuses due to the lack of gravity. The only way to get rid of it is to blow your nose.

2733) Gibraltar has the only wild monkey population in Europe; they are Barbary macaques.

2734) The name Lego is an abbreviation of the Danish words "leg godt," meaning "play well."

2735) In 1952, Mr. Potato Head was the first toy advertised on U.S. television.

2736) Pocahontas is buried along England's Thames River; she died during a visit to England.

2737) Cats have more than 100 vocal sounds; dogs only have about 10.

2738) The world's largest national park is in Greenland. The Northeast Greenland National Park is 375,000 square miles; it is over 100 times bigger than Yellowstone National Park and bigger than all but 29 countries. It only has about 500 visitors per year.

2739) Albert Einstein described it as "spooky action at a distance" and didn't believe nature would be so unreasonable, but quantum entanglement, which occurs when two particles are inextricably linked together no matter their physical separation, has been proven repeatedly. Although entangled particles are not physically connected, they are still able to share information instantaneously, breaking the rule that no information can be transmitted faster than the speed of light. In tests, entangled particles 750 miles apart have shown that any change in one is instantly reflected in the other; this would be true even if they were separated by light-years.

2740) *Law & Order: Special Victims Unit* is the longest-running spinoff in American television history; it debuted in 1999.

2741) On average, Indonesia has the world's shortest people, with an average of 5'2" for men and 4'10" for women.

2742) A polar bear's skin is black.

2743) Mithridatism is the practice of trying to protect yourself against poisoning by taking non-lethal doses of poison to build immunity. Roman emperors adopted the daily habit of taking a small amount of every known poison to gain immunity. It can be effective against some types of poisons, but depending on the poison, it can lead to a lethal accumulation in the body over time.

2744) The first video game console was the 1972 Magnavox Odyssey. It was 5 years before the first Atari and 13 years before the first Nintendo; it had no sound or color and came with 28 games, including hockey, roulette, western shootout, and table tennis.

2745) California is the only state that is at least partially north of the southernmost part of Canada and at least partially south of the northernmost point of Mexico.

2746) In the 18th and 19th centuries, squirrels were popular pets. They were sold in pet shops and were a preferred pet among the wealthy.

2747) "All Too Well" by Taylor Swift is the longest (minutes of playtime) number-one song ever on Billboard's Hot 100. It hit number one in November 2021 and runs for 10 minutes and 13 seconds; it displaced "American Pie" as the longest number-one song ever.

2748) Four U.S. presidents served their entire term without a vice president: John Tyler, Millard Fillmore, Andrew Johnson, and Chester A. Arthur.

2749) It does snow in the Sahara Desert. There have been three recorded episodes of significant snowfall: February 1979, December 2016, and January 2018.

2750) The expression "caught red-handed" originated as a reference to someone killing or poaching an animal that didn't belong to them and getting caught with the blood on their hands.

2751) Until Sunday, September 3, 1967, Sweden drove on the left-hand side. The conversion to the right-hand side was done at 5 p.m. As people switched sides, all traffic stopped. The time and day were chosen to prevent as many accidents as possible.

2752) In 1974, the *Journal of Applied Behavior Analysis* published a paper titled "The Unsuccessful Self-Treatment of a Case of Writer's Block"; it was blank.

2753) About 12% of people dream entirely in black and white. The exposure to color television seems to have had a significant impact on whether people dream in color; people who grew up with little access to color television dream in black and white about 25% of the time. In the 1940s before color television, the numbers were reversed, with about 75% of people reporting they dreamed in black and white.

2754) On average, the Antarctic ice sheet is one mile thick.

2755) At a cost of $160 billion, the International Space Station is the most expensive man-made object ever built.

2756) Actress Mariska Hargitay has played the same character on U.S. primetime live-action television longer than anyone else. She has played Olivia Benson on *Law & Order: Special Victims Unit* since 1999.

2757) At 1,479 miles long, Alaska is the longest state from north to south.

2758) Argentina has the highest number of psychiatrists per capita of any country, about six times more than the United States.

2759) Because of the effect temperature has on how a tennis ball bounces, all 50,000 plus balls used for a Wimbledon tournament are kept at a constant 68 degrees Fahrenheit.

2760) Six American Civil War generals became U.S. presidents: Andrew Johnson, Ulysses S. Grant, Rutherford B. Hayes, James A. Garfield, Chester A. Arthur, and Benjamin Harrison.

2761) Iran has the highest rate of cosmetic nose surgery of any country.

2762) With 28 holidays, Cambodia has the most public holidays of any country.

2763) Lionel and Ethel Barrymore are the only brother and sister to win acting Oscars.

231

2764) When President Harry S. Truman visited Disneyland in 1957, he refused to go on the Dumbo ride because he didn't want to be seen riding in the symbol of the Republican party.

2765) The total mass of the earth's atmosphere is about 5.5 quadrillion tons.

2766) The tallest married couple ever were Canadian Anna Haining Swan, who was 7'11", and American Martin Van Buren Bates, who was 7'9". The couple was married in 1871, and Swan later gave birth to a 22-pound baby.

2767) Lake Maracaibo, Venezuela, has the most lightning strikes of any place in the world. Lightning storms occur about 10 hours a night, 140 to 160 nights a year, for a total of about 1.2 million lightning discharges per year.

2768) Only 5% of the universe is made up of normal matter; 25% is composed of dark matter; 70% is dark energy.

2769) The flag of the Philippines is flown with the blue side up in times of peace and with the red side up in times of war.

2770) Nepal is the only country that doesn't have either a rectangular or square flag; it has a combination of two triangular pennants.

2771) The earth orbits around the sun at 66,600 mph.

2772) A three-year study found that 54% of dog owners were willing to end a relationship if their dog doesn't like their partner, and 94% of dog owners consider their dogs to be part of their family.

2773) Adjusted for inflation, *Waterworld* (1995) was the first film to surpass the budget for *Cleopatra* (1963).

2774) Dung beetles can navigate based on the position of the moon, sun, and stars. Researchers have found that they take a mental snapshot of the night sky and use it to find their way around. The beetles can recall their exact position, and when presented with an artificial sky, they change their course accordingly.

2775) Elvis Presley's natural hair color was sandy blonde.

2776) Pierre, South Dakota, is the only state capital that doesn't share any letters with its state.

2777) Russian astronauts take guns into space to protect themselves from bears if they land off course.

2778) "Fidelity, Bravery, Integrity" is the FBI's motto.

2779) Eight U.S. presidents were born in Virginia, the most of any state.

2780) According to Social Security data, the most popular names for American babies over the last 100 years (1919 to 2018) were James for boys and Mary for girls.

2781) The Milky Way Galaxy weighs about 1.5 trillion times more than the sun.

2782) Aaron Burr was the first U.S. vice president that didn't go on to be president. He was the third vice president and served during Thomas Jefferson's first term.

2783) Adult domestic cats spend up to 50% of their waking time grooming.

2784) Dysania is the state of finding it hard to get out of bed in the morning.

2785) Hawaii has 63.7 inches of average annual rainfall, the most of any state.

2786) A butt is an actual measurement unit for wine; a buttload of wine is 126 U.S. gallons.

2787) *Who Framed Roger Rabbit* (1988) is the only film where cartoon characters from Walt Disney and Warner Brothers appear together.

2788) Rin Tin Tin is often credited with saving Warner Brothers Studio from bankruptcy, and before being eliminated from the ballot, he received the most votes for the Best Actor Oscar at the first Academy Awards in 1929. The Academy wanted to appear more serious and have a human win, so they removed him from the ballot and voted again.

2789) Cate Blanchett is the first person to win an acting Oscar portraying an acting Oscar winner; she won the Best Supporting Actress Oscar portraying Katharine Hepburn in *The Aviator* (2004).

2790) Rats don't sweat; they regulate their temperature by constricting or expanding blood vessels in their tails.

2791) Science Nobel Prize winners are 22 times more likely than their peers to have performed as actors, dancers, or magicians.

2792) If you hear thunder about 15 seconds after seeing lightning, the lightning is about 3 miles away. Sound travels about one mile in five seconds.

2793) The word freelance comes from a knight who was free for hire.

2794) The word stymie originated in golf. Until 1952 when the rules were changed, balls had to remain in place, so you could be stymied by having another player's ball between your ball and the hole; you had to loft your ball over the other ball.

2795) Sudan has more pyramids than any other country; it has almost twice as many as Egypt.

2796) Humans domesticated the horse around 4500 BC; the saddle was invented as early as 800 BC, but the stirrup probably wasn't created until about 300 BC.

2797) The average lightning bolt is about five miles long and one inch wide.

2798) One in 10,000 people has perfect pitch, the ability to identify a musical note just by hearing it with no reference note.

2799) Dallas, Texas, is named after George Mifflin Dallas, U.S. vice president for James K. Polk.

2800) From the Middle Ages until 1809, Finland was part of Sweden.

2801) Mark Twain was the first novelist to present a typed manuscript to their publisher.

2802) Six U.S. presidents didn't have a wife when they took office. Thomas Jefferson, Andrew Jackson, Martin Van Buren, and Chester A. Arthur were all widowers; Grover Cleveland married while in office; James Buchanan never married.

2803) There are an estimated 10,000,000,000,000,000,000 (10 quintillion) insects alive at any given time.

2804) The Red-billed Quelea, a sparrow-sized bird found in sub-Saharan Africa, is the world's most abundant wild bird species. Their population is estimated at 1.5 billion.

2805) For centuries, families in central Europe have eaten carp for Christmas Eve dinner. In Slovakia and some nearby countries, the tradition goes further where the Christmas carp must first swim in the family bathtub for at least a day or two before being killed, cleaned, and prepared.

2806) The acnestis is the part of an animal's skin that it can't scratch itself, usually the area between the shoulder blades.

2807) The creature that most people identify as a daddy longlegs spider is not a spider at all; it is a long-legged harvestman, which is an arachnid. Harvestmen have one body section instead of the two spiders have, two eyes instead of eight, a segmented body instead of unsegmented, no silk, no venom, and a different respiratory system than spiders, among other differences.

2808) In 1990, Pakistan's Benazir Bhutto was the first elected head of a nation to give birth in office.

2809) A starfish is the only creature that can turn its stomach inside out.

2810) Benjamin Franklin was carried to the U.S. Constitutional Convention in a sedan chair carried by prisoners.

2811) A newborn Bactrian camel doesn't have any humps. Baby camels don't get their humps until they start eating solid food.

2812) You would swim the same speed through syrup as you do through water; the additional drag is canceled out by the additional force generated from each stroke.

2813) In humans, night owls tend to have higher IQs and be more creative; they are also mentally alert for a longer portion of the day than early birds.

2814) It wasn't until the Indian Citizenship Act of 1924 that Native Americans were granted full U.S. citizenship. The act was passed partially in recognition of the thousands of Native Americans that served in the military during WWI. The 14th amendment to the U.S. Constitution defines a citizen as any person born in the United States and subject to its jurisdiction, but the amendment had been interpreted to not apply to Native Americans.

2815) George W. Bush is the only U.S. president with an MBA degree.

2816) According to research, zebras likely evolved to have stripes to avoid biting flies. In an experiment, horses wearing a striped pattern coat had far fewer flies land on them than horses wearing a solid color coat. The flies spent the same amount of time circling, but far fewer landed with stripes.

2817) The vinculum is the line between two numbers in a fraction.

2818) Albert Einstein is an anagram for "ten elite brains."

2819) Maryland is the only state with no natural lakes.

2820) The sooty shearwater has the world's longest distance migration. It is a common seabird and has been tracked electronically migrating 40,000 miles.

2821) The Eiffel Tower wasn't intended to be permanent. In 1909, it was scheduled for demolition, but it was saved to be used as a radio tower.

2822) A group of cats is called a clowder.

2823) The dots on dice are called pips.

2824) *Sesame Street*'s Oscar the Grouch was originally orange.

2825) By area, Lake Michigan is the largest lake entirely within the United States.

2826) Arabic numerals originated in India in the 6th or 7th century.

2827) At 92 feet below sea level, Baku, Azerbaijan, is the lowest elevation national capital city.

2828) Beethoven, Brahms, Chopin, Handel, Liszt, and Ravel were all bachelors.

2829) It takes a net worth of $770,000 to be in the top 1% of the world.

2830) Venus and Uranus are the only two planets in our solar system that rotate clockwise.

2831) SOS doesn't stand for "save our ship" or anything else; it was selected as a distress signal because it is easy to transmit: three dots, three dashes, three dots.

2832) The Jeep name comes from the army where "general purpose" was abbreviated as G.P. and phonetically translates to Jeep.

2833) Scorpions can live up to six days without air; they can also go up to a year without eating.

2834) The original Peeping Tom was looking at Lady Godiva.

2835) Congress allocated $2,500 for Meriwether Lewis and William Clark's expedition across America that lasted from May 1804 to September 1806.

2836) When cicadas come in contact with spores of the Massospora fungus, a psychoactive plant, the fungus grows throughout the insect, consuming its organs and converting the rear third of its body into a mass of spores.

The psychoactive nature of the fungus causes the cicada to act as if nothing unusual has happened.

2837) Uzbekistan and Liechtenstein are the only two countries completely surrounded by landlocked countries.

2838) If sound waves could travel through space as they do through air, you would hear the sun burning at a volume of about 100 decibels, about the same volume as a chainsaw or jackhammer. Sound intensity decreases with distance, so the 93 million miles to the sun have a large impact on the volume.

2839) Mosquitoes like blood type O the most. They prefer it twice as much as type A; type B is their second choice.

2840) Franklin D. Roosevelt's armored car previously belonged to Al Capone; he was the first president to use an armored car.

2841) The small bump on the inner corner of your eye is the caruncula.

2842) Writer H.G. Wells coined the term "atomic bomb" over 30 years before the first atomic bomb test.

2843) Grover Cleveland is the only U.S. president to serve two non-consecutive terms; he was the 22nd and 24th president.

2844) After an accident during the race, Tanzanian John Akhwari ran the last 14 miles of the 1968 Olympic marathon with a dislocated knee. When asked later why he kept going, he said, "My country did not send me 9,000 miles to start the race; they sent me 9,000 miles to finish the race." He finished more than an hour behind the winner and was hailed as an Olympic hero and a symbol of the spirit of the games.

2845) A rat's front teeth grow 4½ to 5½ inches each year; like other rodents, they wear them down gnawing.

2846) In an average lifetime, human skin completely replaces itself 900 times.

2847) A polyandric woman has more than one husband.

2848) When the Persians were at war with the Egyptians, they rounded up and released as many cats as they could on the battlefield. Knowing the Egyptian reverence for cats, they knew they would not want to do anything to hurt the cats; the Persians won the battle.

2849) In Victorian London, people were paid to collect dog poop for use in tanning leather.

2850) About 82% of the world's population has never flown on an airplane.

2851) John F. Kennedy had a lifelong struggle with back pain and was wearing a tightly laced back brace that may have kept him from recoiling to the floor of his car after he was hit with the first bullet and made him an easier target for the second shot. The brace was a firmly bound corset around his hips and lower back and higher up; he tightly laced it and put a wide Ace bandage in a figure eight around his trunk, so his movement was significantly restricted.

2852) Australia has the world's highest gambling rate; over 80% of adults gamble in some form.

2853) In 1999, NASA estimated that antimatter cost $28 quadrillion per pound to produce.

2854) In 1938, Nescafe was the first instant coffee.

2855) The tortoise is the longest living land animal of any kind; the oldest known lived to 250.

2856) While there are more than 60 species of eagles worldwide, only two species, the bald eagle and the golden eagle, live in North America.

2857) Scientists believe that it rains diamonds on Jupiter and Saturn. Lightning storms turn methane into soot that under pressure hardens into chunks of graphite and then diamonds as it falls. The largest diamonds would likely be about a centimeter in diameter and would eventually melt in the planet's hot core.

2858) The chemical thought to be responsible for old people smell is 2-nonenal; its production increases with age, starting at about age 40.

2859) Hawaii essentially has its own time zone. It is in the Hawaii-Aleutian Time Zone, which includes Hawaii and Alaska's Aleutian Islands west of 169.5 degrees west longitude.

2860) Queen Elizabeth II doesn't have a passport because passports are issued in her name and on her authority, so it would be superfluous for her to have one.

2861) Christ's name translated directly from Hebrew to English would be Joshua; Jesus comes about by translating Hebrew to Greek to Latin to English.

2862) Harry S. Truman was the first U.S. president paid a salary of $100,000 or more.

2863) When it started, Starbucks only sold whole roasted coffee beans.

2864) Divorce is still illegal in the Philippines and Vatican City.

2865) The United States has more tornadoes than any other country.

2866) The classic film *It's a Wonderful Life* originated from a Christmas card. Philip Van Doren Stern had written a short story, *The Greatest Gift*, and had unsuccessfully tried to get it published. He sent it out as a 21-page Christmas card to his closest friends; a producer at RKO Pictures got hold of it and purchased the movie rights.

2867) There is a chunk of Africa stuck under the United States. When the supercontinent Pangaea broke apart about 250 million years ago, a chunk of Africa was left behind; it is located near Alabama, just off the coast.

2868) *The Simpsons* is the longest-running U.S. scripted primetime show ever; it started in 1989.

2869) During the WWII Battle of Stalingrad, a railway station changed hands between German and Soviet control 14 times in one afternoon.

2870) President Gerald Ford was once a fashion model; in the 1940s, he worked for *Cosmopolitan* and *Look* magazines.

2871) In 1894, boxing was the first sport to be filmed.

2872) Opossums are a great help in preventing the spread of Lyme disease. They are fastidiously clean and spend hours cleaning themselves; as they clean their fur, they pick off and swallow ticks. Studies have shown a single opossum can destroy 5,000 ticks in a season.

2873) Antarctica is the driest continent; it only gets about eight inches of precipitation annually and is considered a desert.

2874) President Richard Nixon was the target of an assassination plot that involved taking over a jet and crashing it into the White House. Samuel Byck successfully managed to take over a Delta Airlines plane, but he didn't get it off the ground. He planned to have the pilots fly it close to the White House where he would take over and crash the plane.

2875) Q is the only letter that doesn't appear in any state name.

2876) The ancient Romans used human urine to wash clothes.

2877) Baby porcupines are called porcupettes.

2878) In 1990, Nicaragua's Violeta Chamorro became the first elected female head of state in the Western Hemisphere.

2879) In Germany, there is no punishment for a prisoner who tries to escape if no other laws are broken. They assume the desire for freedom is natural.

2880) Of the 700 islands in the Bahamas, only 30 are inhabited.

2881) Caterpillars have up to 4,000 muscles, including 248 muscles in their head alone; humans have about 650 total muscles.

2882) Casanova's first profession was a lawyer; he started college at the age of 12 and graduated with a law degree at 17.

2883) The Monday before and the Wednesday after the MLB All-Star game are the only two days during the year where there are no MLB, NFL, NHL or NBA games played. The MLB All-Star game is always played on a Tuesday, and there are no MLB games the day before or after, and MLB is the only professional sport played in July.

2884) Worf, played by Michael Dorn, is the only Star Trek character to appear regularly in two different Star Trek series; he appeared on both *Star Trek: The Next Generation* and *Star Trek: Deep Space Nine*.

2885) About 98% of all the atoms in a human body are replaced every year.

2886) Graham crackers are named after 19th-century evangelical minister Sylvester Graham. He believed that food influenced libido, so he advised a bland diet to suppress lust. He espoused a coarsely ground wheat flour that became known as graham flour and later gave graham crackers their name.

2887) FDA regulations allow a certain amount of foreign animal matter to be present in food. For raisins, 10 insects and 35 fruit fly eggs per 8 ounces are acceptable; for peanut butter, 5 rodent hairs and 150 bug fragments in 1 pound is fine.

2888) In 1913, Adolf Hitler, Sigmund Freud, Marshal Tito, Leon Trotsky, and Joseph Stalin all lived in Vienna within walking distance of each other.

2889) Rats are not likely to blame for transmitting the Black Death bubonic plague that wiped out one-third of Europe's population in the 14th century. Experiments assessing the transmission routes prove that the parasites carrying the disease were much more likely to have come from human fleas and lice.

2890) The ostrich is the fastest two-legged animal; it can reach speeds over 40 mph.

2891) Captain Morgan rum is named after the 17th century Welsh privateer Sir Henry Morgan. A privateer is essentially a pirate who is sanctioned by the government; he was hired by the British to protect their interests in the Caribbean from the Spanish.

2892) Supermodel Cindy Crawford was valedictorian of her high school class and had a scholarship to study chemical engineering at Northwestern University. She dropped out after one semester to pursue modeling full time.

2893) The Incas first domesticated guinea pigs and used them for food, sacrifices, and household pets.

2894) In 1958, Mao Zedong, founding father of the People's Republic of China, initiated a campaign to eliminate sparrows that led to the deaths of 45 million people. He considered sparrows a pest, and through the Great Sparrow Campaign, he ordered all sparrows to be killed. In 1961, up to 45 million people starved to death because the elimination of sparrows led to an explosion in the insect population that ate all the crops.

2895) In 1973, Patsy Cline was the first woman inducted into the Country Music Hall of Fame.

2896) The three-line symbol you typically find in the upper corner of a screen that you click or tap to get to a menu is called the hamburger button because it looks like a hamburger.

2897) At the Palace of Versailles, there were no restrooms, so people would just defecate in the corners. Visitors often complained about how bad the palace smelled, and King Louis XIV ordered that the hallways be cleaned of feces at least once a week. They also brought in potted orange trees to mask the smell.

2898) Scientists have proven that plants can learn and remember. Mimosa pudica, an exotic herb native to South America and Central America, was trained by repeatedly dropping water on it. The Mimosa plants stopped closing their leaves when they learned that there was no damaging consequence. The plants acquired the learned behavior in seconds, and they were able to remember what had been learned for several weeks. Plants lack brains and neural tissues, but they have a sophisticated calcium-based signaling network in their cells, like an animal's memory processes.

2899) Australia's coastline is over 16,000 miles long, and it has over 10,000 beaches, more than any other country.

2900) With about 127 million people, Japan rarely sees more than 10 gun deaths per year.

2901) Popcorn was the first food ever microwaved on purpose. In 1945, Raytheon patented the first microwave oven; engineer Percy Spencer had first discovered the heating powers of microwaves when he accidentally melted a candy bar in his pocket. He tested it out officially on popcorn, which was a success, and on an egg, which exploded.

2902) If you go north, south, east, or west from Stamford, Connecticut, the next state you hit is New York.

2903) At 46.4 degrees south latitude, Invercargill, New Zealand, has the world's southernmost McDonald's.

2904) Metallica is the only music group to play on all seven continents.

2905) More than half of the world's population lives within a 2,500-mile diameter circle in southeastern Asia. The circle incorporates 19 countries and 22 of the 37 cities in the world with a population of 10 million or more.

2906) Birds are essentially immune to the heat of chili peppers; they don't have the right type or number of taste receptors to be affected.

2907) The book title *Fahrenheit 451* is from the temperature book paper catches fire and burns.

2908) Fonts that are harder to read may be more convincing. Psychological research has shown that when readers are forced to slow down to decipher each word, they are forced to spend more time thinking about what they are reading.

2909) Sylvester Stallone holds the record for the most years between Oscar nominations playing the same character; it was 39 years between *Rocky* (1976) and *Creed* (2015).

2910) Of the world's 10 tallest statues, six are Buddhist statues.

2911) Andrew Jackson is the only U.S. president who was held as a prisoner of war; he joined the Revolutionary War at age 13 and was captured by the British.

2912) Fylfot is the heraldic name for the symbol that was later known as the swastika.

2913) Trees can tell if a deer is trying to eat them and defend themselves by producing astringent tannins that taste bad and put the deer off. When a bud is damaged, the tree can sense the animal's saliva in the wound, which triggers a hormone that causes it to increase the concentration of tannins in that part of the tree. It also spurs the tree to produce more growth hormones that cause the remaining buds to grow more vigorously and make up for those that have been lost to the deer.

2914) If you define a mountain as an elevation of 2,000 feet or more, 13 states don't have any mountains: Delaware, Florida, Illinois, Indiana, Iowa, Louisiana, Michigan, Mississippi, Missouri, New Jersey, Ohio, Rhode Island, and Wisconsin.

2915) A group of bears is called a sloth.

2916) In case their pants split, Major League Baseball umpires are required to wear black underwear.

2917) Worldwide, the average human body has a volume of about 2.22 cubic feet.

2918) California's name comes from the Spanish legend of Queen Califa, who ruled an island called California. When Cortéz landed in Baja California, he believed he had found the island of Queen Califa, which was supposed to be populated only by women who used gold to make tools and weapons.

2919) Israel is the only country with a net gain of trees in the last 100 years.

2920) It only takes 23 people in a group to have a 50% chance that two will have the same birthday. This is known as the Birthday Paradox; the probability goes up to 99.9% with just 70 people.

2921) In 1884, Mount Rushmore got its name from New York attorney Charles Edward Rushmore, who visited the Black Hills area on business. He asked a guide what the name of the mountain was, and the guide said they would name it now. The name somehow stuck.

2922) At age 59, Sean Connery is the oldest man to win *People* magazine's sexiest man alive.

2923) During the Cold War, the Soviets could tell if a passport was fake by looking at the staples; the staples in real Soviet passports corroded quickly because of low-quality metal.

2924) In 1976, the Coast Guard was the first U.S. military academy to admit women.

2925) If you average out the colors of all the stars we can see, you get beige, so the average color of the observable universe is beige.

2926) South Africa's Barberton Greenstone Belt is the world's oldest mountain range. The range is 3.6 billion years old, and the highest peak is 5,900 feet.

2927) Abraham Lincoln and John F. Kennedy share some striking similarities, although a century apart. Lincoln was elected to Congress in 1846; Kennedy was elected to Congress in 1946. Lincoln became President in 1860; Kennedy became president in 1960. Both were assassinated on a Friday and were sitting next to their wives when it happened, and both were succeeded by a vice president named Johnson. Vice President Andrew Johnson was born in 1808; Vice President Lyndon Johnson was born in 1908.

2928) The expression "worth one's salt" originated in ancient Rome because soldiers were sometimes paid in salt or given an allowance to purchase it. The word salary derives from the Latin "salarium," referring to a soldier's allowance to buy salt.

2929) Walking takes about 200 muscles to take a single step.

2930) Uruguay is the first country to fully legalize marijuana; it took full effect in 2017.

2931) *The Addams Family* was the first television family with a computer in their home; they had a huge UNIVAC computer.

2932) At 64.9 degrees north latitude, Fairbanks, Alaska, has the world's northernmost Walmart.

2933) Human babies have 300 bones; some fuse together to form the 206 bones in adults.

2934) President Herbert Hoover was known as "The Great Engineer"; he was a mining engineer and owned a large engineering consulting company.

2935) On average, sharks kill 12 people annually worldwide.

2936) Less than 10% of legally blind Americans can read Braille.

2937) London taxi drivers must pass possibly the world's hardest test. They need to know all of London's 25,000 streets, which way they run, which are one way, and everything on them down to the smallest pub, restaurant, and shop. Drivers study for years to pass.

2938) Daniel Day-Lewis is the only three-time Best Actor Oscar winner; he won for *My Left Foot*, *There Will Be Blood*, and *Lincoln*.

2939) In August 1954, baseball's Eddie Mathews was on the cover of the very first *Sports Illustrated* ever published.

2940) The U.S. Department of Defense is the world's largest employer.

2941) The first email was sent in 1971.

2942) Cerebral hypoxia is the end cause of every human death. Lack of oxygen to the brain is the final cause of death, regardless of what initiates it.

2943) Czech Republic's Ester Ledecka is the first woman to win gold medals in two different sports at the same Winter Olympics. At the 2018 PyeongChang Olympics, she won in skiing and snowboarding.

2944) There is an area of over 100 volcanoes under the ice sheet in western Antarctica.

2945) The tardigrade is a water-dwelling, eight-legged, micro animal about 0.02 inches long that can survive extreme conditions that would kill most life forms. They can survive temperatures from -458 to 300 degrees Fahrenheit, pressures from the vacuum of space to more than 1,000 atmospheres, and radiation 1,000 times higher than other animals. They can also live for 30 years without food or water. They were discovered in 1773 and are found everywhere from mountain tops to deep sea and tropical areas to the Antarctic.

2946) Antarctica has an average elevation of 8,200 feet, the highest of any continent.

2947) Of all the senses, smell is most closely linked to memory.

2948) In Michigan, you are never more than six miles from a body of water. Michigan has over 11,000 inland lakes plus four of the five Great Lakes.

2949) Sometime between 1268 and 1300, the first pair of corrective eyeglasses were invented in Italy; they were two reading stones (magnifying glasses) connected with a hinge.

2950) According to Ernest Hemmingway, the only three sports are bullfighting, motor racing, and mountaineering, and "All the rest are merely games."

2951) The term "slush fund" was originally used by sailors to refer to the side money they made selling animal fat; sailors sold the fat from the meat cooked on board to tallow makers.

2952) In the 1830s, ketchup was sold as a cure for diarrhea, jaundice, indigestion, and rheumatism; they even made ketchup pills. In 1834, a medical paper was published that claimed tomatoes could treat digestive problems.

2953) At 69.0 degrees north latitude, Murmansk, Russia, has the world's northernmost McDonald's.

2954) The word "robot" was first used in a 1920 play called *Rossum's Universal Robots*. It comes from the Slavic word "rabota," meaning slave labor.

2955) A priest was the first person to propose the big bang origin of the universe; Georges Lemaitre's work preceded Edwin Hubble.

2956) In 1983, Guion Bluford was the first African American in space.

2957) If you've ever yawned and had saliva shoot out your mouth, it is called gleeking. The salivary glands underneath your tongue become stimulated and shoot a concentrated jet of pure saliva; it typically happens when yawning.

2958) You can always see your nose, but you don't see it unless you think about it. The process is called unconscious selective attention and allows the brain to block out distractions.

2959) Originally, the term third world country did not mean a developing country. A French demographer coined the term in 1952 during the Cold War, and it referred to countries that weren't aligned with either the United States or the Soviet Union.

2960) Founded about 2000 BC, Cholula, Mexico, is believed to be the oldest continuously inhabited North American city.

2961) To protect children from being given names that may adversely affect them, Denmark has one of the world's strictest child naming laws. Parents can only choose a name from a list of 7,000 approved names; the name must show the gender of the child and not be unusual, and surnames cannot be used as first names. Alternative spellings of usual names are also not allowed.

2962) Venus is often called the Earth's twin because it is nearly the same size and mass and has a similar composition.

2963) The ostrich is the only bird with two toes on each foot.

2964) In 1888, the first vending machine in the United States dispensed Tutti-Frutti gum.

2965) The first cell phone call was made in 1973.

2966) At 54.8 degrees south latitude, the National University of Tierra del Fuego in Ushuaia, Argentina, is the world's southernmost university.

2967) *Toy Story* (1995) was the word's first computer-animated feature film.

2968) Whispering is harder on your vocal cords than normal speech.

2969) The average American professional football game lasts 3 hours and 12 minutes but only has about 11 minutes when the ball is in play.

2970) Switzerland and Vatican City are the only two countries with square flags.

2971) A combination of two words to make a new word, such as breakfast and lunch into brunch, is called a portmanteau.

2972) River and Joaquin Phoenix are the only brothers to receive acting Oscar nominations.

2973) You can't hum while holding your nose; to create the humming sound, air must escape through your nose.

2974) Litmus paper can change color when exposed to an acid or base because it is infused with lichens.

2975) Worldwide, about 24,000 people are killed by lightning annually.

2976) The earth's surface curves out of sight at about 3.1 miles.

2977) Based on AKC registrations, the three most popular purebred dogs in the United States are the Labrador Retriever, German Shepherd, and Golden Retriever.

2978) The earth's continental plates drift about as fast as human fingernails grow.

2979) Camel hair brushes are typically made from squirrel hair.

2980) The Eiffel Tower was originally intended for Barcelona; Spain rejected the project.

2981) France and its territories cover more time zones than any other country. France covers 12 times zones; the United States and Russia and their territories each cover 11 time zones.

2982) Twelve languages are written right to left: Arabic, Aramaic, Azeri, Divehi, Fula, Hebrew, Kurdish, N'ko, Persian, Rohingya, Syriac, and Urdu.

2983) When a woodpecker's beak hits a tree, it experiences 1,000 times the force of gravity.

2984) Researchers locate penguin colonies by looking for the stain trail from their droppings via satellite. It is easier to see than looking for the penguins themselves.

2985) *It Happened One Night* (1934), *One Flew Over the Cuckoo's Nest* (1975), and *The Silence of the Lambs* (1991) are the only three films to win all five major Academy Awards (best picture, director, actor, actress, and screenplay).

2986) In 1841, Edgar Allan Poe created mystery fiction's first detective in *The Murders in the Rue Morgue*.

2987) Alaska is the only state name that can be typed on one row of a standard keyboard.

2988) Adjusted for inflation, *The Exorcist* is the only horror film to gross $1 billion in the United States.

2989) Without the impact of gravity, astronauts are up to two inches taller in space.

2990) Kathryn Bigelow was the first female Best Director Oscar winner for *The Hurt Locker* (2008).

2991) Including U.S. territories, the greatest distance between any two points in the United States is between Guam and the U.S. Virgin Islands; it is 9,514 miles from Point Udall, Guam, to Point Udall, St. Croix, U.S. Virgin Islands.

2992) Forks were first introduced in Italy in the 11th century; however, they were originally seen as an offense to God since they were considered artificial hands and therefore sacrilegious.

2993) Until 1934, sheep grazed in New York's Central Park; for fear they would be eaten, they were moved during the Great Depression.

2994) To make customers drink more, caviar was served free in old west saloons.

2995) A 2018 study found that bees stop buzzing abruptly during a total solar eclipse.

2996) Five European countries have the same name as their capital city: Vatican City, Monaco, Luxembourg, Andorra, and San Marino.

2997) To produce one pound of honey, a hive of bees must visit 2 million flowers and fly about 55,000 miles. One bee colony can produce 60-100 pounds of honey annually. An average worker bee makes only about 1/12 of a teaspoon of honey in its lifetime and has a lifespan of about two months; queen bees typically live for three to five years.

2998) The tarsier has the largest eye relative to its body of any mammal. It is a small primate found on various Southeast Asian islands, including the Philippines. It is known for its extremely large eyes; even though it is about the size of a squirrel, each eye has a diameter of about 0.6 inches, as large as its brain.

2999) If a patient died during surgery in ancient Egypt, the surgeon's hands were cut off.

3000) The world's most popular first name is Mohammed and its variations.

3001) In 1974, Argentina's Isabel Peron became the first female head of state in the Western Hemisphere.

3002) In his duty as a sheriff, President Grover Cleveland twice served as an executioner.

3003) Chris Elliot was the first *Saturday Night Live* cast member to also have their child become a cast member.

3004) George Washington and James Monroe are the only two U.S. presidential candidates who have run effectively unopposed.

3005) When threatened, ladybugs release a foul-smelling chemical from their knees that can repulse predators. The substance is a mix of alkaloids and can also ooze from their abdomens.

3006) The Chinese giant salamander is the world's largest amphibian and can be almost six feet long.

3007) The concept of giving a key to the city comes from medieval times where walled cities were locked at night, but someone with the key could come and go as they liked.

3008) Queen is the only music group where every member has written more than one number-one single; all four members have been inducted into the Songwriters Hall of Fame.

3009) The short, erect tail of a hare, rabbit, or deer is called a scut.

3010) A group of Purdue engineering students made a licking machine, modeled after a human tongue, and found that it took an average of 364 licks to get to the center of a Tootsie Pop.

3011) In 1838, Edgar Allan Poe published the novel *The Narrative of Arthur Gordon Pym of Nantucket*, which describes how the crew of a ship called the *Grampus* were adrift in the ocean and drew straws to decide who would be eaten. The losing crew member was Richard Parker, who was killed and eaten. Forty-six years later in 1884, a yacht called the *Mignonette* sank, and its four surviving crew escaped in a lifeboat. They eventually decided they were going to have to eat one of their own to survive. They killed and ate a crew member named Richard Parker.

3012) Hippos sleep in the water; they surface automatically and breathe without waking up.

3013) To help keep the president fit, Herbert Hoover's physician invented a sport known as Hooverball. It is a combination of volleyball and tennis and is played with a six-pound medicine ball. The Hoover Presidential Library Association and the city of West Branch, Iowa, still co-host a national Hooverball championship each year.

3014) With the dissolution of the Soviet Union, 15 independent republics were created: Russia, Ukraine, Georgia, Belarus, Uzbekistan, Armenia, Azerbaijan, Kazakhstan, Kyrgyzstan, Moldova, Turkmenistan, Tajikistan, Latvia, Lithuania, and Estonia.

3015) A spider's muscles pull its legs inward, but they can't push them out again. To push them out, it must pump a watery liquid into its legs.

3016) At 19,551 feet, Mount Logan, in the Saint Elias range in the Yukon province of Canada, is the world's highest coastal mountain.

3017) Actor Sean Connery competed in the 1953 Mr. Universe bodybuilding competition.

3018) Balloons were originally made from animal bladders.

3019) Dogs tend to wag their tails more towards their right when they are relaxed and more to their left when they are afraid or insecure.

3020) The first print appearance of OMG was in a letter from Lord Fisher to Winston Churchill in 1917. Fisher wrote to Churchill, "I hear that a new order of Knighthood is on the tapis—O.M.G. (Oh! My God!)—Shower it on the Admiralty!!"

3021) Without even flapping their wings, the wandering albatross can travel 500-600 miles in a single day and maintain speeds higher than 79 mph for more than 8 hours. They do it through a cycle called dynamic soaring that has four major components: a windward climb, a turn from windward to leeward at the flight's peak, a leeward descent, and a curve from leeward to windward at the flight's base.

3022) New Zealand bans television advertising on Christmas, Easter, and Good Friday.

3023) The movie *Limelight* by Charlie Chaplin had a 20-year gap between its release and winning an Oscar. It was officially released in 1952, but it was not released in Los Angeles County and eligible for an Oscar until 1972. It won a Best Original Score Oscar in 1973 and is Charlie Chaplin's only competitive Oscar win.

3024) Lobsters have urine release nozzles right under their eyes, and they urinate as a way of communicating with each other.

3025) The word deadline originated in American Civil War prison camps; it was the line that prisoners couldn't go beyond, or they would be shot.

3026) Despite being a ruthless warlord, Genghis Khan was a very enlightened ruler. He established freedom of religion, banned torture of prisoners, outlawed slavery, promoted people based on individual merit rather than birth, established universal law, created a writing system, instituted an international postal system, and redistributed the wealth he gained.

3027) Oxford University existed about 350 years before the start of the Inca and Aztec empires. As early as 1096, there was teaching at Oxford, making it the world's third-oldest university in continuous operation and the oldest English-speaking university. The Aztec and Incan empires weren't founded until the 1430s.

3028) *60 Minutes* was the first U.S. network television show without a theme song.

3029) Cats are crepuscular animals, which means that they are active primarily during twilight hours, just after dawn and before dusk.

3030) In 1816, the stethoscope was invented because Rene Laennec, a French doctor, felt uncomfortable placing his ear directly to a woman's chest to hear her heartbeat. The first stethoscope was just a little wooden tube.

3031) Gymnast Cathy Rigby was the first woman to pose nude for *Sports Illustrated*.

3032) The Arctic Desert is the largest desert at least partially in North America. It covers 5.4 million square miles in Canada, Greenland, Norway, Russia, Sweden, and the United States.

3033) American savant Kim Peek was the inspiration for the movie *Rain Man*; among his many abilities, he could read two pages of a book simultaneously. His left eye read the left page, and his right eye read the right page. Scans of his brain indicated that he didn't have the normal connections that transfer information between the left and right hemispheres, which may have been the reason for some of his abilities.

3034) Men account for about 90% of all the world's shark attacks. The reason is behavioral; men more frequently participate in the activities that put you at greatest risk for shark attacks, such as surfing, diving, and long-distance swimming. As women participate more in these risker activities, the number of female attacks is on the rise.

3035) *The Wolf of Wall Street* used the "F" word more times than any other Best Picture Oscar nominee.

3036) At an elevation of 8,596 feet, Bogota, Colombia, is the world's highest elevation city with a population of over 5 million.

3037) The Colorado River of Texas is the longest river that flows entirely within one state; it flows for 970 miles, entirely within Texas, and it is the 11th longest river in the United States.

3038) Giraffes can't cough because their lungs are too far away from their epiglottis, and coughing is a combination movement of the lungs and epiglottis.

3039) Venus could have maintained an Earth-like environment for 2 to 3 billion years. Despite its current blazing temperatures and sulfuric acid clouds, simulations show that it could have maintained moderate temperatures and liquid water until 700 million years ago.

3040) Cleopatra was born 2,500 years after the Great Pyramid of Giza was built; she was closer to our current time than she was to the pyramids.

3041) Franklin D. Roosevelt is the only U.S. president that has ever been inside Fort Knox.

3042) India spends more time reading than any other country. Its citizens reported an average of 10 hours 42 minutes per week reading.

3043) In the sport of curling, pebbling the rink ice is done to create friction for the stone to curl. Ice preparers sprinkle the ice with tiny water droplets that freeze on the surface of the ice, creating a pebbled texture.

3044) A mondegreen is a mishearing or misinterpretation of a phrase in a way that gives it a new meaning, such as when you mishear the lyrics of a song and insert words that sound similar and make sense.

3045) Five countries don't have any airports within their boundaries: Vatican City, San Marino, Liechtenstein, Andorra, and Monaco.

3046) In 1964, the world record for a human going without sleep was set by 17-year-old Randy Gardner; he was intentionally awake for 11 days 25 minutes without any stimulants.

3047) William Shakespeare was the first person other than royalty to appear on a British stamp.

3048) On average, humans can remember the faces of about 5,000 people.

3049) At 82.5 degrees north latitude, Alert, Nunavut, Canada, is the world's northernmost permanent settlement; it is about 508 miles from the North Pole.

3050) In 1748, Scottish scientist William Cullen invented and demonstrated the basis of modern refrigeration. He boiled diethyl ether that absorbed heat from a space and cooled it to the point that he could create ice. Refrigerators wouldn't enter the home until 1913.

3051) At 5'4", James Madison was the shortest U.S. president.

3052) A Shabbat elevator works in a special mode and stops at every floor; it avoids pushing buttons, which is considered doing work on the Sabbath.

3053) In Denmark, a svangerskabsforebyggendemiddel is a condom. This is the official term; there is a shorter more common term, gummimand.

3054) Worker ants, the most common and smallest ants in any colony who do most of the work, are all sterile females.

3055) A day on Mars is 40 minutes longer than a day on Earth.

3056) Due to air resistance, the fastest a human body can fall is about 120 mph; this is known as terminal velocity.

3057) Fruit flies were the very first animal to go into space. In 1947, they went up in a captured German V2 rocket; they were recovered alive.

3058) Pittsburgh is the only city where all the major sports teams have the same colors; the Pirates, Penguins, and Steelers all use black and gold colors.

3059) The Twinkie filling flavor was originally banana cream.

3060) None of the Beatles could read or write music. When they needed to write music for others to play, arrangers at sheet music publishing companies would do it.

3061) No witches were burned at the stake during the Salem witch trials; 20 were executed, but most were hung, and none were burned.

3062) If California was a country, it would have the world's 8th largest economy.

3063) Compared to humans, cats have six to eight times more rod cells in their eyes; the rods are sensitive to low light, giving them their superior night vision. Their elliptical eye shape and larger corneas also help gather more light.

3064) The human eye has enough visual acuity that you could see a candle flame 30 miles away on a dark night if the earth were flat.

3065) The black mamba is the fastest moving land snake; it can move at speeds up to 12 mph.

3066) Until they are about four months old, babies only see in black and white with shades of gray.

3067) Although official records don't exist for safety reasons, 7'4" actor and professional wrestler Andre the Giant, who weighed over 500 pounds and had an incredible tolerance for alcohol, drank 156 beers in a single sitting. That is over 14.5 gallons.

3068) Blood can be used as an egg substitute in cooking. Blood and eggs have a similar protein composition, particularly with albumin that gives both their coagulant properties. In tests, 65 grams of blood substituted for one egg.

3069) The Mississippi River flows through more states than any other river; it flows through or along 10 states: Arkansas, Illinois, Iowa, Kentucky, Louisiana, Minnesota, Mississippi, Missouri, Tennessee, and Wisconsin.

3070) Before alarm clocks were invented, knocker-ups were people who would tap on the client's windows with a long stick until they were awake.

3071) In 1977, the show *Soap* featured the first openly gay character on U.S. television.

3072) The Cadillac car brand was named for the founder of Detroit, Michigan; in 1701, the French explorer Antoine Laumet de la Mothe, sieur de Cadillac founded Detroit.

3073) Karl Marx was once a foreign correspondent for Horace Greeley's *New York Daily Tribune* newspaper.

3074) The youngest Olympic medalist in an individual event was 12 years old in the 1936 200-meter women's breaststroke swimming.

3075) During WWII, Private Wojtek in the Polish army carried ammunition to the frontline and was later promoted to corporal; he was a bear. He was also taught to salute.

3076) On July 16, 1439, England banned kissing to stop the spread of the plague.

3077) The word sarcasm can be traced back to the Greek verb "sarkazein," which initially meant "to tear flesh like a dog."

3078) A pirate who is yelling "Avast, ye mateys" is telling his mates to stop or cease.

3079) You could fit 1.3 million Earths inside the sun, an average-size star.

3080) Joseph Stalin plotted to kill John Wayne and sent two men posing as FBI agents to assassinate him. Stalin was a big film fan and considered Wayne a threat to the Soviet Union because of his strong anti-communist beliefs.

3081) Urohidrosis is the habit of some birds of defecating onto their legs and feet to cool themselves. For birds, solid and liquid wastes are expelled together, so it is a liquid mixture of feces and urine. Flamingos, several species of storks, and some vultures exhibit this behavior.

3082) Theodore Roosevelt was the first American to win a Nobel Prize of any kind. He won the 1906 Nobel Peace Prize; the Nobel Prizes started in 1901.

3083) Today's average American woman weighs as much as the average American man from the 1960s.

3084) Ancient Roman public toilets had a long marble bench with holes on top, where you sat, and holes in the front, for the sponge on a stick used to clean yourself after. There were no doors or dividing walls; you sat right next to someone else. Once you had done your business, you would rinse the sponge in the channel of running water at your feet, push the sponge on a stick through the hole in the front and wipe yourself, and then rinse off the sponge and leave it in a basin for the next person.

3085) Captain James Cook was the first man to set foot on all the continents other than Antarctica.

3086) At 55.8 degrees south latitude, Cabo de Hornos National Park, Tierra Del Fuego, Chile, is the world's southernmost national park.

3087) A catfish is the only animal that naturally has an odd number of whiskers.

3088) In ancient Rome, gladiators were huge celebrities; wealthy women would buy vials of their sweat and use it as face cream.

3089) The swastika has been around for over 3,000 years and commonly symbolized goodness and luck until its use by the Nazis. It has been used by cultures all over the world, including early Christians, Jews, Hindus, and Buddhists.

3090) In 1935, Iceland was the first country to legalize abortion.

3091) The probability of a human living to 110 years or more is about 1 in 7 million.

3092) Underneath their scales, Komodo dragons have a layer of tiny bones from head to tail that protects them like chain mail or armor.

3093) Quito, Ecuador, is closer to the equator than any other national capital city; it is 15.9 miles south of the equator.

3094) The Challenger Deep is the deepest known location in the oceans; it is in the Pacific Ocean's Mariana Trench and is 36,070 feet deep.

3095) Mexico City has the world's largest taxi fleet, over 140,000 taxis.

3096) In his writings, William Shakespeare created over 1,700 of our common words and phrases, more than anyone else by far. He did it by changing nouns into verbs, changing verbs into adjectives, connecting words never used together, adding prefixes and suffixes, and creating original words. Some examples of his creations include: fancy-free, lie low, foregone conclusion, a sorry sight, for goodness sake, good riddance, mum's the word, what's done is done, scuffle, uncomfortable, manager, dishearten, eventful, new-fangled, hot-blooded, rant, with bated breath, laughable, negotiate, jaded, a wild goose chase, a heart of gold, fashionable, puking, dead as a doornail, obscene, bedazzled, addiction, faint-hearted, one fell swoop, vanish into thin air, swagger, zany, grovel, unreal, spotless reputation, full circle, arch-villain, bloodstained, and all of a sudden.

3097) During WWII, India had a volunteer army of 2.5 million soldiers, the largest in history.

3098) Ketchup originated in China many centuries ago; the original sauce was derived from fermented fish. The British picked it up and altered it to be more like a Worcestershire sauce. Tomatoes weren't used in ketchup until the early 19th century in the United States.

3099) By mass, the Etruscan shrew is the smallest mammal, weighing about 0.06 ounces on average. It has a very fast metabolism and eats 1.5 to 2 times its body weight per day. Its heart beats about 1,500 times per minute, the fastest of any mammal.

3100) Genghis Khan once ordered his army to eat every tenth man. In 1214, Khan laid siege to the city of Chengdu, the capital of the Chinese Jin empire. The siege went on for a long time, and supplies were short; they were also ravaged by the plague. Khan ordered that every tenth man be sacrificed to feed the others. Khan personally abandoned the siege, leaving it to one of his generals, and Chengdu eventually fell in 1215.

If you enjoyed this book and learned a little and would like others to enjoy it also, please put out a review or rating. If you scan the QR code below, it will take you directly to the Amazon review and rating page.

Made in United States
Orlando, FL
23 December 2024

56072498R00147